The Naples Riviera

THE NAPLES RIVIERA

THE WATCHER REMITTED.

CHARCOAL CARRIERS, AMALFI

THE
NAPLES RIVIERA

BY

HERBERT M. VAUGHAN, B.A. (Oxon.)

AUTHOR OF " THE LAST OF THE ROYAL STUARTS "
ETC.

WITH TWENTY-FIVE ILLUSTRATIONS IN COLOUR BY
MAURICE GREIFFENHAGEN

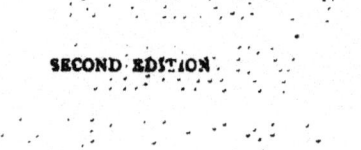

SECOND EDITION

NEW YORK
FREDERICK A. STOKES COMPANY
1908

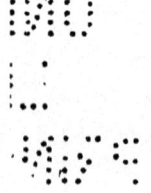

TO

G. L. L.

IN MEMORY OF

MANY PLEASANT DAYS IN THE SUNNY SOUTH

THIS BOOK IS

AFFECTIONATELY DEDICATED

BY THE AUTHOR

CONTENTS

LIST OF ILLUSTRATIONS

THE NAPLES RIVIERA

CHAPTER I

INTRODUCTORY

"In otia natam
Parthenopen."

THAT the city of Naples can prove very delightful, very amusing, and very instructive for a
week or ten days no one will attempt to dispute.
There are long mornings to be spent in inspecting
the churches scattered throughout the narrow streets
of the old town,—harlequins in coloured marble and
painted stucco though they be, they are yet treasure-
houses containing some of the most precious monuments of Gothic and Renaissance art that all Italy
can display. There are afternoon hours that can be
passed pleasantly amidst the endless halls and galleries
of the great Museo Nazionale, where the antiquities
of Pompeii and Herculaneum may be studied in
advance, for the wise traveller will not rush headlong
into the sacred precincts of the buried cities on the
Vesuvian shore, before he has first made himself
thoroughly acquainted with the wonderful collections
preserved in the Museum. Then comes the evening
drive along the gentle winding ascent towards Posilipo
with its glorious views over bay and mountains, all

tinged with the deep rose and violet of a Neapolitan
sunset ; or the stroll along the fashionable sea front,
named after the luckless Caracciolo the modern hero
of Naples, where in endless succession the carriages
pass backwards and forwards within the limited space
between the sea and the greenery of the Villa Reale.
Or it may be that our more active feet may entice
us to mount the winding flights of stone steps leading
to the heights of Sant' Elmo, where from the windows
of the monastery of San Martino there is spread out
before us an entrancing view that has but two possible
rivals for extent and interest in all Italy :—the
panorama of the Eternal City from the hill of San
Pietro in Montorio, and that of Florence with the
valley of the Arno from the lofty terrace of San
Miniato.   We can while away many hours leisurely in
wandering on the bustling Chiaja or Toledo with
their shops and their amusing scenes of city life, or
in the poorer quarters around the Mercato, where
the inhabitants ply their daily avocations in the open
air, and eat, play, quarrel, flirt, fight or gossip—do
everything in short save go to bed—quite uncon-
cernedly before the critical and non-admiring eyes
of casual strangers.   Pleasant it is to hunt for old
prints, books and other treasures amongst the dark
unwholesome dens that lie in the shadow of the
gorgeous church of Santa Chiara or in the musty-
smelling shops of the curiosity dealers in the Strada
Costantinopoli, picking up here a volume of some
cinque-cento classic and there a piece of old china that
may or may not have had its birth in the famous
factory of Capodimonte.   All this studying of historic
sculpture in the churches and of antiquities in the

Museum, this observing the daily life of the populace, and bargain-hunting in the Strada de' Tribunali, are agreeable enough for a while, but of necessity there comes a time when the mind grows weary of yelling people and of jostling crowds, of stuffy churches and of the chilly halls of the Museum, of steep dirty streets and of glaring boulevards, so that we begin to sigh for fresh air and a change of scene. Nor is there any means of escape within the precincts of the city itself from the eternal cracking of whips, from the insulting compliments (or complimentary insults) of the incorrigible cabmen, from the continuous babel of unmusical voices, and from the reiterated strains of "Santa Lucia" or "Margari" howled from raucous throats or strummed from rickety street-organs. Oh for peace, and rest, and a whiff of pure country air! For there are no walks in or around the City of the Siren, where there is nowhere to stroll save the narrow strip of the much-vaunted Villa (which is either damp or dusty according to weather) or the fatiguing ascent amidst walled gardens and newly built houses to the heights of the Vomero, which are covered with a raw suburb. Moreover our pristine delight in the place is beginning to flag, as we gradually realise that the city, like the majority of great modern towns, is being practically rebuilt to the annihilation of its old-world features, which used to give to Naples its peculiar charm and its marked individuality amongst large sea-ports. Long ago has disappeared Santa Brigida, that picturesque high-coloured slum, on whose site stands the garish domed gallery of which the Neapolitans are so proud ; gone in these latter days is classic Santa Lucia with its

water-gate and its fountain, its vendors of medicated
water and *frutti di mare*, those toothsome shell fish of
the unsavoury beach ; vanished for ever is many a landmark of old Naples, and new buildings, streets and
squares, blank, dreary, pretentious and staring, have
arisen in their places. This thorough *sventramento di
Napoli*, as the citizens graphically term this drastic
reconstruction of the old capital of the Kingdom of
the Two Sicilies, is no doubt beneficial, not to say
necessary, and we make no protest against these
wholesale changes, which have certainly tended to
destroy utterly its ancient character and appearance.
But all seems commonplace, new, smart, and unpoetic,
and we quickly grow weary of Naples now that it
has been turned into a Liverpool of the South without
the local colour and the peculiar attributes of which
author and artist have so often raved. The life of
the people, picturesque enough in its old setting, now
appears mean and squalid ; the toilers in the streets
look jaded, oppressed and discontented ; we search
in vain for the spontaneous gaiety of which we have
heard so much. We feel disappointed, cheated even,
in our expectations of Naples, and we begin to understand that its chief attraction consists in its proximity
to the scenes of beauty that mark the course of its
Riviera.

The Riviera of Naples may be said to extend from
the heights of Cumae, at the end of the Bay of Gaeta
to the north, as far as Salerno in a southerly direction,
whilst, lying close to this stretch of shore, are included
the three populous islands of Capri, Procida and
Ischia, which in prehistoric times doubtless formed

part and parcel of the Parthenopean coast itself. Our pleasant task it is to write of these classic shores and islands, where the beauties of nature contend for pre-eminence with the glorious traditions of the past that centre round them. What spot on earth can surpass, or even be compared with, Amalfi in the perfect lustre of its setting? What loftier or bolder cliffs than those of Capri can the wild bleak headlands of the North Sea exhibit? The fertile lands of France cannot vie with the richness of the Sorrentine Plain, nor can any mountain on the face of the globe rival in human interest the peak of Vesuvius; Pompeii is unique, the most precious storehouse of ancient knowledge the world possesses; whilst the Bay of Baia recalls the days of Roman power and luxury more vividly to our minds than any place save the Eternal City itself. And again: what illustrious names in history and in literature—classical, medieval, modern—are for ever associated with these smiling shores! Robert Guiscard and Hildebrand in quiet Salerno, Tasso at health-giving Sorrento, Vittoria Colonna in her palace-fortress on the crags of Ischia, the great Apostle of the west at Puteoli :— these are but a few of the more eminent and gracious figures that arise before us at the casual bidding of memory. Then there are the infamous, as well as the virtuous and the gallant, whose misdeeds are still freshly remembered upon these coasts or in their fertile valleys. The sinister Tiberius, the half-crazy and wholly vicious Caligula, many a king and queen of evil repute that ruled Naples, the vile Pier-Luigi Farnese, the adventurer Joachim Murat, all have left the marks of their personality upon the

coveted shores of the Neapolitan Riviera. From
the days of the Sibyl and of the Trojan hero to
the stirring times of Garibaldi and of King Bomba,
which were but of yesterday, Naples and its environs
have played a prominent part in the annals and
development of the civilised western world ; Roman
emperors, Pagan statesmen and poets, Norman, French
and Spanish princes, popes, saints and theologians,
merchants and scientists of the Middle Ages, writers
of the Renaissance and heroes of the *Risorgimento*,
all have combined to shed a halo of historical romance
upon Naples and its Riviera, where there is scarcely
a sea-girt town or a crumbling fortress that is not
redolent of the memory of some personage whose
name is inscribed on the roll of European history.
It seems but right, therefore, that many works should
have been written concerning this favoured corner of
Italy, so replete with natural charm and with historical
interest ; and in truth multitudes of books, large and
small, witty and dull, erudite and empty, light and
heavy, prosaic and rhapsodical, have poured forth
from the prolific pens of generations of authors. We
feel sincerely the need of an apology for making a
fresh addition to the ever-increasing pile of Neapolitan
literature, and we can only urge in extenuation of
our crime of authorship that the same scene appeals
in varied ways to different persons, and that every
fresh description is apt to shed additional light upon
old familiar subjects. In the following pages we
make no profession to act the part of a guide to
the neighbourhood of Naples, for are there not the
carefully prepared pages of Murray and Baedeker, to
say nothing of the works of such writers as Augustus

Hare, to lead the wanderer into every church and castle, to show him every nook in valley and mountain, and to supply him thoroughly with accurate dates and facts? No, our treatment of this theme may be deemed a poor one, but it has at least the merit and the courage of following its own peculiar lines. For we pursue our own course, and we touch lightly here and omit there ; we run to dissertation in this place, we glide by silently in another. We take our own views of people and places, and give them for what they are worth to our readers to approve or to condemn, as they think fit. We offer a medley of history and of imagination, of biography and of private comment; and we crave indulgence for our shortcomings by observing that any deficiencies in these pages can easily be remedied by application to the abundant literature upon Naples and its surrounding districts which every good library is presumed to contain.

CHAPTER II

THAT little stream the Sebeto, which is indeed, as the courtly Metastasio observes, " scanty in depth of water though overflowing with honour," may be considered as the boundary line that divides the city of Naples from its eastern environs, although it is evident that the whole stretch of coast from Posilipo to Torre del Greco is covered with an unbroken line of houses. Past the highly cultivated *Paduli*, the chief market-gardens on this side of the city, with the town of La Barra on the fertile slopes to our left, we pass by way of San Giovanni a Teduccio to Portici, once a favourite resort of royalty. Here the dilettante Charles III., first Bourbon King of Naples, built a palace and laid out gardens in the days of patches and powder, constructing a royal pleasaunce that was destined to become the chief residence of the temporary supplanter of his own family, Joachim Murat, the citizen king of Naples and brother-in-law of the great Napoleon. Villa and gardens still remain, but monarchs have ceased to visit Portici since the days of Bomba, and the old royal demesne has been turned into an agricultural college. Adjoining and practically forming part of Portici is the town of Resina, which preserves almost intact the old classical name of Retina

8

that it bore in the distant days when it served as the port of Herculaneum. Here then in the mean streets of Resina we find ourselves standing above, though certainly not upon, historic ground, for the temples and villas, the theatres and private houses of the famous buried city lie far below the surface trodden by our feet. To visit Herculaneum it is necessary for us to descend some seventy to a hundred feet into the depths of the earth, passing more than one layer of ancient lava, for Resina and Portici themselves are but modern editions of former towns that have been engulfed in the course of ages. If the stranger can derive any solid satisfaction from the descent by a gloomy underground passage and from fleeting glimpses of ancient walls and dwellings seen through a forest of wooden baulks, which serve to support the spaces excavated, he must indeed be an enthusiast. But most people, perhaps all sensible people, will be content to take the undoubted interest of Herculaneum on trust, probably agreeing (at any rate after their visit) that the inspection of this subterranean city is not worth the candle, by whose flickering beams alone can objects be distinguished in the oppressive darkness. Personally we strongly hold to the expressed opinion of Alexandre Dumas, who declared that even the most hardened antiquary could not desire more than one hour's contemplation of this hidden mass of shapeless wreckage. " Herculaneum," writes that genial Frenchman, " but wearies our curiosity instead of exciting it. We descend into the excavated city as into a mine by a species of shaft ; then come corridors beneath the earth which can only be entered by the light of tapers ; and these smoke-grimed passages allow us from time to time to obtain a momentary glimpse of the angle of a house, the colonnade of some temple, the steps of a theatre. Everything is fragmentary, mutilated, dingy, uncertain, confused, and therefore unsatisfactory. Well, at the end of an hour spent in wandering amongst these abysmal recesses, the most hardened archæologist, the most dry-as-dust antiquary, the most inquisitive of tourists begins to experience only one feeling—an intense desire to ascend to the light of day and to breathe once more the fresh air of the upper world."

Nevertheless, it was from these dismal caverns, black as Erebus, that some of the choicest marbles and bronzes that now adorn the Museum at Naples were originally extracted. From a villa at Herculaneum also was taken the famous collection of 3000 rolls of papyrus, chiefly filled with the writings of the Epicurean philosopher Philodemus, perhaps the greatest "find" of ancient literature that has yet been made, although the contents of this damaged library, deciphered with equal toil and ingenuity, have not proved to be of the value originally set upon them by expectant scholars. But much of the city itself has yet hardly been touched since the days when it was destroyed in the reign of Titus, so that far below the squalid lanes of Portici and Resina there must still exist acres upon acres of undisturbed buildings, public and private, many of them perhaps filled with priceless works of Greek and Roman art, for Herculaneum, unlike Pompeii, was never tampered with by the ancients themselves, for the coating of volcanic mud, which filled the whole area of the city, made impracticable a systematic searching of its ruins by the despoiled citizens. Then, as if nature had not already buried the city sufficiently deep, subsequent eruptions of Vesuvius have super-imposed additional layers of lava, whilst confiding human beings have in their turn built habitations upon the volcanic crust.

We all know the story, perhaps mythical, of the discovery of Herculaneum at the beginning of the eighteenth century by the accidental sinking of a well upon its long-forgotten site and of the subsequent excavations made by the Prince d'Elbœuf. These so-called explorations were, however, made in the most greedy and destructive spirit, for the prince's sole object was to obtain antique works of art for his private collection, not to make intelligent enquiries about the dead and buried city lying beneath his estate. Ignorant workmen were despatched to hew and hack wholesale in the mirky depths in order to discover statuary and paintings, and since there was no receptacle at hand to contain the *débris*, they took the simple course of filling in each hollow made with the masses of rubbish already excavated. Later in the same century the Bourbon king was induced by Neapolitan savants to take some interest in the work, but, strange to relate, the superintendent appointed, a certain Spanish officer named Alcubier, was so ignorant and careless that half the objects found under his supervision were broken or lost before they reached Naples ; this ignoramus, it was said, even went so far as to order whole architraves to be smashed up and their bronze lettering to be picked out before making a copy of the original inscription ! Under these circumstances the marvel is that anything of beauty or value should have survived at all, for this selfish plundering of Herculaneum, in strong contrast with the reverent treatment meted out to Pompeii, may be considered one of the greatest pieces of vandalism ever perpetrated. In spite of this wholesale destruction, however, there must remain untouched, as we have said, a vast quantity of objects, beautiful, useful or curious, yet it is extremely doubtful if we shall live to see any serious and intelligent effort made to bring these hidden treasures forth to the light of day. The expense of working this buried hoard would be enormous in any case, whilst the existence of the houses of Resina and Portici overhead necessitates special measures of precaution on the part of the excavators. The only method of examining Herculaneum properly would be in fact to treat the buried site like an immense mine by the construction of regular galleries and shafts for the entrance of skilled workmen, and to remove the rubbish displaced to the outer air. Perhaps some multi-millionaire might be found ready to undertake so arduous, yet so fascinating a task, though we fear that the Italian Government, which has always shown itself as tenacious of its subterranean wealth of antiquity as it appears languid in the work of quarrying it, would indignantly refuse to accede to any such offer. As regards the ancient city of Hercules, therefore, we must perforce remain content to inspect the magnificent bronzes and the other objects of interest that are to be found in the Museum of Naples, for we are not likely to see any further researches just at present, more's the pity, since there is every reason to suppose that a thorough investigation conducted regardless of cost would yield up to the world the most marvellous and valuable results.

Some two miles of dusty suburb lie between Resina and Torre del Greco, which has been destroyed time after time by the lava streams descending from "that peak of Hell rising out of Paradise," as Goethe once named the burning mountain overhead. Nevertheless, the Torrese continue to sit patiently at the feet of the fire-spouting monster, trembling when he is angry, pleased when he is quiescent, and ready to abandon meekly their homes when he renders them insupportable by his furious outbursts. Yet these people never fail to return and risk the ever-present chances of death and destruction. And little can we blame them for their fatalism, when we gaze upon the glorious views that reveal themselves at this spot, whence Naples rising proudly from the sea, the rocky islands of Ischia and Capri, the aerial heights of Monte Sant' Angelo and all the features of the placid bay are seen spread around us in a panorama of unsurpassed loveliness. Beneath lava rocks, black and sinister, that contrast strangely in their sombre hues with the brilliant tints of sea and sky, lie little beaches of glittering gravel that would afford delightful retreats for meditation, were it not for the dozens of half-naked brown-skinned imps, children of the fisher-folk of Torre del Greco, who wallow in the warm sand or rush with joyful screams into the tepid surf. The population must have increased not a little since those days, nearly a century ago, when the unhappy Shelley could find peace and solitude in his darkest hours of unrest upon these shores, where it would be well-nigh impossible for a twentieth-century poet to espy a retreat for soothing his soul in verse. Yet somehow, during the drowsy noontide rest when the

active life of the South ceases, if only for an hour or
so, it is still possible to catch the spirit in which that
melancholy wanderer indited one of his most exquisite
lyrics :—sunshine, clear sky, murmuring seas, the
fragrance of the Italian spring, all are present to our
reverie ; and how true and perfect a picture has the
poet-artist drawn for us of this beautiful Vesuvian
shore !

"The sun is warm, the sky is clear,
    The waves are dancing fast and bright,
Blue isles and snowy mountains wear
    The purple noon's transparent light :
The breath of the moist earth is light
    Around its unexpanded buds ;
Like many a voice of one delight,
    The winds, the birds, the ocean floods,
The City's voice itself is soft, like Solitude's.

I see the Deep's untrampled floor
    With green and purple seaweeds strown ;
I see the waves upon the shore,
    Like light dissolved in star-showers, thrown :
I sit upon the sands alone ;
    The lightning of the noontide ocean
Is flashing round me, and a tone
    Arises from its measured motion,
How sweet ! did any heart now share in my emotion ? "

But it must be admitted that the seashore by
Torre del Greco does not often lend itself as a
suitable spot for romantic or solitary communings
with nature ; it is a busy place where the struggle
for life is keen and practical enough, and its inhabitants have little time or inclination to bestow on the
pursuit of poetry.   As in all the towns of the *Terra
di Lavoro*, as this collection of human ant-hills on

the eastern side of Naples is sometimes designated,
the old command given to the first parents of mankind—" by the sweat of thy brow shalt thou eat
bread "—is scrupulously observed in Torre del Greco.
It is little enough, however, that these frugal people
demand, for a hunk of coarse bread, tempered with a
handful of beans or an orange in winter or with a
slice of luscious pink water-melon or a few figs in
summer, is thought to constitute a full meal in this
climate ; nor are these simple viands washed down by
anything more potent than a draught of *mezzo-vino*,
the weak sour wine of the country.   A dish of
maccaroni or a plateful of kid or veal garnished with
vegetables is a treat to be reserved for a marriage or
some great Church festival, whilst a chicken is regarded as a luxury in which only *gran' signori* of
boundless wealth can afford to indulge.   Amongst the
many classes of toilers with which populous Torre del
Greco abounds, that of the coral-fishers is perhaps the
most interesting.   There is pure romance in the very
notion of hunting for the beautiful coloured substance
lying hidden in the crystalline depths of the Mediterranean, and its quest is not a little suggestive of
azure caverns beneath the waves, peopled by soft-eyed
mermaids and strange iridescent fishes.   As a matter
of fact, it would be difficult to name a harder occupation or a more dismal monotonous existence than that
of the coral-fishers, many hundreds of whom leave
this little port every spring in order to spend the
summer months on the coasts of Tripoli, Sardinia, or
Sicily.   The men employed, who work under contract
during some six months of unending drudgery, are by
no means all natives of Torre del Greco, but are

collected from various places of the neighbourhood,
not a few of them being thrifty youths from Capri,
who are eager to amass as quickly as possible the
lump sum of money requisite to permit of marriage.
It is true that the amount actually paid by the
owners of the coral fleet sounds proportionately large,
yet it is in reality poor enough recompense when
measured by the ceaseless toil, the burning heat and
the wretched food, which the venture entails.   The
lot of the coral-fisher has however much improved of
late years, partly by measures of government which
now compel the contractors to treat their servants
more humanely, and partly by the fact that the
practice of emigration in Southern Italy has reduced
the numbers of applicants for the coral-fishing business
and has thereby, indirectly at least, raised wages and
bettered the old conditions of service.   A truly pitiable
account is given of these poor creatures some thirty
years ago by an English writer, whose knowledge of
the Neapolitan people and character remains probably
unsurpassed ; and it is some satisfaction to reflect that
even in Mr Stamer's day the bad old oppressive system
had already been somewhat tempered for the benefit
of these white slaves, who for nearly half the round of
the year were worse treated than King Bomba's unhappy victims in the pestilent prisons of Naples and
Gaeta.

"Badly paid, badly fed, and hard worked is the poor
coral-fisher.   Compared with his, the life of a galley-
slave is one of sybaritical indolence.   His treatment
was, until very recently, not one whit better than that
of the poor oppressed negro as he existed in the vivid
imagination of Mrs Harriet Beecher Stowe ; im-

A CAPRIOTE FISHERMAN'S WIFE

measurably worse than that of the real Simon Pure. The thirty ducats for which he sold his seven months' services once paid, he was just as much a slave as Uncle Tom of pious memory, harder worked, more brutally handled. His *padrone* was a sea-monster, alongside of whom Mr Legree would have seemed a paragon of Quaker-like gentleness and amiability. His word was law, and a rope's end well laid on his sole reply to any remonstrance on the part of his bondsmen. For six days out of the seven he kept them working incessantly, not unfrequently on the seventh into the bargain, if the weather was favourable; and that they might be strong, hearty and able to haul away, their food consisted of dry biscuits; a dish of maccaroni with just sufficient oil to make the sign of the cross being served out for the Sunday's dinner." *

In those "good old days," not so very far distant, the dredging nets were coarse and weighty, and the capstan of the clumsiest and most primitive description, so that the coral-seeking serfs under contract were worked like bullocks until they were often wont to fall asleep out of sheer exhaustion as they hauled away mechanically. We can imagine then with what raptures of joy these ill-treated mortals must have hailed the advent of October, the month that terminated their long spell of suffering and semi-starvation, and with what eagerness they must have returned homewards, the more industrious to perform odd jobs during the winter season on farms or in factories; the lazier to enjoy a well-earned holiday of loafing on the quay or in the piazza. And although times have changed for the better in the eyes of the coral-fisher,

* W. J. A. Stamer: *Dolce Napoli.*

B

his lot still remains hard enough, even in the present days of grace; whilst any employment that saps the workman's strength during the hot summer months and leaves him idle or unemployed in winter time cannot well be described as a desirable trade. Yet the temptation to obtain a considerable sum of money in advance, as is the case in this particular industry, often proves overwhelming to the young man of the Torres or of Castellamare, imprudently married before he is out of his teens and with an ever-increasing family. It is so easy to accept the proffered gold, which will keep wife and babies in comparative comfort throughout the long hot summer; unskilled labour is paid so lightly on these teeming shores of the Terra di Lavoro; saddled already with children he cannot make up his feeble mind to emigrate; in short, to go a-coralling is his sole chance, if he wishes to keep his home together and to stave off charity or starvation from his young wife and family.

Beyond Torre del Greco we seem to escape to a certain extent from the enveloping network of human dwellings, so that we are at last enabled to gain some idea of the natural features of the country. The oriental character of the landscape, which marks more or less distinctly the whole of the Neapolitan coast-line, will at once be noticed in the domed farm buildings, not unlike Mahommedan *koubbas*, washed a glistening white, that stand out sharply against the lugubrious tints of the lava beds. Above us, crowning a bosky hillock that juts forth from the mountain flank, stands one of the many convents of the monks of Camaldoli, whose houses are scattered throughout the breadth of Southern Italy.

The position of their Vesuvian settlement is certainly unique, for the rising ground on which it is perched appears like some verdant oasis amid the arid fields of sable lava. Secure in its commanding site, the monastery has many a time been completely surrounded by burning streams, which have invariably left the building and its woody demesne unscathed. More than once have the good brethren, who wear the white robe of St Romualdo of Ravenna, looked down from their convent walls upon the work of destruction below, and have watched the waves of liquid fire surging angrily but uselessly round the rocky base of their retreat. Hard manual labour, prayer, solitude and contemplation : these are the chief duties enjoined by the famous Tuscan order, and surely no more suitable place for carrying out such precepts could have been chosen by the pious founder of this Vesuvian convent. For what scenes on earth could be deemed more beautiful to contemplate, we wonder, than the wide stretches of heaven and ocean, of fertile plain and of rugged mountain, that are ever before the eyes of the brethren ; or more instructive than the constant spectacle of disappointed human ambition and energy, which is afforded by the barren lava beds and the ruined cities close at hand !

Descending from the slopes of Camaldoli, we cross a tract of country wherein black lava alternates with patches of rich cultivation and of thriving vineyards, and gaining the high road we soon reach Torre Annunziata. Here it is evident that the manufacture of maccaroni forms the chief industry of its population, for on all sides are to be seen the frames filled with the golden coloured strings of *pasta* that have been hung up to dry in the sunshine. Every flat roof in the place, moreover, is covered with smooth concrete and protected by a low parapet for the spreading of the grain, and on the beach are laid huge cloths of coarse brown material that are heaped with masses of the crude corn, whilst men with their naked feet from time to time turn the grain so as to dry the whole bulk. Torre Annunziata and its inland neighbour, Gragnano, are in fact the two chief local scenes of this industry with which the Bay of Naples has always been so closely associated, and it is here that we can best make ourselves acquainted with the process of manufacturing maccaroni. By following any one of the tall brown-skinned fellows, stripped to the waist and bare-legged, who have been breathing the fresh air of the street for a few moments, we quickly arrive at the entrance of one of the many small factories with which the town abounds. In spite of open doors and windows its atmosphere feels hot and stifling, for it is impregnated with tiny particles of flour dust, which too often, alas! are apt to affect permanently the lungs of the workmen. The dough of maccaroni is obtained by mixing pure wheaten flour with semolina in certain proportions, only water being used for the purpose, whilst the task of kneading is carried out in primitive fashion by means of a lever worked continuously by two or more men. When the dough has at length arrived at the required consistency after some hours of steady kneading, it is placed in a large perforated copper cylinder, each hole having a central pin at the bottom and a valve on top. A powerful screw is then employed to press down upon the dough, which is thus squeezed out of the imprisoning cylinder through the holes in the serpentine shape that is so familiar to us. On reaching a certain length these pipes, issuing from the holes, are twisted off and are then removed for drying to the frames in the open air. Maccaroni has, of course, many varieties of form and quality, from the thin fluffy vermicelli, known under the poetical name of *Capilli degli Angeli*, to the great thick pipe-stem-like article of ordinary commerce. There are endless means of cooking and dressing this, the national dish of Italy, but perhaps the most popular of all is *alla Napolitana*, wherein it is served with tomato sauce, to which a sprinkling of grated Parmesan cheese is frequently added. A compound of eggs and maccaroni, sometimes known as a Neapolitan omelette, likewise makes an appetising dish, though it is one that is little known to foreigners. One circumstance is patent; the dismal so-called "maccaroni pudding" one meets with in England seems to have nothing in common with the delicately flavoured, sustaining dish that can be obtained for a few pence in any Southern restaurant.

Torre Annunziata has the reputation of being a dirty malodorous town, composed of shabby stone houses and full of quarrelsome people. Well, perhaps there is a scintilla of truth in the sweeping observation, yet if we can contrive to endure the smells and racket of the place for a brief space of time, there is much of human interest to be observed in the daily scenes of its crowded beach and its noisy streets. After all, no odours of the South can compare in all-pervading intensity with the blended aroma of fried fish and London fog that old Drury Lane can often produce ; nor are the Torrese more dangerous to strangers or

more objectionable in their habits than the crowds of
Lambeth or Seven Dials.   In strength of lungs, it
must be granted, the Italian easily surpasses the
Londoner, for the Southern voice is positively alarming in its vigour and its far-reaching power.   No one
—man, woman or child—can apparently speak below
a scream ; even the most amiable or trivial of con-
versations seems to our unaccustomed ears to portend
an imminent quarrel, to so high a pitch are the
naturally harsh voices strained.   Morning, noon and
night the same hubbub of men shouting, of women
screeching, and of children yelling continues for
nobody minds noise in Italy, where people are
troubled with no nerves of their own and consequently
have no consideration for those of strangers.   And
why, therefore, should they suspend their native habits
to please a handful of cavilling *forestieri* ?

A stroll through Torre Annunziata, although it
possesses not a few drawbacks, can be made both
amusing and instructive ; we can even find something
attractive in the quality of the local atmosphere, which
suggests at one and the same time sunshine, garlic,
incense, stale fish and wood smoke ; it is the pungent
but characteristic aroma of the South, filled "with
spicy odours Time can never mar."   And what truly
charming pictures do the family groups present in
the wide archways giving on the untidy courts within,
full of sun and shadow and gay with bright-coloured
garments swaying in the wind !   The ebon-haired
young mother with teeth like pearls and with warm-
tinted cheeks sits fondling the last helpless little
addition to her growing family, whilst toddlers of any
age from two to seven, unkempt but bright-eyed and

engaging, play around the door-step, watched over by
their grandmother, or may be their great-grandam,
who with her wizened face enfolded in her yellow
kerchief, her skinny neck, and her distaff in the bony
fingers, looks as if she had stepped out of some
Renaissance painting of the Three Fates in a Florentine
gallery. Crimson carnations in earthenware pots stand
on the steps of the outside staircase, giving a touch of
refinement to the squalid home, and from the balcony
overhead the glossy-black, yellow-billed *passer solitario*,
the favourite cage-bird of the Neapolitan poor, chirrups
with apparent cheerfulness in his wicker-work prison.
Behind, in the dim shadows of the large room, which
serves as sole habitation, we can espy the inevitable
household altar with the oil lamp glimmering before
the little crude-coloured print of the Virgin and Child,
and its usual accessory, the piece of palm or olive
that was blessed by the priest last Palm Sunday ;
poor and mean though the chamber be, its bed linen
and simple appointments are more cleanly than might
perhaps be inferred from the appearance of the family
itself. In a shady corner close by, three or four young
labourers at their mid-day rest have finished their
frugal repast of bread and beans, and are now playing
eagerly the popular game of *secchinetto* with a frayed
and grimy pack of cards. Wives or sweethearts
watch with anxious faces from a respectful distance,
for it is not meet to disturb the lords of creation when
they happen to be engaged in a game of chance.
What possibilities of farce and tragedy can be drawn
from so simple, so common a scene upon these shores,
where human life is less artificially conducted than
elsewhere in Europe, and where human passions are

kept under less restraint? Terrible are the tales of
jealousy and revenge, of deliberate treachery and of
uncontrolled violence, which are related of these quick-
tempered grown-up children of the South, who seem
to love and hate with the blind intensity of untutored
savages.

> " Lo 'nnamorato' mmio sse chiammo Peppo,
>   Lo capo jocatore de le carte ;
>   Ss' ha jocato 'sto core a zecchinetto,
>   Dice ca mo' lo venne, e mo' lo parte.
>   Che n'agg' io a fare lo caro de carte ?
>   Vogho lo core che tinite 'm pietto ! "

> (" That lover of mine is called Handsome Beppo,
>   The best player of cards all around this way ;
>   He's been playing on Hearts at *zecchinetto*,
>   And says now they turn up, now are sorted away.
>   What matters the heart in the card-pack to me?
>   The heart in his bosom's the heart for me ! ")

Here lies the sleeping fisherman, worn out probably
with hours of hauling at the heavy nets, who is snatch-
ing a chance hour of repose, prone upon his chest with
face buried in his crossed arms. Little he seems to
reck of the damp of the soil or the heat of the sun,
nor can a noisy game of *mora* played by a couple of
his companions beside him disturb his deep slumber.
Mora has ever been the classic game of the South,
and indeed, there is abundant evidence to show that
it was played by the ancestors of these dwellers in
Magna Graecia hundreds of years before Pompeii was
overthrown. The game, which requires nothing but
the human fingers, bears no little resemblance to our
own humble pastime of " Up Jenkin ! " which may
almost be described as a species of drawing-room *mora*;

perhaps some Italian traveller in a past age may actually have introduced this form of the southern diversion into prosaic England. The two players, face to face and craning forward with outstretched necks, simultaneously extend their right hands with one or more fingers pointing upward, the aim of each man being to guess the exact number, from two to ten, jointly displayed by both right hands. If one of them hit upon the correct figure, then he gains one point towards the stakes, which are usually made in *centesimi* rather than in *soldi*. How rapidly do the lean supple brown fingers flash backwards and forwards, and with what gusto do the two frenzied combatants yell out their numbers! *Mora* has been a favourite recreation with these people almost from their cradles, and he would be a bold man indeed who would venture to challenge a Torrese at this game, for the native's skill and experience are almost bound to tell eventually in his favour, and the odds are " Lombard Street to a China orange " against the outside player. There are certain maxims too with regard to the game which are closely observed by those who play it, as well as peculiar expressions, such as *tutte* to denote that all ten fingers are being shown, or *chiarella* for all but one. Five points usually make the game, and these are commonly marked by holding up one or more fingers of the disengaged left hand.—These are a few of the many sights to be witnessed by those who can afford to endure the pestering attentions of small boys, and the uncomplimentary staring of the adult population in such places as the Torres or Castellamare ; and such as wish to make themselves acquainted with the details of southern life and manners cannot do better than pass an idle hour in the fishmarket or the piazza of these little industrial towns of the Vesuvian shore. For to regard Southern Italy from the majestic isolation of a railway compartment or a hired carriage cannot possibly give the traveller the smallest insight into the ordinary phases of local life ; for he is ever looking, as it were, into a picture from which all trace of colour has vanished.

It is but a short quarter of an hour by train from Torre Annunziata to Castellamare di Stabia, the ill-fated Stabiae of the Romans, which shared the evil lot of Pompeii and Herculaneum. On our right we have the sea, with the castle-topped islet of Revigliano, whilst on looking to the left we can survey the fertile valley of the Sarno, and the shapeless mounds which hide that precious goal of every traveller to these shores, the buried city of Pompeii. Everywhere thrives sub-tropical vegetation :—cactus and aloe draped in wreaths of smilax ; tall straggling masses of scarlet geranium that cling for protection to the Indian fig, and blossom in security amid their spiky but safe retreats ; shrubs of fragrant yellow genista ; clumps of purple-leaved *ricini*, as the Italians name the castor-oil plant. If it were summer time, the daturas would be covered with their great white floral trumpets, and every oleander bush would be one blaze of the coarse carmine blossoms that are here called *Mazza di San Giuseppe*, or St Joseph's nosegay, and a very gaudy rank bouquet they make. But in spring-time the oleander can but display long greyish leaves and pods of snowy fluff, which is blown hither and thither like thistle-down on the air ; and it is only in flaming summer that these regions are brightened by St

Joseph's flower, or by the still more gorgeous masses of the mesembryanthemum, which clambers on all sides over the lava rock and hangs in crimson festoons from tufa cliffs, making impossibly splendid splashes of colour in the landscape.

So many writers have expatiated upon the sordid ugliness of Castellamare and upon the beauty of the wooded slopes above the town, that a further description of the place may well be dispensed with. Uninteresting, however, as this industrial town appears, it boasts a long historical record, to which its crumbling medieval castle bears witness. The great Emperor Frederick the Second, the scholar-pope Pius the Second, and all the monarchs of the Angevin, Aragonese and Bourbon dynasties have been associated with this "castle by the sea." The whole district was once the property of that human monster Pier-Luigi Farnese, duke of Parma, heir of Pope Paul the Third, of whose demoniacal cruelty and treachery the racy pages of Cellini's Memoirs give so vivid an account, and whose repulsive face has grown familiar to us from Titian's famous portraits in the gallery of Naples. It was the evil Pier-Luigi's descendant and heiress-general of the family, Elizabeth Farnese, Queen of Spain, who conveyed the beautiful villa and woods of Quisisana to the Bourbon kings, and here the Neapolitan royal family for several generations sought health (as the name of the place implies) and repose upon the breezy heights that lie so conveniently near to the great city in full view to the west. Nowadays the old royal villa, deserted by crowned heads since Ferdinand's days and fallen from its high estate to its present use of a hotel and pension, forms with its park the chief attraction of Castellamare, where English travellers are wont to congregate in winter, and Neapolitan and Greek seekers of pleasure or drinkers of medicinal waters resort in the hot summer months. The Southerners who come here for their *villeggiatura* certainly enjoy a better time than the winter visitors, for the bulky form of Monte Sant' Angelo intercepts much of the sunshine, thereby rendering the place damp and chilly in the cold season of the year. Nominally it is the mineral springs that attract the Neapolitan folk, wherein they have a fine choice of health-giving beverages, varying from the *acqua ferrata*, a mild chalybeate that is found useful as a tonic, to the powerful *acqua del Muraglione*, that is warranted to reduce the stoutest mortal to a mere shadow of his former self in a trice. But though the waters may be occasionally sipped of a morning and wry faces made, it is in reality the warm sea-bathing on the shore, where people spend hours pickling in tepid salt water, and also the cool rides or walks amongst the shady alleys of sweet chestnut and ilex woods of Quisisana and Monte Coppola, which draw hither in summer the elegant world of Naples, and even of Athens, to visit Castellamare. The leafy groves on the zephyr-swept hill sides, once sacred to the pleasures of Bourbon tyrants, now ring with peals of noisy laughter, with gallant compliments, and with the harsh shouting of the *ciucciari*, the leaders of the poor over-driven donkeys. Unhappy patient beasts! usually covered with raws and galls, that are urged forward at a gallop by the remorseless stick, or even by the goad, for the Neapolitan donkey-boy is absolutely callous to the feelings of his animal. Not that he is cruel out of sheer cussedness, for cruelty's sake, for he can be really kind to his dog or his cat ; but the beast of burden, the helpless uncomplaining servant of man, suffers terribly at his hands. It is useless to remonstrate or argue with the young ruffian, who at our sharp reprimand will merely open wide his big black eyes and stare in genuine amazement. *Non sono Cristiani*—they have no souls, and the beasts are their property and not yours ; what does it matter then to you how they are treated, provided they carry you properly? That is the sum total of the donkey-boy's argument, and he has high ecclesiastical authority to back up his private theory, if he had the wit to enter into a discussion with us on the subject. Almost equally hopeless is it to point to the simple fact that a well-groomed, well-treated animal lasts longer than a half-starved, mutilated scare-crow. " How old is your horse ? " we once asked a driver in the south. " He is very old indeed, *eccelenza*," was the reply ; " he must be nearly twelve!" On being informed that horses often worked well up to twenty years old and over in England, he let us infer, quite politely, that he thought we were romancing. Tenderness towards the dumb creation is a common, not to say a prevailing characteristic of the Anglo-Saxon race, and it must be confessed that the thoughtless and horrible cruelty towards animals witnessed on all sides in the Neapolitan Riviera amounts to a serious drawback to the full enjoyment of its many beauties and amenities. Matters are improving a little of late, it is only fair to add.   There is an Italian Society for the Prevention of Cruelty to Animals, and its officials have done some good in the streets of Naples itself, but naturally its new ideas have not yet penetrated far into the country districts.

To the healthy and energetic the most delightful excursion that Castellamare can offer is the ascent to the summit of Monte Sant' Angelo, that monarch of the Bay of Naples, whose lofty crest gleams with snowy streaks until the spring be well advanced.   The lazy or the feeble can make use of one of the poor oppressed donkeys, but it is better to engage its ragged master, who without his four-footed drudge to whack and kick is a harmless enough being, to act as guide over the steep ill-defined pathway that leads ever upwards.   As we slowly ascend through the sub-tropical region of fig and vine, of olive and carouba, we question our guide, who in spite of his bright eyes and well-knit frame seems about as intelligent a companion as the poor ass left behind in the stall, where he is enjoying, let us hope, an unexpected holiday.   It is not easy to extract information from our native attendant, yet with a little judicious pressing we learn from him that the top of the mountain, which is our bourne, was once inhabited by evil spirits, until a holy hermit took up his abode on the peak, since when his sanctity has kept the place tolerably clear of witches and foul incubi.   Wicked sprites, however, still haunt the spreading woods of beech and chestnut which we must presently traverse, and our guide (whose name is Vincenzo) admits to us that he would not care to venture there alone, even in broad daylight.   There is, he tells us, warming up at

ROAD NEAR CASTELLAMARE

last to the subject, much gold hidden there, which the spirits guard so jealously that they are ready to tear in pieces any mortal who is clever enough to find and bold enough to rifle their secret hoards. Only a priest, on account of his sacred office, is reckoned safe from their iniquitous spells. "But has not any one dared," we ask, "to go in company with a holy man, to search for this hidden treasure?" Well, yes, he had been told that men from Vico had once ventured up into the woods to search for the gold. With a little encouragement Vincenzo is finally prevailed upon to give us the whole story, which is evidently of somewhat recent date.

Once upon a time there were four men, one of them being a priest, who lived in Vico, and one of these men had often been told by his father that in the forests near the top of Monte Sant' Angelo there lay buried a chest full of gold—*molto! molto!* The father of the man had been himself in his youth to search for the treasure, but find it he never could, for he would never take a priest with him to avert the spells of the evil spirits of the mountain sides, who kept the place hidden. So this time the man chose two out of his friends, the boldest and the trustiest he could fix upon, to accompany him, and at the same time he obtained the promise of a cousin, who was a priest, to assist in the undertaking. All four made their way up to the woods, and whilst the three men were digging and searching, the priest continued to read aloud the incantations out of a certain book he had brought with him for the purpose. In course of time the chest was discovered to the joy of all, and sure enough it was bulging with the desired gold pieces. They opened it without difficulty, and the four friends divided its contents in equal shares. Scarcely had the work of division been carried out, than there came a loud voice issuing from the unknown, calling out the question :— " *Che ferete con questo tesoro ?* " " *Mangeremo, beveremo !* " boldly replied one of the group, to whom this sudden accession of wealth offered dreams of unlimited platters of maccaroni and countless flasks of ruby-red Gragnano in the future. " We shall eat, we shall drink, but we shall also make abundant alms ! " called out another—let us hope it was the priest !—but no sooner had the word *elemosina* (alms) been uttered than there was heard a most terrific rattling of chains, the gold pieces turned to dead leaves in the affrighted mortals' hands, and the four men took to their heels and fled in alarm down the mountain flank.

Vincenzo believes this tale implicitly, just as it was related to him, and he adds to combat our own incredulity that the priest and one of the men who took part in this strange adventure were still living and ready to confirm the story, but that of the remaining two, one was now dead, and the other had been deaf and dumb ever since the event. It seem a pity to criticise Vincenzo's simple little narrative, which makes a pretty fairy-story and points a sound moral, as it stands.

We enter the fresh scented woods that have now replaced in our climb the rich cultivated crops and terraced gardens, and here amidst the clumps of ancient chestnuts our guide points out to us the great snow-pits, the contents of which are used to cool the water sold by the *acquaioli* during hot summer nights in the sultry streets of Naples. These pits are dug about fifty feet deep, and half as much across, being conical in shape with a grating placed a short distance above the tapering base to allow the melted snow to drain off into the soil. The sides of each pit are first well lined with straw and leafy branches, and the new-fallen snow shovelled in and forced into a solid mass by pressure from above, whilst on top is placed a sound thatched roof. As we wander through the silent woods we see patches of anemones, white and blue, lying upon the leaf-strewn ground, and beside them in many places are tufts of the pale starry prim-roses ; coarse spurge, and lush masses of the helle-bore with its large pale green flowers and dark leaves are common enough on all sides. From amongst the naked trees we emerge into the bare bleak stony stretches that lead to the summit, covered with the coarse but aromatic vegetation that clothes the dry limestone wastes of the south. How truly marvellous is the description of these wind-swept, weed-grown solitudes that Robert Browning presents to us in what is perhaps the most truly Italian in feeling of all his poems, " The Englishman in Italy ! " For here with the rich imagination, worthy of some of Shelley's finest flights, is mingled an accurate appreciation of Nature, of which Wordsworth might well be proud ; for the Lake poet himself could not have improved upon this exquisite description of the various shrubs and plants of a limestone hill-top in Italy.

> " The wild path grew wilder each instant,
>   And place was e'en grudged
> 'Mid the rock-chasms and piles of loose stones,
>   Like the loose broken teeth
> Of some monster which climbed there to die
>   From the ocean beneath—

c

Place was grudged to the silver-grey fume-weed
    That clung to the path,
And dark rosemary ever a-dying,
    That, spite the wind's wrath,
So loves the salt rock's face to seaward,
    And lentisks as staunch
To the stone where they root and bear berries,
    And . . . what shows a branch
Coral-coloured, transparent, with circlets
    Of pale sea-green leaves."

Above our heads hovers a kite, performing graceful circles in the keen clear air and breaking the oppressive silence of the place with his shrill screams, for his mate must have her nest hidden in some cleft of yon grey towering cliff. A pair of crested hoopoes with brown plumage and ruddy breasts keep fluttering a little way before us, uttering from time to time their curious notes of alarm. Mercifully these handsome birds have escaped the fowler, who lays his snares even amongst the spirit-haunted crags of this desolate region. The hoopoe, though a very rare visitor to our northern shores, is fairly common on the Mediterranean coast, and he would be still more frequently encountered, were it not for his hereditary enemy, Man. There is a venerable legend concerning this interesting bird — *bubbola*, the Italians call him — which relates how ages ago on the scorching plains of Palestine a number of hoopoes once followed King Solomon as he was riding, and in order to protect the great king from the fierce rays of the sun, they formed themselves into a living screen to shelter the royal head. Grateful for this welcome attention, Solomon Ben David at eventide sent for the king of the Hoopoes to ask him what reward he would like to receive for this service, and the answer was promptly made that a crown of pure gold on the head would be acceptable. The Jewish monarch smiled grimly as he granted the request, whereupon immediately each bird found his poll decorated with a tuft of pure golden feathers, and mightily pleased with their new magnificence were the conceited hoopoes. But alas! the news was quickly spread abroad that there were to be seen strange birds with plumes of real gold, and the eternal lust of gain at once set men in quest of the hoopoes, whom they began to slay wholesale with stones, arrows, and traps in order to obtain the coveted precious metal they bore on their heads. In despair, the king of the hoopoes then flew to the monarch sitting on his ivory throne at Jerusalem, and begged him to change their golden crowns for crests of feathers. Solomon the Wise smilingly gave the order ; at once lovely red and black feathers took the place of the golden plumes, and the slaughter of the hoopoes in Palestine forthwith ceased. And the story, argues the recorder of this lesson upon the folly of personal adornment, must of necessity be true, for it is certain that the hoopoes bear a crown of feathers upon their heads unto this day.

Slowly we toil up the last portion of the peak, until we reach the ruined chapel of St Michael upon its summit, which is still a resort of local pilgrims, although in these days of doubt and avarice, when "sins are so many and saints so few," the statue of the Archangel since its removal from this spot no longer perspires with the sacred dew, which the priests used to collect with cotton wool on the first day of August and distribute to the peasants of the district.

Like the oil that was once wont to exude from the blessed relics of St Andrew in the Cathedral of Amalfi, *non c'è più;* we may possess motor cars and radium, but we must contrive to exist without these precious exhibitions of the miraculous.

It would be sheer folly to attempt a full description of that glorious view, comprising the bays of Gaeta, Naples, and Salerno; of Vesuvius with his ascending smoky clouds; of the endless chain of the snow-tipped Abruzzi Mountains that bound the vision to the east; of the vast expanse of the Mediterranean, stretching in one unbroken sheet of turquoise to the west, varied by violet patches of reflected cloud, and studded by innumerable ships, from the vast liners to the tiny fishing craft with their glistening sails, like snow-white sea-swallows resting on the calm waters. Again we turn to Robert Browning, most human of poets and most kindly of philosophers, to find adequate expression for the thoughts we dare not, cannot utter.

> " Oh, heaven and the terrible crystal !
>   No rampart excludes
> Your eye from the life to be lived
>   In the blue solitudes.
> Oh, those mountains, their infinite movement !
>   Still moving with you ;
> For ever some new head and breast of them
>   Thrusts into view
> To observe the intruder ; you see it
>   If quickly you turn,
> And before they escape you surprise them.
>   They grudge you should learn
> How the soft plains they look on, lean over
>   And love (they pretend)
> —Cower beneath them, the flat sea-pine crouches,
>   The wild fruit-trees bend ;

MONTE FAITO, CASTELLAMARE

E'en the myrtle leaves curl, shrink and shut,
  All is silent and grave :
'Tis a sensual and timorous beauty.
  How fair ! but a slave."

We descend by the slopes of Monte Faito in the quiet of the evening, facing the distant headland of Posilipo and the sunset, where above the horizon we see collecting thick masses of dark purple cloud, which augur a stormy morrow. Above us the peak of the Archangel is already wreathed in garlands of white mist, a sure sign of coming tempest, and it is amid a lurid light from the sinking sun that we hasten downwards, bending our steps in the direction of Pozzano, where the form of its convent stands out sharply defined against the background of the Bay. Night is rapidly approaching, and in the gathering darkness as we strike the road below the convent, we can already hear the ominous roaring and seething of the waters under the cliff, lashed to fury by the first deep breaths of the coming squall. Hurrying along the broad smooth roadway it is not long before we reach our hotel door, where we bid good night to Vincenzo, just as the first heavy drops of rain have begun to fall ; pleasantly exhausted after our long excursion, we are ready to appreciate to the full the warmth and good cheer of the hospitable Hotel Quisisana.

CHAPTER III

LA CITTÀ MORTA

POMPEII can never be visited without the same
haunting conviction, the same oppressive thought:
how terribly difficult it is to understand the City of
the Dead which holds in so small a space the whole
secret of the antique world! There are far more
grandiose and impressive ruins to be seen in Rome;
the city of Timgad in Northern Africa is more complete as a specimen of a Roman settlement than the
half-excavated town near Vesuvius; yet here, and here
only, can the men of the past stretch hands, as it were,
across the barrier of eighteen intervening centuries to
the dweller of to-day, and the dead-and-gone spirits
of a highly organized civilization can whisper into the
living ears of the twentieth century. For Pompeii
will speak to us, if we will take the trouble to learn the
tongue in which alone she can convey the secret of
her story. It is needless to say that this language is
not obtainable by one or two cursory visits to the
Naples Museum, and a few hurried half-hours given to
the contents of the guide-book; no, the language of
Pompeii, which constitutes the key of access to the
hidden chambers of the Roman world, can only be
acquired with much expenditure of precious time and
with infinite trouble. But "life is short and time is

fleeting," and our bustling age expects to seize its required knowledge in the twinkling of an eye ; well, in that case the story of Pompeii must remain a sealed volume to the traveller, who is conveyed to the City of the Dead in a train crammed with fellow-tourists ; who eats a heavy unwholesome luncheon to the sound of mandoline-players twanging sprightly Neapolitan airs ; and who is finally piloted round the sacred area by a chattering guide in the oppressive heat and glare of a sunny afternoon. Fatigued in mind and body, such an one will sink with ill-concealed relief upon the dusty velvet cushions of the returning train, thoroughly disappointed in the vaunted marvels of Pompeii, which his imagination had led him to expect. A vague impression of low broken walls, of narrow—to his eyes absurdly narrow—streets, of broken columns and of peeling frescoes fills his tired brain, as he is borne back to his hotel in Naples. But this disenchantment is his own fault, for no one who sets foot within the Sea Gate of the buried city in the proper spirit of know-ledge and appreciation can possibly fail to enjoy the privilege which has thus been afforded him—

> "to stand within the City Disinterred ;
> And hear the autumnal leaves like light footfalls
> Of spirits passing through the streets ; and hear
> The Mountain's slumberous voice at intervals
> Thrill through those roofless halls."

Before passing through the Porta Marina into the purlieus of the city, let us first of all instil into our minds the essential difference that exists between the ruins of Pompeii and the historic fragments of Rome or Athens. When we gaze upon the well-known sites of the vanished glories of the Palatine or the Acropolis, we experience no effort in looking backward through the vista of the past and in conjuring up some vague representation of the scenes that were once enacted in these places ; the more imaginative feel the very air vibrating with the unseen spirits of men and women famous in the world's history.   He must be indeed a Philistine or a dullard who cannot contrive to arouse a passing exaltation at the thought of treading in the footsteps of Cicero and the Caesars in Rome, of Pericles and Socrates in Athens, for the very soil of the Forum and the stones of the citadel of Pallas seem impregnated with the very essence of history.   But this is far from being the case at Pompeii, where long careful study of details and a grasp of hard facts are really of more avail than a poetic imagination in reclothing with flesh the dry bones of the past, for the importance of the Campanian city is almost purely social.   The *names* of many of its prominent citizens are certainly familiar to us from inscriptions found, yet who were these persons that we should take so deep an interest in their lives and fates ?   Who were Pansa the ædile, Eumachia the priestess, Caecilius Jucundus, Aulus Vettius and Epidius Rufus, and a score of other Pompeian worthies ?   The answer is, they were officials or simple dwellers in a flourishing provincial town ; they had no especial literary or public reputation ; their names were probably little known beyond the walls of their own city.   Imagine an English country town, such as Exeter or Shrewsbury, suddenly overwhelmed by some unforeseen freak of Nature and afterwards embalmed in the manner of Pompeii as a curiosity for the edification of future ages.   To what extent, we ask, would the discovery of a place of this

size and population supply the existing dweller with
a complete impression of our national life and civilization in the opening years of the twentieth century?
The reply will be that it would give a very good idea
of the average provincial town, but that it would
hardly serve as a fair criterion to judge of the life
pursued in the capital, or in the really large cities.
Such a comparison will afford us a certain clue to the
unveiling of the mysteries of Pompeii.

For the city at the mouth of the Sarno was an
ancient Campanian settlement, founded long before the
days wherein Greek adventurers beached their triremes
on the shores of the Siren. It was a native community
of Oscans, deriving its name from the Oscan word
pompe (five), and, unlike Paestum, it appears to have
retained its original appellation under all its successive
masters. Its primitive inhabitants seem to have intermingled with their Hellenic victors, and to have grown
civilized by intercourse with them. Temples of heavy
Doric architecture were raised; walls and watch-towers
were built; and by the time the city fell into the
hands of the encroaching Romans, it had become a
flourishing place with some twenty to thirty thousand
inhabitants, owing its prosperity to its excellent situation at the mouth of the river, which made Pompeii a
convenient port to serve the rich district of Campania
that lies eastward of Vesuvius. Nuceria (the modern
Nocera) and the larger city of Nola were both dependent
on it, for the Sarno was in those days navigable, so that
ships bringing Egyptian corn and Eastern merchandise
frequently left the Pompeian harbour and sailed up
stream to unload their cargoes at these cities. Let us
picture then to ourselves a compact town, an irregular

oval in form, surrounded by walls pierced by eight gates and embellished with twelve towers ; its eastern extremity towards Nocera containing the Amphitheatre, and its most westerly point marked by the Herculaneum gate leading to the Street of Tombs.   Southward, we must imagine the sea much closer to its walls than at the present day, for the alluvial deposits have in the course of nearly two thousand years added many acres of solid ground to the shores of the Bay.   Behind the city to the north rose the mountain side, not seared with the traces of lava as in these days, nor surmounted by a smoking cone, but radiant with vineyards and gardens which extended unbroken up to the very rim of the ancient crater.   Amidst the greenery of the luxuriant slopes peeped forth innumerable farms and villas of wealthy Romans, for this exquisite spot had long become an abode of cultured leisure.   Within the closely packed streets of the town itself there were to be found few open spaces except the Forum, and perhaps a small park in front of the amphitheatre, for the place was prosperous, though not wealthy, and its chief citizens were forced to remain content with the tiny gardens enclosed within the walls of their own dwellings.

Internally Pompeii presented, like many another Roman town, marks of its six hundred years of existence.   There was at least one perfect Doric temple ; there were Oscan-Grecian buildings, notably the so-called "House of the Surgeon," with its air of old-fashioned simplicity ; there were houses of the Republican period ; there were numberless dwellings of the Imperial era ; there were unfinished structures that were being completed at the time of the city's overthrow. For, sixteen years before Vesuvius suddenly awoke from its long sleep, the neighbourhood had been visited by the severe earthquake shock of 63, and the effects produced by this disaster had not nearly been effaced, when the great event of 79 transformed the town into a huge museum for the delight and instruction of future generations. Pompeii therefore preserves the marks of more than half a thousand years of civilization, so that those who will take the necessary trouble can trace within its area the gradual progress of its social and political life from the far-off days of Greeks and Oscans to the reign of the Emperor Titus. The case of a ruined Exeter or Shrewsbury could not be widely different. The students of ensuing ages would be able to find in the dead town one or two churches of Norman or Plantagenet times ; portions of medieval city walls and gateways, perhaps even some undoubted traces of Roman baths or fortifications ; some few public buildings erected under Tudor or Stuart sovereigns ; a large number of the plain roomy mansions of the Georgian period ; and, last of all, a preponderating quantity of nineteenth century structures of every description—churches, warehouses, factories, inns, barracks, shops, dwelling-houses. Many would be the inscriptions and monuments we should find in such a town, alluding to private and public persons utterly unknown to English history, but more or less noteworthy in local annals : grandees of civic life, soldiers, philanthropists, clergymen, *et hoc genus omne*. Future generations of scholars would doubtless strive eagerly to obtain details of the careers of these provincial worthies, who filled municipal offices in the reigns of Queen Victoria and King Edward, in order to throw more light upon the period wherein they flourished. Let us apply then the same principles to the study of Pompeii *mutatis mutandis*, for in our quest of better knowledge of the old Roman life we fix anxiously upon every detail concerning the leading personages of the dead city. Nevertheless, it is its existence in the aggregate that proves of surpassing interest to us; we desire to learn of the daily tasks and occupations of the mass of its population, rather than to become acquainted with the private histories of its leading individuals; we study the former, in fact, only as a means to a definite end. We cry for information, which to a certain extent we can secure, as to how an average Roman city was administered, provisioned, drained; how its inhabitants passed their time both in leisure and in business; how they amused themselves in their homes and in the theatre; what they ate and what they drank—the endless trifles of human life, in short, which like the *tesseræ*, the tiny cubes of their own mosaic pavements, go to make up a complete picture out of a thousand fragments. Not a few of the cubes in this case are missing, it is true, nor are they ever likely to be found; nevertheless, we own an abundant supply wherewith we can piece together a tolerably accurate picture of the life of a Roman provincial city during the first century of the Christian era.

It is of course quite outside our province to attempt any detailed account of the wonders of Pompeii. The reader who desires full information must turn to the elaborate works of Mau and Helbig, of Gell and Overbeck, to say nothing of the descriptive pages, full of condensed knowledge, contained in Murray's and Baedeker's guide-books in order to obtain a clear impression of all he wishes to inspect. We can but dwell on a point here and there, and even then but lightly and superficially, for any endeavour on our part to add to the statements and theories of the great archaeologists already cited would be indeed a matter of supererogation and presumption.

Entering then by the Marine Gate, and pursuing our course eastwards along the lines of naked broken house-fronts, we reach the great rectangular space of the Forum. Here at its southern extremity let us select a shady corner, for the sun beats down fiercely upon the bare ruins at every season of the year, and even on a winter's afternoon the air often shimmers with the heat haze, so that in no place on earth is the use of an umbrella so necessary or desirable as at Pompeii.

What an ideal spot for the founding of a city! That is our first impression, as we glance across the broad sunlit enclosure on to the empurpled slopes of Vesuvius rising grandly above the broken columns of the great temple of the Capitoline Jove; behind us, we know, is the azure Bay with Capri and the Sorrentine cape lying on its unruffled bosom, so that we stand between sea and mountain to north and south, whilst we have the luxuriant slopes of Vesuvius to westward, and to the east the rich valley of the Sarno, thickly dotted with groves and hamlets. One element alone is wanting in the glorious scene before us— Life; it will be our duty and pleasure to re-invest as far as possible this empty space before us with the semblance of the busy crowds that once flitted in and out of its colonnades and porticoes; to rebuild in imagination its shapeless ruins, so that we may obtain a fleeting picture of the Pompeian Forum in early Imperial days.

Conceive, then, in front of us, instead of this long bare stretch flanked by broken walls and strewn with shapeless fragments of brick and stone, an immense double arcade, two stories in height, affording ample protection against sun or rain and enclosing an oblong pavement whereon are set numerous statues of emperors or private citizens, occupying lofty positions of honour above the heads of the surging throng below.   Imagine that group of shattered pillars, which obstructs our full view of the distant cone of Vesuvius, transformed into an imposing temple, covered with polychrome decoration, not in the best of taste according to our modern ideas of art, but gorgeous and cheerful in the clear atmosphere of the south.   Rebuild, in the mind's eye, the Basilica and the temple of Apollo on the left, and straight before us, as we look forward from our coign of vantage at the narrow southern end of the colonnade, let us plant the three dominant statues of Augustus, Claudius and Agrippina to form our foreground.   If we can construct by stress of fancy some such setting of classical architecture, gay with primary colours and gilding and graceful in design, it is easier to people the Pompeian Forum with the masses of humanity that once mingled here.   For we have the knowledge of modern Italian life to guide us to a certain extent ; we have seen the swarms of citizens who to-day fill the main piazzas of the towns, especially those of the provincial type, where the morning market is held and the chief cafés and shops are situated.   But if the general use

THE FORUM, POMPEII

of the piazza is characteristic of the modern second-
class Italian city, this concentration of life was far
more marked in the ancient Roman town, wherein
the Forum must have appeared as the very heart of
the whole body social and politic.   Roman city life
indeed displayed two strongly antagonistic phases :—
the utmost privacy in the home, the most public
exhibition in the Forum, where every trade and form
of business were carried on in the open air, and
whither pursuit of gain, or pleasure, or religious duty
led all the citizens to direct their steps.   For, as we
have already shown, almost all the public life of the
place was concentrated within this space and its
surroundings ; temples, markets, shops, law courts,
municipal offices, all abutted on the Forum ; it was
not merely the chief, but the only place that drew
together the daily crowd, bent alike on business or
amusement.   No chariots were permitted to cross the
area sacred to the claims of money-making, of gossip,
and of worship ; so that we must picture to ourselves
a great mass of people undisturbed by the passing of
vehicles, or by the shouts and whip-crackings of the
noisy charioteers—was ever such a thing as a quiet
Italian coachman, ancient or modern, we digress to
wonder!   All was orderly and decorous when compared with the quarrelling, screaming groups of
citizens that block the congested streets of modern
Naples.   Happily for us various paintings of the
Forum of Pompeii have been discovered, and these
are naturally of immense value in helping us to a
proper understanding of the habits and methods of
the people, and of the general appearance of the
Forum itself during its busiest hours.   The costumes

of men, women and children ; the articles of clothing
and of food ready for sale ; the little knots of loiterers
or gossips ; the citizens intent on reading the municipal
notices that are herein portrayed, all combine to
present us with an authentic picture of Pompeian and
therefore of Roman civic life.   " There is nothing new
under the sun," grumbled the Preacher many centuries
before the city under Vesuvius had reached its zenith
of civilization, and it must be confessed that the
general impression conveyed after studying the contemporary pictures of antique life does not differ very
widely from that which we obtain by observing present
Italian conditions.   For the frescoes in the Naples
Museum and in certain of the Pompeian houses seem
to recall strongly the scenes of the piazza, where all
the elements of society, irrespective of rank or station,
are still wont to congregate.   Differences of dress, of
manner, of custom are doubtless evident enough, yet
somehow we perceive an essential sameness in these
two representations of classical and modern Italy.
Nevertheless, these simple and often rude wall-
paintings furnish us with many pieces of information
that we search for in vain amidst the ancient authors,
who naturally considered the commonplace everyday
scenes of life beneath the notice of contemporary
record.   We are enabled to learn, for instance, how
the citizens were usually dressed in the Forum, and
how, in an age when hats and umbrellas were practically non-existent, the pointed hood, like that of the
Arab burnous, was often used to cover the head in
cold or wet weather.   Again, it is easy to perceive
from the same source that the diet of the Pompeians
must have resembled closely that of their present

descendants; even the shape of the loaves has in most cases continued unchanged to the present day. And one curious coincidence is certainly worth mentioning, in that a peculiar method of preparing figs with caraway seeds, which was long supposed to be a local speciality of a remote town in Central Italy, has now been recognized as a common method of dressing this fruit for the table at Pompeii, for large quantities of figs so treated have been unearthed in shops and kitchens. Such grains of information as the wearing of hoods and the preserving of figs may appear trifling enough at first sight, yet it is from a number of petty details such as these that we are assisted to an intimate understanding of a state of society extinct nearly two thousand years ago.

Close beside us on the eastern side of the Forum is set the Chalcidicum, the large building of the priestess Eumachia, one of the most gracious personalities of Pompeii with which the modern world has become acquainted. It was this lady who generously presented this structure, one of the handsomest and most solid of the public buildings of the city, to the fullers to serve as their exchange, wherein goods might be exposed upon benches and tables for the convenience alike of sellers and purchasers. "Priestess Eumachia," remarks a modern critic, "has done the thing well; no expense has been spared in the building and its decorations. The columns of the portico are of white marble; the statues of Piety and Concord, works of art; and the flower-borders along the panelled walls, prettily conceived and carefully executed. After so much plaster and stucco, it is a relief to see something so solid and genuine. When a third-rate city apes

D

the capital, there must needs be a certain amount of sham. But at Pompeii it is all sham, or next door to it. In the entire city are not more than half a dozen edifices whose columns are of real marble, the bas-reliefs and cornices of anything more solid than stucco ; and of these half-dozen, the Exchange heads the list."

We feel tolerably secure in assigning this fine building to the early years of the Emperor Tiberius, and in naming the Emperor's mother, Livia, as the divinity to whom it was dedicated. The statue of Concord with the golden horn of plenty doubtless once adorned the large pedestal which still stands in the eastern apse of the Exchange, but though the figure and emblem were those of Concordia, the face bore certainly the features of Imperial Livia. Yet more interesting than the various speculations as to the actual uses of this edifice and the different names of the statues which once embellished its alcoves, is the circumstance that the marble portrait of the foundress herself has been discovered. It is true that only a copy in plaster now occupies the pedestal at the back of the apse where Eumachia's statue once stood, for the original has been removed for safety to Naples, but it is not difficult to call to mind the calm gentle face of this Pompeian Lady Bountiful, and her graceful figure in its flowing robes. The existence of this statue adds undoubtedly a touch of special human interest to the whole building, and we find our minds excited by the brief inscription which still informs the curious that the fullers of Pompeii erected this portrait in marble in grateful appreciation " to Eumachia, a city - priestess, daughter of Lucius Eumachius."

Outside the Chalcidicum, at the corner of the lane usually termed Via dell' Abbondanza, is to be seen a pathetic little memorial of the working life of the city : the fountain of Concordia Augusta, the divinity of Eumachia's noble building hard by. Dusty and heating is the business of fulling cloth, and it generates thirst, so that it is but natural to find a fountain close at hand, whereat the labourers could refresh their parched throats. With what eagerness must the exhausted toilers during those long summers of centuries past have leaned forward to press their human lips to the cool mouth of the sculptured goddess that ejected with pleasing gurgles a volume of water into the basin below! That this fountain proved a boon to weary citizens is evident enough, for the features of water-spouting Concordia are half worn away by thirsty human kisses, and her suppliants' hands have left deep smooth furrows in the stonework of the basin, whereon they were wont to support their bodies, so as to direct the cooling draught into the dry and dusty gullet. In Italian cities to-day we can frequently observe some exhausted labourer bend deftly downwards to snatch a drink of water from the mouth of some fantastic figure in a public fountain. Who has not paused, for instance, beside Tacca's famous bronze boar in the Florentine market-place without noting an incident of this kind? If we ourselves are· too dainty to place our own aristocratic lips where our fellow-mortals have pressed theirs, not so are the abstemious descendants of the ancient Romans, the Italians, whose minds remain untroubled by any nasty-nice qualms of possible infection.

Here then is the setting of the picture, and we

must ourselves endeavour to repeople the empty
space with the crowds of high and low that once
collected here.

" It is high change, and the Forum is crowded.
All Pompeii is here, and his wife. *Patres conscripti*,
inclined to corpulence, taking their constitutional,
exquisites lazily sauntering up and down the pavements ; decurions discussing the affairs of the nation,
and the last news from Rome ; city magnates fussing,
merchants chaffering, clients petitioning, parasites
fawning, soldiers swaggering, and Belisarius begging
at the gate. . . . It is a bright and animated scene.
Beneath, the crowded Forum, with its colonnades and
statues, at one end a broad flight of steps leading
to the Temple of Jupiter, at the other a triumphal
arch ; on one side the Temple of Venus and the
Basilica ; on the other the Macellum, the Temple of
Mercury, the Chalcidicum ; overhead the deep blue
sky. Mingled with the hum of many voices and
the patter of feet on the travertine pavement are the
ringing sounds of the stonemasons' chisels and
hammers, for the Forum is undergoing a complete
restoration. Although fifteen years have elapsed
since the city was last visited by earthquake, the
damage then done to the public buildings has not
been entirely repaired. First the Gods, then the
people. The temples of Jupiter, Venus, and Mercury
are completed, but the Forum and Chalcidicum are
still in the workmen's hands." *

With this fleeting glimpse at the public life of the
city, let us now turn our attention to its domestic
arrangements. Of the many houses which have been

* W. J. A. Stamer : *Dolce Napoli.*

excavated of recent years under the truly admirable superintendence of Signor Fiorelli, none is better calculated to give us a striking impression of the working details of an upper-class Roman household than the private dwelling which is known equally under the two names of the Casa Nuova and the House of the Vettii ;—perhaps the former name has now ceased to own any significance, since the buildings were laid bare as far back as the winter of 1894-5.   An hour or two spent in a careful inspection of this house and its contents is to most persons worth four times the same amount of time occupied in aimless wandering amongst the hot glaring streets of the city, peeping into this courtyard and that, and listening to the interminable tales of guide or custodian.   If we study the Casa Nuova intelligently, lovingly and minutely, it will not be long before we obtain a tolerable grasp of Roman life and manners, which will prove of immense service and of genuine delight.   What then is it, the question will be asked, that makes the House of the Vettii so valuable as an example of antique architecture and decoration, in preference to other mansions which can boast an equal and often a greater distinction ?   The answer is simple enough : it is because this particular group of buildings has been allowed to remain as far as practicable in the exact condition wherein it was originally unearthed, when its various rooms and courts were once more exposed to the light of day. For until the clearing of this " new house " a decade or so ago, no proper opportunity had so far been afforded to the amateur of our own times of judging for himself the interior of a Roman dwelling in full working order, and with all its furniture, paintings, and utensils complete. Up to this, almost every object of value had been removed at once for safety, every fresco even of importance had been cut bodily out of its setting and placed in one of those immense halls on the ground floor of the Museum in Naples. How well do we remember those gaunt chilly chambers, filled from pavement to ceiling with painted fragments of all sizes, a medley of domestic subjects and of classical myths ! Torn from the walls they were specially executed to adorn, divorced from their proper scheme of surrounding ornament, these wan dejected ghosts stare at us like faces out of a mist. The uninitiated cannot find pleasure in them, for they have no pretention to be called works of art ; on the contrary they form an inherent part of a conventional system of house decoration. The classical student can of course find many points of interest in the incidents portrayed, but all charm of local environment is absent ;—it is, in short, impossible to judge of Roman decoration from this collection of crumbling, fading pieces of painted stucco. It would be as easy to imagine the effect of a rose-bush in full bloom from the sight of a few withered rose-buds, pressed until every vestige of colour had left their petals, as to understand the significance of antique domestic art from the contents of the Museo Nazionale.

But here, in the House of the Vettii, the public was for the first time initiated into the mysteries of true Roman life ; here it was admitted to gaze upon the fruits of classical taste and refinement, and to contrast them, favourably or unfavourably, with prevailing modern standards. The Casa Nuova has been left as an object lesson, a complete museum in itself, wherein every daily incident of Pompeian life, every domestic secret, reveal themselves to our inquisitive eyes. Here in the roofless halls we can be taken from entrance to dining-hall, from *atrium* to sleeping rooms, spying into the minutest detail of shape, size and colour, as though we were seriously intending to rent the house for our own habitation. The last tenant has even left his money-chest in his hall, his pots and pans in the kitchen, and as we inspect his utensils, we wonder if they would suit our own requirements to-day. Of portable objects of value—plate, jewels, statuettes of precious metals and the like—belonging to the late owner, there is certainly no trace, for Signor Fiorelli's labourers were not the first to break the deep silence of this buried mansion. For it was the survivors of the stricken town, the citizens of Pompeii themselves, who were the foremost pioneers to excavate, and they carried off every work of art they could conveniently remove. Cutting from above into the deposit of ashes that filled the streets, they managed to reach in course of time the level of the ground, after which they tunnelled from room to room, from house to house, collecting every object they thought worth the trouble of transporting. Perhaps the owners of the house, the Vettii themselves, presuming they escaped in the general castastrophe, may have returned with skilled workmen to recover some of their treasures ; perhaps some " man of three letters "—the colloquial Roman term for thief (*fur*)—may have forestalled the masters' efforts—who knows ?   And at this distance of time, who cares ?

The house once occupied by Aulus Vettius Restitutus and Aulus Vettius Corvina stands in a quiet district not far from the Capuan Gate, and consequently at some distance from the Forum. Like all Roman habitations it was essentially Oriental in its outward aspect, and must have resembled closely any one of those mysterious dwellings of wealthy Arab citizens which we constantly encounter in the native quarters of Algiers or Tunis. The gateway giving on the street was wide, certainly, but it was well defended both by human and canine porters ; its windows were few and small, and were probably closely latticed like those of the nunneries which we sometimes perceive overhead in the crowded streets of Naples. There must have been something austere, even suspicious, in the external appearance of the Casa de' Vettii, but snarling dog and grim janitor have long since disappeared, and we pass unmolested through the *atrium* and thence into the Great Peristyle, which is perhaps the most remarkable feature of this house. The peristyle, as its name implies, is a Greek importation in a Roman city, and its use would have been scorned by the old-fashioned citizens, such as the master of the " House of the Surgeon " ; yet it was in truth admirably suited to the character of Southern Italy, where it afforded shelter from sun and wind, and its arcades protected from the rainfall. The peristyle of the Vettii, with its gaudily tinted pillars of stucco, is highly ornate ; perhaps it passes the limits of good taste in certain points of colour and æsthetic decoration, yet the general effect is undoubtedly pleasing to the eye. This courtyard is at once a lounge open to the sky ; it is a garden ; it is an art-gallery ; for the cheerful court of Greek domestic architecture had nothing in common with its successor of the Middle

Ages, the monastic cloister of religious meditation. Cannot we imagine to ourselves the goodman of the house proudly leading his guests after a sumptuous meal in the adjacent dining-room into the cool corridors of his peristyle, in order to point out to them his statues and vases of bronze or porphyry, and to expatiate upon their value or elegance of form? On such a festive occasion these great shallow basins of pure white marble before us would be heaped high with fragrant pyramids of red and white roses, roses that were perhaps plucked all dewy in the famous gardens of Paestum on the other side of Mons Gaurus. For the flowering shrubs in the tiny pleasaunce itself are far too precious to be stripped of their blossoms in so lavish a manner, and perhaps if Vettius be anything of an amateur gardener, he may comment to his visitors upon the rare plants that fill his diminutive flower-beds. Careful and reverent hands have restored the little garden as near as possible to its pristine plan and appearance. There are still standing the two bronze statues of urchins holding in their chubby arms ducks from whose bills once gushed the limpid water, making a soothing sound amidst the alleys of the peristyle; corroded and injured they certainly appear, yet here they hold their original positions in Vettius' domain long after temple and tower have fallen to the ground. The marble chairs and tripod tables likewise remain, and around them still thrive the very plants that the servants of the house were wont to tend in the days of Titus. For, by a rare chance, we find depicted on the walls of the excavated house the actual flowers and herbs that were popular during Vettius' lifetime, and these have been replanted by modern hands in the garden of the peristyle. There are clumps of papyrus, the strange mop-headed rush from the banks of the Nile, introduced into Italy as. a botanical novelty after the conquest of Egypt ; there are rose-bushes, of course ; and also masses of shining ivy trained in the ancient Roman manner upon a cage of wicker-work fixed into the soil. As we watch the verdure-clad sunlit space there descends, delicately fluttering, one of those splendid pale yellow brimstone butterflies of the South with flame-coloured blushes on its wings, and after some moments of graceful hesitation, this new visitor settles upon the purple head of an iris bloom. With its vivid colouring and its quick movements the butterfly brings an atmosphere of life into the courtyard that was hitherto lacking. Its appearance too suggests the famous allegory, the unsolved riddle of human existence which so puzzled the divine Plato and the ancient philosophers of Athens and Syracuse. Here are we, the living men of to-day, watching the corpse of a departed world upon which the mystic symbol of Psyche has just alighted. *Tempus breve est* is the simple little truism that rises to our reflecting minds. Eighteen centuries between the Vettii and ourselves ! They are gone like a flash, and we are amazed to note how little has our nature altered either for the better or the worse within that space of time, long enough if we measure its limit by the standard of history, trivial if we reckon it by the progress made in human ethics and human understanding. Surely there are lessons to be learned in the silent city ; Pompeii, we realize, is not merely a heap of antique dross whence

LA CASA DEI VETTII, POMPEII

we can pick up precious grains of knowledge, but it is an oracle in itself, which, if properly consulted, will give us plain answers to our modern speculations, and will possibly reprove us for our conceited assumption of omniscience.

Still brilliant in their strong prevailing tints of black, yellow and vermilion are the decorative schemes which make a visit to the house of the Vettii of such supreme importance for those who wish to understand fully the artistic tastes of the Romans, and also their artistic limitations. If the contents of the Museum seem colourless and cold, and prove unsatisfying and disappointing, here the eye of the artist can feast upon the classical ornamentation which remains fairly fresh in spite of a dozen years of exposure to daylight. For this province of art is peculiarly associated with the opening years of the Empire, and Pompeii is naturally the chief place for its study, and in Pompeii the untouched Casa Nuova is all important for the student. According to Pliny, the inventor of this pleasing style of decoration was a certain Ludius, who flourished in the reign of Augustus, and first persuaded the Romans to embellish their flat wall-surfaces with designs of " villas and halls, artificial gardens, hedges, woods, hills, water basins, tombs, rivers, shores, in as great a variety as could be desired ; figures sitting at ease, mariners, and those who, riding upon donkeys or in waggons, look after their farms ; fishermen, snarers of birds, hunters and vine-dressers ; also swampy passages before beautiful villas, and women borne by men who stagger under their burdens, and other witty things of this nature ; finally, views of sea-ports, everything charming and suitable ":—a fairly long and comprehensive list of subjects, truly, from which a patron might pick and choose, or an artist might execute!

Although the great architect Vitruvius strongly denounced this new striving after scenic effect and characterized it as petty and false, yet none can deny that these cheerful scenes with their bright colours and their agreeable if trivial subjects were singularly well adapted to improve the appearance of the bare narrow rooms, the meagre proportions of which seem to us absolutely incompatible with plain comfort, to say nothing of luxury. Space may be increased, so far as the eye is concerned, by an architectural or landscape painting ingeniously conceived, and thus the restricted rooms seem to obtain by means of this new system of decoration a wider expansion, and with it an increased sense of ease and lightness. The invention of Ludius became at once the fashion, the rage; and all Rome began to cover the walls of its narrow chambers with these novel designs, which had already found favour in Imperial circles. Campania, where the old Greek love for polychrome still lingered, was not slow in imitating the new taste of the Capital, so that Pompeii bears undoubted testimony to the popularity of this revolution in artistic ideas, which substituted a lighter freer method for the old conventional severity of treatment. Experts profess to trace—and none will endeavour to gainsay them— a marked difference between the frescoes executed before the earthquake of 63 and those undertaken subsequent to that date. The wall paintings of the first group, carried out when the art was comparatively novel, are superior in harmony of colour, in choice of themes and in technical finish to those which belong to the latter period, the sixteen years that intervened between the earthquake and the eruption of Vesuvius. From this circumstance it has been inferred, not without reason, that this particular house must have passed some time before the year 63 out of the possession of people of good taste into the hands of vulgarians, ignorant of the fundamental principles of art and anxious only to obtain what was startling and garish. As freedmen, the two Vettii would naturally belong to a class which was not remarkable for culture; nevertheless, they seem to have had the good sense to leave intact some of their predecessor's most cherished works of decoration, and for this exhibition of restraint we must feel duly grateful towards our dead-and-gone hosts, the maligned Vettii.

But it is not only for purposes of examining Roman internal decoration *in situ* that this art gallery of the Casa Nuova is available. Below the painted panels of the dining-room runs a long string of ornament, whereon are represented Cupids and Psyches engaged in the various occupations of Pompeian daily life. Full of dainty grace and of lively expression, these little winged figures initiate us into a number of the trades and customs of the ancients. For they are made to appear before us as goldsmiths, vine-dressers, makers and sellers of olive oil, dealers in wine, fullers of cloth, and as partakers in a dozen other scenes of town or country life. Where learned antiquaries had hitherto doubted and disputed, the discovery of the paintings of these celestial little mechanics and merchants helped to solve many a difficulty, for the secret of half the arts and crafts of Pompeii is revealed to us in this playful guise. Nor are the designs themselves contemptible from an artistic point of view ; look how intent, for example, is the pose of the tiny jeweller working with a graver's tool upon the gold vessel before him ; how steadily he bears himself at a task which requires at once strength of hand and delicacy of workmanship. Look again at the nervous pose of the pretty elf who is gingerly pouring wine out of a huge amphora, which he holds in his arms, into a shallow tasting cup offered by a brother Cupid. How thoroughly must the unknown artist have enjoyed the task of painting this frieze ! How unfettered his fancy, as his brush glided smoothly and deftly over the carefully prepared wall-surface ! Excellent, no doubt, he thought his work at the time of execution, but even the most conceited of Campanian artists could hardly have dreamed that these creations of his brush would still at the end of two thousand years be admired, commented upon and even reproduced in thousands, by a process he never dreamed of, for the benefit of citizens of nations as yet unborn or unforeseen.

As the spring evening softly steals over the city and the shadows of the colonnades lengthen, let us leave the silent halls and chambers of the Casa dei Vettii and turn our footsteps westward ; and issuing out of the Gate of Herculaneum, let us traverse the famous Street of Tombs, that extends along the road leading to the sister buried city. In ancient times this was the Via Domitiana, a branch road of the Appian Way, and it formed the most frequented entrance into Pompeii. To Roman ideas, therefore, it was but natural that tombs should be erected alongside its borders, whilst the spirits of the passing and repassing crowds were in no wise affected by the memorials of death attending their exits and entrances. And with the surging human tide that was ever flowing in this thoroughfare the funeral processions must constantly have mingled, the wailing of the hired mourners rising sharply above the din of harsh voices, the creaking of clumsy wooden wheels and the braying of the heavily laden asses. Now over all reigns a decorous silence, such as we moderns deem fitting for a cemetery; only the hum of insects breaks the deep quiet of the atmosphere, nor are there any living creatures visible at this late hour save the bats which flit restlessly in and out of the weed-grown piles of brick or stone that once were stately monuments of wealth or piety. Above our heads the tall sombre cypresses shoot upward like gigantic spear-heads into the crystal-clear air, pointing heavenward like our own church spires in a rural English landscape. This Street of the Dead in the City of the Dead is in truth a solemn and a soothing spot; nor can we find its precincts melancholy, when we stand in the midst of such glorious scenery. For Monte Sant' Angelo towers to our left against the mellow evening sky, flecked with lines of peach-blossom cloud, whilst in front of us the dark form of Capri seems to float in a golden haze between firmament and ocean. Behind us the dark mass of the Mountain with its breath of ascending smoke seems like an eternal funeral pyre in honour of the Dead, who were spared the horrors of that fearful disaster which overwhelmed the living. Upon the broken tombs and altars the light from the setting sun falls with warm cheerful radiance, flushing

stone and brick-work with a ruddy glow like jasper;
whilst, high in the heavens above the cypress tops,
the crescent moon prepares to turn to gold from
silver.

Beati sunt mortui : here rest, we know, the priestess
Mammia, the decemvir Aricius, Libella the aedile, and
a host of other citizens with whose names the student
or the lover of Pompeii is familiar. How many a
time has this line of roadway rung with the sound of
the last sad appeal, the thrice repeated valediction :
" *Vale, vale, vale!* farewell until the day when Nature
will allow us to follow thee!" How often have the
wooden pyres flung up in these precincts their clouds
of perfumed smoke into the clear air, now redolent
with the aroma of yellow broom, of dewy thyme and
of sweet marigolds! Perhaps it was amidst these
lines of cypress-set tombs by the Herculaneum Gate
that the poetic genius, whose verses were spurned by
his own generation, composed his famous Ode to
Naples, for in its opening lines Shelley tells us it was
the aspect of the " city disinterred " that gave him
inspiration :—

"Around me gleamed many a bright sepulchre
Of whose pure beauty, Time, as if his pleasure
Were to spare Death, had never made erasure ;
    But every living lineament was clear
    As in the sculptor's thought ; and there
The wreaths of stony myrtle, ivy and pine,
Like winter-leaves o'ergrown by moulded snow,
Seemed only not to move and grow,
Because the crystal silence of the air
Weighed on their life. . . ."

Tranquilly and slowly descends night upon the
untenanted city, as one by one the stars begin to peep

forth like chrysolites in the heavens, which have changed from azure to a deep indigo during the sunset hour. Amid chilly dews, to the sound of the evening bell from the distant church of Santa Maria di Pompeii, we hasten in the growing darkness from the Street of the Tombs towards our modest inn outside the Marine Gate, anticipating with delight a ramble in the city in the freshness of the coming morning.

E

CHAPTER IV

VESUVIUS: THE STORY OF THE MOUNTAIN

THE first appearance of Vesuvius, whether viewed from the deck of a steamer entering the Bay of Naples or espied from the window of a railway carriage on the main line running southward from Rome, makes an impression that will linger for ever in the memory. It is open to argument which is the more striking of the two experiences: the Mountain rising proudly from the deep blue waters into the paler shade of the upper air, or its graceful broken contour seen from the landward side to the north across the green fertile plains of the Campagna Felice. From a long acquaintance with both ways of approaching Naples, we are inclined to prefer the latter view. Travelling in an express train from Rome we find ourselves whirled suddenly, by magic as it were, into the atmosphere of the South, when with the sight of the domes and towers of Capua, the ancient capital of Campania the Prosperous, we first note the presence of orange trees and hedges of aloe, of white lupin crops and clumps of prickly pear, and we feel we are nearing Naples with "its burning mountain and its tideless sea," so that we eagerly strain our eyes in a southerly direction to catch our first glimpse of Vesuvius, with whose shape and history we have been so familiar since our childhood's days. At length we perceive its double summit, with smoke tranquilly issuing from the cone and obscuring the clarity of the air, and as we hurry forward towards our destination, through the plains studded with elm-trees festooned with vines, we have the satisfaction of observing its form grow larger and more distinct in outline.

On our arrival at Naples, in course of time we grow more intimately acquainted with the peculiar attractions of "the Mountain," as the Neapolitans always designate their treacherous but fascinating neighbour, of whose near existence they have every reason to be proud, for certainly Vesuvius, though barely as lofty as Ben Nevis, *is* to us westerns the most famous mountain upon earth. Regarding Vesuvius both from the land and the sea, we note that it rises in solitary majesty from an extended base some thirty miles in circumference, and that it sweeps upwards in graceful curving lines until at a distance of about 3000 feet from sea level its summit is cleft into two peaks; that to the north being a rocky ridge which catches our eye as we gaze eastward from the heights of Sant' Elmo or the Corso at Naples, the other point being the actual cone of the volcano itself. The upper part of the Mountain has in fact two aspects; in other words, Vesuvius is double, being composed of the ridge of Monte Somma to the north, 3760 feet in height, which is pre-historic; and the ever-shifting modern dome of Vesuvius to the south, which is *about* 4000 feet high. We say "about" purposely, for Vesuvius proper sometimes over-tops, sometimes equals, and sometimes even crouches under its immovable sister-peak, according to the effect produced by volcanic action. Monte Somma, which is one of the everlasting hills, is the parent, and Vesuvius is the child, born but yesterday from a geological point of view, for it is not so old as the Christian era ;—" it is a variable heap thrown up from time to time, and again, not seldom, by a greater effort of the same force, tossed away into the air, and scattered in clouds of dust over far-away countries. Thus it has happened often, in the course of these variations of energy, that Vesuvius has risen to a conical height exceeding that of Somma by 500 or 600 feet, and again, the top has been truncated to a level as low as Somma, or even as much below that mountain as we now behold it above." *

To understand the story of the Mountain, therefore, it is necessary for us to travel back in retrospect to ancient Roman days. In the first place, however, one word as to its present name that we use to-day, for all are familiar with Vesuvius, but comparatively few, until they visit Naples, have heard mention made of Monte Somma. The name of Vesuvius, then, though strictly applicable only to the volcanic and modern portion of the Mountain, is not a recent appellation ; on the contrary, it is probably of far more ancient origin than *Mons Summanus* by which the whole was known to the Romans. The point is by no means unimportant, for etymologists derive Vesuvius from the Syriac " Vo Seevev, the abode of flame," thereby proving to us that whatever opinions may have been held as to the nature of the Mountain in the century preceding the Christian era, its volcanic

* Professor John Phillips : *Vesuvius.*

nature must have been perfectly well understood
by those who gave it this suggestive title in a more
remote age. But the secret locked up in Mons
Summanus was not altogether unsuspected by the
Roman scientists. Strabo, the geographer, writing
about thirty years before the birth of Christ, made a
careful examination of the crest of Mons Summanus,
then a saucer-shaped hollow surrounded by a steep
rocky edge and occupied by a flat plain covered with
cinders and void of grass, although the flanks of
the Mountain were extraordinarily fertile. From what
he saw during his visit, Strabo conjectured the
Mountain to be an extinct volcano, in which surmise
he was destined to be proved partly in the right and
partly in the wrong ; whilst Vitruvius, the famous
architect of the Emperor Augustus, "who found Rome
of brick and left it of marble," as well as Tacitus the
historian, shared the same opinion. About a century
and a half before the first recorded eruption in 79,
Mons Summanus figures prominently in Roman
history as the scene of a curious incident during
the Servile War, so that in the pages of the old
chronicler Florus we obtain an interesting description
—especially interesting because it was not given for
scientific purposes—of the condition of the mountain
top at that period. The brave gladiator Spartacus
and his intrepid band of revolted slaves, seeking
a place of safety from the pursuing Roman legions,
not very wisely selected the top of this isolated peak,
which, although affording a good position of defence
and possessing a wide outlook over the Campanian
plain, had only one narrow passage in its rocky rim
to serve as entrance or outlet. Followed hither by the

Roman forces and caught like rats in a trap, Spartacus and his men were doomed either to be reduced by starvation, or else to run the gauntlet of the sole narrow exit, which the Senate's commander, Clodius Glabrus, was already guarding. The story of Spartacus' escape from his terrible dilemma is told in the history of Florus, and repeated with further details by Plutarch in his Life of Crassus.

"Clodius the Prætor, with three thousand men, besieged them in a mountain, having but one narrow and difficult passage, which Clodius kept guarded ; all the rest was encompassed with broken and slippery precipices, but upon the top grew a great many wild vines : they cast down as many of these boughs as they had need of, and twisted them into ladders long enough to reach from thence to the bottom, by which, without any danger, all got down save one, who stayed behind to throw them their arms, after which he saved himself with the rest."

A dozen learned statements of a scientific nature as to the ancient appearance and slumbering condition of the Mountain could not impress our imagination more vividly with its subsequent natural changes than the account of this episode of Spartacus and his handful of rebels, beleaguered by Clodius within the very crater of the volcano. We can see the Mountain in the last years of the Roman Republic before us, with its truncated cone encircled by a low rampart of rock half hidden by wild vine, ivy, eglantine, honeysuckle and all the creeping plants whose tough trailing stems enabled the besieged gladiators to effect their escape from the snare into which they had unwittingly fallen. We can understand from this event

how utterly remote was the idea of any upheaval of
nature to the dwellers on these shores, whose ancestors
remembered the crest of the mountain as the scene of
a military operation.

The first warning of a coming eruption after
unnumbered centuries of quiet was given by a series
of earthquakes which did an immense amount of
damage at Herculaneum and Pompeii; yet in a
district which had from time immemorial been subject
to similar convulsions of nature, the shocks, though
unusually distressing and destructive to life and
property, were evidently unconnected in the popular
mind with their true cause: the reawakening to life
of the mountain overhead. The mischief done by the
earthquakes was accordingly repaired as quickly as
possible, and the normal course of life was resumed
until the terrific and wholly unexpected outbreak of
August 24th 79, during the reign of the Emperor
Titus. Of this, the first recorded eruption of Vesuvius,
we are exceptionally fortunate in possessing the
testimony of a credible eye-witness, who was no less
a personage than Caius Plinius Caecilius Secundus,
better known to the modern world as Pliny the
Younger, who wrote two lengthy letters to Tacitus
on the subject of this event, the first describing the
fate of his uncle, the Elder Pliny, most eminent of
Roman naturalists, who perished during this period of
terror; and the second containing a more detailed
account of the eruption itself. For it so happened—
luckily for posterity—that at the time of this sudden
outburst of Mons Summanus, the Elder Pliny was in
command of the Roman fleet at Misenum on the Bay
of Naples, where his young nephew (who was also his

adopted son) was living with his mother in a villa. "On the 24th of August," writes Pliny the Younger some eleven years after the event he is about to describe, "about one in the afternoon, my mother desired my uncle to observe a cloud which appeared of a very unusual size and shape. He had just returned from taking the benefit of the sun, and after bathing himself in cold water, and taking a slight repast, was retired to his study. He immediately arose and went out upon an eminence, from whence he might more distinctly view this very uncommon appearance. It was not at that distance discernible from what mountain this cloud issued, but it was found afterwards to ascend from Mount Vesuvius. I cannot give a more exact description of its figure than by resembling it to that of a pine-tree, for it shot up to a great height in the form of a trunk, which extended itself on the top into a sort of branches, occasioned, I imagine, either by a sudden gust of air that impelled it, the force of which decreased as it advanced upwards, or the cloud itself being pressed back again by its own weight, expanded in this manner ; it appeared sometimes bright, and sometimes dark and spotted, as it was more or less impregnated with earth and cinders. This extraordinary phenomenon excited my uncle's philosophical curiosity to take a nearer view of it." The nephew then proceeds to relate how his uncle sailed by way of Retina, the port of Herculaneum, to Stabiae, where he met with his second in command, one Pomponianus. Meanwhile the Younger Pliny, who had declined to accompany his uncle's expedition on the plea of having to pursue the studies with which as a hard-working youth of seventeen he was evidently engrossed, became alarmed during the night for the Elder Pliny's safety. His own and his mother's terrible experiences are vividly portrayed in the second letter, which, at the historian's special request, the Younger Pliny wrote to Tacitus in later years.

"When my uncle had started, I spent such time as was left on my studies—it was on their account, indeed, that I had stopped behind. Then followed the bath, dinner and sleep, this last disturbed and brief. There had been noticed for many days before a trembling of the earth, which had caused, however, but little fear, because it is not unusual in Campania. But that night it was so violent, that one thought everything was being not merely moved, but absolutely overturned. My mother rushed into my chamber; I was in the act of rising, with the same intention of awaking her, should she have been asleep. We sat down in the open court of the house, which occupied a small space between the buildings and the sea. And now—I do not know whether to call it courage or folly, for I was but in my eighteenth year—I called for a volume of Livy, read it as if I were perfectly at leisure, and even continued to make some extracts which I had begun. Just then arrived a friend of my uncle, who had lately come to him from Spain; when he saw that we were sitting down—that I was even reading—he rebuked my mother for her patience, and me for my blindness to the danger. Still I bent myself as industriously as ever over my book. It was now seven o'clock in the morning, but the daylight was still faint and doubtful. The surrounding buildings were now so shattered, that in the place where we were, which though open was small, the danger that

they might fall on us was imminent and unmistakable.
So we at last determined to quit the town. A panic-
stricken crowd followed us. . . . We saw the sea retire
into itself, seeming, as it were, to be driven back by
the trembling movement of the earth. The shore had
distinctly advanced, and many marine animals were
left high and dry upon the sands. Behind us was a
dark and dreadful cloud, which, as it was broken with
rapid zig-zag flashes, revealed behind it variously shaped
masses of flame ; these last were like sheet lightning,
though on a larger scale. . . . It was not long before
the cloud that we saw began to descend upon the
earth and cover the sea. It had already surrounded
and concealed the island of Capreae, and had made
invisible the promontory of Misenum. My mother
besought, urged, even commanded me to fly as best I
could ; ' I might do so,' she said, ' for I was young ;
she, from age and corpulence, could move but slowly,
but would be content to die, if she did not bring death
upon me.' I replied that I would not seek safety
except in her company ; I clasped her hand and
compelled her to go with me. She reluctantly obeyed,
but continually reproached herself for delaying me.
Ashes now began to fall—still, however, in small
quantities. I looked behind me ; a dense dark mist
seemed to be following us, spreading itself over the
country like a cloud. ' Let us turn out of the way,'
I said, ' whilst we can still see, for fear that, should we
fall in the road, we should be trodden under foot in
the darkness by the throngs that accompany us.' We
had scarcely sat down when night was upon us,—not
such as we have seen when there is no moon, or when
the sky is cloudy, but such as there is in some closed

room where the lights are extinguished. You might hear the shrieks of women, the monotonous wailing of children, the shouts of men. Many were raising their voices, and seeking to recognise by the voices that replied, parents, children, husbands or wives. Some were loudly lamenting their own fate, others the fate of those dear to them. Some even prayed for death, in their fear of what they prayed for. Many lifted their hands in prayer to the gods; more were convinced that there were now no gods at all, and that the final endless night of which we have heard had come upon the world. . . . It now grew somewhat light again; we felt sure that this was not the light of day, but a proof that fire was approaching us. Fire there was, but it stopped at a considerable distance from us; then came darkness again, and a thick, heavy fall of ashes. Again and again we stood up and shook them off; otherwise, we should have been covered by them, and even crushed by the weight. At last the black mist I had spoken of seemed to shade off into smoke or cloud, and broke away. Then came genuine daylight, and the sun shone out with a lurid light, such as it is wont to have in an eclipse. Our eyes, which had not yet recovered from the effects of fear, saw everything changed, everything covered deep with ashes as if with snow. We returned to Misenum, and after refreshing ourselves as best we could, spent a night of anxiety in mingled hope and fear. Fear, however, was still the stronger feeling; for the trembling of the earth continued, while many frenzied persons, with their terrific predictions, gave an exaggeration that was even ludicrous to the calamities of themselves and of their friends. Even then, in spite of all the perils which we had experienced, and which we still expected, we had not a thought of going away till we could hear news of my uncle." *

As to the fate of the Elder Pliny, it seems that the old man had been obliged together with his friends and servants to fly from the villa at Stabiae where he was resting. The sea being too agitated to allow of an embarkation, the fugitives turned their steps towards the slopes of Mons Gaurus, the present Monte Sant' Angelo, with pillows bound over their heads to serve as protection against the showers of hot cinders that were falling thickly on all sides. At length the famous old writer, who was somewhat plethoric and unwieldy, sank exhausted to the ground, never to rise again, and shortly expired in an attack of heart failure, induced by the unusual excitement and fatigue he had lately been called upon to endure. At any rate, it appears fairly certain that the Elder Pliny did not perish, as is still sometimes asserted, by the direct effects of the eruption, but rather through an ordinary collapse of nature—syncope, perhaps. Three days later his body was found lying not far from Stabiae by his grief-stricken nephew, who describes his uncle's corpse as looking " more like that of a sleeping than of a dead man."

This then was the first, as it was also the most violent, of the many outbreaks of Vesuvius which our own age has witnessed, and with this eruption of 79 in the reign of Titus, the Mountain, as we have already said, greatly altered its shape. More than half the rim of the ancient crater that had enclosed Spartacus and his men less than two hundred

* Pliny's Letters. (*Church's and Brodribb's Translation.*)

years before had been torn away and destroyed, its remaining portion on the landward side retaining the old name of Mons Summanus.   Between this remnant of the old wall of the crater and the scene of wreckage on the southern face of the Mountain, there now appeared the great cleft, the horse-shoe shaped valley called the Atrio del Cavallo, which separates the two peaks of the whole summit.   A fragment only of the original crater, known as the Pedimentina, still remains on the seaward side above Torre del Greco. From that terrible day, so vividly described by the Younger Pliny, to our own times, a period stretching over 1800 years, a vast number of eruptions, great and small, have been enumerated, for owing to the nearness of Vesuvius to one of the largest cities in Europe, every incident connected with its activity has been carefully noted, at least since the time of the Renaissance.   Out of the many upheavals we propose to select the eruptions of 1631 and 1779, as being amongst the most significant.

Ever since an outburst in the year 1500, the Mountain appears to have lapsed into a remarkable condition of quietude, even of apparent extinction, for over a century and a quarter, during which period, it may be remarked, the Sicilian volcano of Etna was unusually active.   Once more the summit of Vesuvius was beginning to assume the form it had borne in the days previous to the overthrow of Pompeii ; the riven crater was becoming filled with dense undergrowth and even with forest trees, amidst which wild boar made their lairs and were occasionally hunted.   The learned Abate Giulio Braccini, whose account of the eruption of 1631 is the most graphic

and accurate we possess, explored the crater shortly
before the outbreak of the volcano, but found little
to suggest any idea of an approaching convulsion.
He reckoned the deep depression occupying the crest
of the mountain to be about five miles in circumference, and to take about a thousand paces of walking
so as to reach the lowest point within its area.   He
remarked abundance of brushwood on its sides, and
observed cattle grazing peacefully upon the open
grassy patches in the midst of the over-grown space.
A deep crack, however, ran from end to end of the
whole crater, which allowed persons so minded to
descend amidst rocks and boulders to a large plain
below the surface, whereon Braccini found three pools
of hot steamy water, of a saline and sulphureous
taste.   Such was the tranquil aspect of the Mountain
as surveyed by the Abate Braccini in the first half
of the seventeenth century ; to men of science signs
of latent energy were certainly not wanting, yet to
the ignorant, careless peasants of the hill-side and the
scarcely less ignorant dwellers of the towns on the
seashore, the state of repose in which the Mountain
had continued for four or five generations suggested
no fears or suspicions.   Tilling of vineyards, building
of new houses, sinking of wells, went on apace as
cheerfully as though an eruption were an impossibility,
till certain unmistakable portents that occurred
towards the close of the year 1631 roughly dissipated this spell of fancied security.   Earthquakes,
more or less severe, began at this time to be felt
along the whole of the volcanic line stretching from
Ischia to the eastern slopes of Vesuvius ; the plain
within the crater of the Mountain began to heave

and rise in an alarming fashion, and the water in all
the local wells sank mysteriously below ground.
The signs of some impending disaster coming from
the heights above were too strongly marked to be
lightly disregarded ; the idea of a volcanic convulsion,
though by this time a long-distant and vague memory,
became so terrifying to the dwellers on the mountain's
flanks and in Torre del Greco, Resina and the various
towns that line the seaward base of the Mountain,
that the majority of the people removed themselves
and their property with all speed to places of safety.
Nevertheless, despite the warnings given by Nature
and also by men of science and the royal officials,
many remained behind in their houses, and in consequence perished, to the immense number, it is surmised,
of 18,000.   On the morning of Wednesday, December
16th, the long threatened eruption burst forth in
earnest upon an expectant world. Amidst crashes
like prolonged volleys of artillery the people of
Naples and the surrounding district beheld the terrible
pine-tree of smoke and ashes, described centuries ago
by Pliny, ascend from the south-western side of the
summit of the Mountain, veiling the sky for miles
around, and so charged with electricity, that many
were even killed by the *ferilli*, or lightning flashes,
that darted from the smoking mass. The spectacle
of the ominous pine-tree was at once followed by a
terrific rumbling and an ejection of lava, which after
flowing down the southern flank in several streams
finally reached the sea, making the waters hiss and
boil at the moment of contact. Slowly but surely
these relentless red-hot rivers of lava crept like
serpents along the hill-side, destroying vineyard and

garden, cottage and chapel, on their downward path. Resina shared the fate of its ancient forerunner Herculaneum, whilst Torre del Greco and Portici suffered severely, as we can see to-day by noting the great masses of lava flung on to the strand at various points. To add to the universal confusion of Nature, the sea, which had now become extraordinarily tempestuous, probably owing to some submarine earthquake-shock, suddenly retreated half a mile from the coast, and then as suddenly returned in a tidal wave more than a hundred feet beyond its normal limits. Such were the main features of the second great eruption of Vesuvius, wherein the ashes ejected by the Mountain were wafted by the wind beyond the Adriatic, to the Greek islands and even to Constantinople itself.

From this date onward the Mountain became very active in contrast with its previous condition of lethargy, and throughout the whole of the eighteenth century there were frequent eruptions, many of them on a vast scale. All these outbursts have been carefully recorded and commented upon, for naturally the scientists of a great city like Naples were intensely interested in the passing phases of their own volcano. During the latter half of this century all the phenomena have been described for us by Sir William Hamilton, British ambassador at the Court of the Two Sicilies, the versatile diplomatist who eventually married the beautiful but frail Emma Hart. During his long period of residence in Naples, Sir William made no fewer than fifty-eight explorations of the crater alone, besides carefully studying every peculiarity visible upon the sides of the Mountain. He was,

of course, a close observer of the great eruptions of 1766-7, and also of the still greater convulsion of 1779, which, strangely enough, occurred on the seventeenth centenary of the awakening of the Mountain from its pre-historic slumbers. On this occasion, Hamilton, accompanied by a Mr Bowdler of Bath, had the temerity to track the streams of flowing lava to their hidden source by walking over the rough unyielding crust of stones and earth that had formed upon the surface of the molten stream, as it slowly trickled down hill at the rate of about a mile an hour. The adventurous pair of Englishmen were successful in their quest, and Sir William thus describes the fountain-head of the fiery streams that he found a quarter of a mile distant from the top of the cone.

" The liquid and red-hot matter bubbled up violently, with a hissing and crackling noise, like that which attends the playing off of an artificial firework ; and by the continued splashing up of the vitrified matter, a kind of arch, or dome, was formed over the crevice from whence the lava issued ; it was cracked in many parts, and appeared red-hot within, like a heated oven. This hollowed hillock might be about fifteen feet high, and the lava that ran from under it was received into a regular channel, raised upon a sort of wall of scoriæ and cinders, almost perpendicularly, of about a height of eight or ten feet, resembling much an ancient aqueduct."

Some days later, at midnight on August 7th, a veritable fountain of red fire shot up from the crest of Vesuvius, illuminating all the surrounding country; and on the following night a still more marvellous sheet of flame appeared, hanging like a fiery veil

F

between heaven and earth, and reaching to a height (so Sir William Hamilton guessed) of about 10,000 feet above the summit, affording a wonderfully grand but terrible spectacle.   This great curtain of fiery particles, accompanied by inky black clouds from which were darting continual flashes of lightning, was reflected clearly on the smooth surface of the Bay, delighting the Court and the scientific world of Naples, but inspiring, as may well be imagined, the mass of superstitious inhabitants with the direst alarm. The theatres were closed and the churches were opened ; above the rumblings and explosions of the agonised volcano could be heard the tolling of the bells.   Maddened by terror, the Neapolitan mob rushed to the Archbishop's palace to demand the immediate production of the holy relics of St Januarius, the protector of the city, and on this request being refused, set fire to the entrance gates, a forcible argument that soon persuaded his Eminence of the propriety of the people's demand.   Thereupon the head of the Saint, enclosed in its case of solid silver, was accordingly borne in solemn procession with wailing and repentant crowds behind it to an im- provised shrine, hung with garlands, on the Ponte della Maddalena, at the extreme eastern boundary of the city.   Nor was the confidence reposed by the Neapolitans in their patron Saint misplaced, for except from the stifling smells and the dense rain of ashes, the terror-stricken capital suffered not a whit, whilst the general alarm inspired its inhabitants with a revival of religious fervour which was by no means insalutary.   As usual, the old cynical proverb was once more justified :—*Napoli fa gli peccati, e la*

Torre gli paga, for of course poor Torre del Greco was grievously affected by the lava streams. In this case, however, even Torre del Greco and Resina did not fare so badly as did the towns on the northern slopes of Monte Somma, a district which is of course perfectly immune from lava inundations owing to the protecting rocky ridge of the Atrio del Cavallo. But it seems that the great veil of clouds and fire, extending some thousands of feet from the crest of the mountain to the heavens above, was swayed by a chance current of air, so that its component red-hot dust, ashes and stones were emptied in one fatal shower upon the northern flank of the Mountain. Whole villages were ruined, hundreds of acres of vines and crops were scorched and burned ; the smiling peaceful hillside was in a few minutes converted into a parched wilderness. Ottajano, a large town of some 12,000 inhabitants, was the place most seriously injured by this wholly unexpected rain of destruction, for a tempestuous fall of red-hot stones, some of immense size, and a shower of ashes killed hundreds of the terrified and suffocating citizens, and blocked up the streets with smoking débris to a depth of four feet.

Of the recent eruptions of Vesuvius, which have been pretty frequent during the latter half of last century, that of April 1872, so carefully recorded by Professor Palmieri, who in spite of imminent danger never abandoned his post in the Observatory, is the most notable. It is remembered also owing to the catastrophe whereby some twenty persons out of a large crowd of strangers, who had imprudently ascended to the Atrio del Cavallo to get a closer

view of the phenomenon, were suddenly caught by the
lava stream and enfolded in its burning clutches.
For if ignorance and superstition seem to make the
poor fisherman or peasant unduly alarmed on such
occasions, curiosity and self-confidence are sometimes
apt to lead the educated or scientific into unnecessary
peril.   Naples itself was once more alarmed in 1872,
so that the relics of St Januarius at the furious
demand of the populace were again brought forth in
solemn procession, and exposed towards the face
of the Mountain on the Ponte della Maddalena.
Thousands of quaking mortals gathered near this
spot, joining in the chanting of the priests and
watching with pallid anxious faces the fiery currents
of lava slowly trickling down the south-western flank
of Vesuvius towards the city itself.   A certain number
of attendants meanwhile were engaged in perpetually
brushing away from the image of the Saint, from his
improvised altar, and from its votive garlands the
ever-accumulating mantle of grey dust, and it is
scarcely to be wondered at that a certain cool-headed
Neapolitan artist, Il Vaccaro, should all this time
have been busily engaged in painting so characteristic
and highly picturesque a scene.   Within the churches,
and particularly in St Januarius' own cathedral,
enormous crowds of hysterical men and women had
collected, loudly bewailing their past sins and implor-
ing the Divine mercy, for

> " E belle son le supplice
> Pompe di penitenza, in alto lutto."

Again the historic *palladium* proved effectual, and
the city, that was never for a moment in danger, was

once more saved! Naples received no damage
beyond a temporary panic and a heavy fall of ashes,
which covered every street and flat surface within the
town to a depth of some inches and which it took
many days of enforced labour to remove. Again
it was the poor confiding vine-dressers and tillers of
the Vesuvian soil who suffered in this upheaval, for
though the loss of life was very slight indeed, yet
numerous houses, fields and vineyards were totally
destroyed and many more were injured. Truly it is
a maxim well proven by time :—*Napoli fa gli peccati,
e Torre gli paga.*

Such, told baldly and briefly, is the history of the
Mountain, which forms the most conspicuous feature
of the Bay of Naples and dominates one of the
fairest and most populous districts on the face of the
globe. But it does not take long to make visitors
to the Neapolitan shore understand the mysterious
charm, not unmixed with awe, and the all-pervading
influence of Vesuvius. Go where we will within the
circuit of the Bay of Naples and even outside it, we
are never out of sight of the obtruding Mountain
and its smoky wreath. We begin to feel that the
Mountain is an animated thing, that the destiny of
the Parthenopean shore is locked up in the breast of
the Demon who has his dwelling within its red-hot
caverns. So sudden are the actions, and so capricious
the moods of this Monster of the Burning Mountain,
that no one can tell the day, or even the hour, wherein
he will give us an exhibition of his fiery temper,
though, it is true, in the case of violent eruptions he
is kind enough to afford timely warning by means

of a succession of earthquakes and other signals almost equally alarming. His Majesty's presence is felt everywhere ; each morning as we open our window upon the dazzling waters of the Bay, we note with relief his tranquil aspect ; each night, ere we retire to sleep, we find ourselves inevitably drawn to watch the glare thrown by the molten lava within the crater upon the thick vapour overhead. The nightly expectation of this aerial bonfire possesses an extraordinary fascination for the stranger. Some times the lurid glare is continuous ; at other times there are long intervals of waiting, and even then the reflected light is very faint, a mere speck of reddish glow in the surrounding blackness, gone in the twinkling of an eye. But, strangely enough, one grows to understand the Mountain better from a distance and by watching its moods from afar, like the Neapolitans themselves, who never ascend to probe its mysteries, except a few vulgar guides and touts who batten on the curiosity of the foreigner.

On clear windless days the intermittent clouds of vapour sent up from the crater assume the most fantastic shapes—trees, ships, men, birds, animals— ever changing like the forms of Proteus. It would seem as if the Spirit of the Mountain were idly amusing himself, like a child blowing bubbles, or a vendor at a fair-stall carving out little figures of gingerbread to tickle the fancy of country boys and girls. The clouds so formed sometimes cause amuse- ment by their uncanny shapes, but not unfrequently they inspire alarm. The superstitious peasant of the *Paduli*, looking up suddenly from his work amidst the early peas or tomatoes, beholds against the blue sky a vague nebulous form that to his untutored mind suggests a gigantic crucifix upheld in mid-air above the Mountain, and he crosses himself devoutly ere he bends down to earth once more to his work in the rich dark soil. "Such stuff as dreams are made of" appear in truth the weird phantoms that the sly Demon of Vesuvius flings up into the pure aether, and if credulous mankind likes to draw inferences for good or bad from these unsubstantial creations of his fancy, he laughs to himself with a hollow reverberating sound. It must, however, have been in the true spirit of prophecy on the occasion of King Manfred's birth, that the genius of the Mountain despatched two cloud-forms into the sky (so the unabashed old chroniclers gravely relate), one having the appearance of a warrior armed cap-à-pie, and the other that of a fully vested priest. The affrighted gazers below, struck with the strange phenomenon, beheld the two figures sway towards each other and finally become locked together in deadly aerial combat, until all resemblance to human shape had vanished from the pair. Then, after an interval of time, men perceived the cloudy mass once more assume a mortal shape, and a huge towering priest with flowing robes and tiara on head was left in solitary and victorious possession of the sky. The Churchman had swallowed up the soldier; the Pontiff had vanquished the King; it was a true premonition of the fatal field of Benevento, which saw the ultimate triumph of the Papal over the Imperial cause.

But if the near presence of the burning mountain has tended to make the inhabitants of its immediate zone the slaves of superstitious awe, the disasters of

generations have likewise imbued them with a spirit of
fatalism, that appears even stronger than their outward
show of credulity.   Life is not so sweet nor so dear
apparently to these children of the South, but that
they can afford to take their chance of disturbance or
death with a true philosophic calm.   The fisher-folk
and maccaroni workers of Resina, Portici and the two
Torres have, it is true, little to lose ; a small boat can
at the last moment easily convey their families and
slender stock of household furniture to a place of
temporary safety, and when the danger is over-past,
the same shallop can bring back the refugees and their
belongings.   But with the husbandmen the case is
different.   Not only has he to fear the actual stream
of lava, which may or may not overwhelm his house
and farm in its slow inevitable course, but there are
also the showers of hot ashes and of scalding water
that will frizzle up in a few seconds every green blade
and leaf upon his tiny domain, for which he pays an
enormous rental, sometimes as much as £12 sterling
an acre.   Yet the *contadino* takes his chances with a
seraphic resignation that we do not usually attribute
to the southern temperament.   After the eruption of
1872, which covered the rich *Paduli* with a deep
coating of grey ashes, a young peasant girl was heard
deploring the loss of her carefully tended gourds and
melons ; " *Oh come volimme fa ?   Addio, pummarole !
addio, cucuzzielle !* " whereupon an older woman, wit-
nessing these useless tears, upbraided her with the
words : " Do not complain, child, lest worse befall you ! "
And indeed the whole population of the *Paduli*, instead
of lamenting over their scorched and spoiled crops,
were jubilant at the thought that the havoc done was

only partial, not irrevocable ;—a few months of in-
cessant labour, said they, would bring back the holdings to their former state of perfection. Yet a general
opinion prevails among foreigners that the Neapolitans
are lazy, thriftless and helpless! They indeed rely
to a certain extent upon St Januarius to protect their
crops from the efforts of Nature, over which, they
argue, the Saint is more likely to possess control than
his human applicants, but when once the fatal shower
of ashes has fallen, they do not expect " San Gennaro "
to set their injured acres to rights again, but with a
rare patience turn to the task themselves. A more
industrious, and at the same time a more capable and
practical race of agriculturists than the tillers of the
slopes of Vesuvius, it would be hard to match. And
thus in the sunshine of the south, yet ever under the
shadow of death and destruction, dwell many thousands
of human beings, as unconcerned as though Vesuvius
were miles and miles away. Not unconscious, but
fully conscious of their doom, the victims of the
Mountain toil and moil upon the fertile farms (in
many cases risen phoenix-like from their own ashes)
that grow the early beans and tomatoes, the egg-
plants and the white fennel roots (*finocchi*) that well-
fed travellers devour in the hotels of Naples. Or else
they tend the vines that yield the generous *Lagrima
Christi*, of which imprudent and heated visitors drink
long draughts unmixed with water, and then complain
of ensuing languor and pains beneath their waistcoats.
Luscious, yet seductive wine! Counsellor of moderation after a first experience of excess! Essence of
Vesuvius, whose strange name so puzzled the poet
Chiabrera!

" Chi fu de' contadini il si indiscreto,
  Ch' a sbigottir la gente
  Diede nome dolente
  Al vin' che sovra gli altri il cuor fa lieto?
  Lagrima dunque appellerassi un riso
  Parte di nobilissima vendemmia ? "

(Who was the jesting countryman, I cry,
  That gave so fearsome and so dour a name
  To that choice vintage, which of all think I
  Most warms the heart's blood with its genial flame?
  Smiles, and not tears, the epithet should be
  Of juice wrung from so fair a vinery.)

Scarcely had the above pages been written, than
the Mountain, which had been drowsing for more than
thirty years, suddenly awakened to give appalling evidence of its latent activity and powers of mischief.
The eruption of April 1906 has, in fact, surpassed all
previous outbursts within living memory, and it may
probably be reckoned amongst the most violent of all
hitherto recorded.   Many of the details of this event
doubtless remain fresh in the memory, and in any case
the sad condition of numerous towns and villages, and
of the beautiful Vesuvian districts, the *paesi ridenti*, as
the Neapolitans affectionately term these fertile lands,
will serve for some years to come as a sinister and
ever-present reminder of the horrors of the past and
of the dread possibilities of the future.   All vegetation
for miles around the volcano has been injured or
destroyed, for not only was the Mountain itself
covered deep with grit and ashes, but the streets and
gardens of Naples, the luxuriant plain of Sorrento, and
even the heights of Capri, twenty miles distant across
the Bay, were shrouded in a funereal mantle of the

greyish-yellow dust that Vesuvius had flung into the
air to let fall like a shower of parching and destructive
rain upon the earth. How vast was the amount of
matter ejected from the crater and scattered in this
form over the surrounding country, we may judge from
the scientific calculation that 315,000 tons fell in
Naples alone! Everywhere appeared the same scenes
of desolation, the same dreary tint, for so thickly had
this aerial torrent of ashes descended, that buildings, trees and plants were completely hidden by
it, the whole landscape suggesting the idea of a
recent heavy fall of dirty-coloured snow. *Paesi
ridenti*, indeed! It was a land of ugliness and
mourning, a city of stifling air and of human
terror.

A few days previous to the eruption, which began
on April 5th, the island of Ustica, which lies some
forty miles north of Palermo, had been visited by
earthquake shocks of such violence that the Italian
Government at last decided to remove the greater
part of its population to the mainland, as well as the
convicts attached to the penal settlements on the
island. Scarcely had these manifestations ceased at
Ustica, than Vesuvius began to show signs of
increased activity; the supplies in the wells on the
mountain sides began to fail, and there was observed
a strong taste of sulphur in the drinking water;
whilst—most dreaded phenomenon of all—the ever-
active crater of Stromboli, that lies midway between
Naples and Messina, suddenly lapsed into quiescence.
We all know the subsequent story of the outbreak;
of the thousands of fugitives flying into Naples or
other places of refuge; of the utter destruction of

houses and cultivated lands;—the doleful scenes of a
Vesuvian eruption have been enacted and described
time after time in the history of the Mountain, and
there is every reason to suppose they will be repeated
at intervals for centuries to come. The marvel is
how human beings can calmly settle down and pass
their lives so close to the jaws of the fire-spouting
monster, and why an intelligent Government permits
its subjects to dwell in places which are ever exposed
to catastrophes such as that which we have just
witnessed. Well, it is the natural temperament of
the Vesuviani to be fatalistic, despite their religious
fervour ; and acts of legislature cannot force them to
abandon their old deep-rooted notions ; all that the
Italian Government can do therefore is to stand ready
prepared to help, when the upheaval *does* occur, as it
inevitably must.

It is always a matter of speculation on these
occasions as to what course the ejected lava will
pursue ; whose turn, of the many settlements on the
southern slopes of the Mountain, will it be to suffer?
This time it was Bosco-Trecase, a village above Torre
Annunziata, that was devastated by the sinuous
masses of incandescent matter, high as a house and
broad as a river. Torre Annunziata itself, as also
ruined Pompeii were threatened, but the red-hot
streams of destruction mercifully stopped short of
their expected prey. The story of horrors and panic
in the overthrow of Bosco-Trecase is happily relieved
by many a recorded incident of valour and unselfish-
ness. The royal *Carabinieri*, that splendid body of
mounted police, who in their cocked hats and volumi-
nous cloaks appear as ornamental in times of quiet as

they prove themselves useful in the stormy hours of peril, acquitted themselves, as usual, like heroes. It was they who guided away the trembling peasants before the advance of the lava, searching the doomed houses for sick and crippled, whom they carried on their shoulders to places of security. Working, too, with almost equal zeal and practical good sense were the Italian soldiers, who richly deserved the praise that their royal commander, the Duke of Aosta, subsequently bestowed upon them for their invaluable services rendered during these fearful days of darkness and danger. "Soldiers!" declared the Duke, in his address to the troops on April 23rd, "I have seen you calm and happy in the work of alleviating the misfortunes of others, and I put on record the praise you have won. By promptly appearing at the places distressed by the eruption, you have encouraged the people by your presence and your example; you have maintained order and have safe-guarded property. Helping the local authorities, and even in some instances filling their offices, you have carried out the most urgent and dangerous duties in order to save the houses and to keep clear the roads. In the spots most heavily afflicted you have lent your assistance in removing and caring for the injured, and in searching for and burying the dead you have given proofs of great self-sacrifice and reverence (*pietà*). Not a few of the refugees have obtained food and shelter in your barracks, and whole communities without means of existence have been provided by you with the necessaries of life. Everywhere and from all your conduct has gained you loud applause. Nevertheless, your task is not yet ended ; continue at it out of love for your country and devotion to your King ! " *

With such a reputation for kindness of heart and energy in time of need, no wonder that the Army is popular with all classes in Italy !

Nor did the King and Queen hold aloof from the scene of disaster, for they hurried from Rome at midnight of that terrible Palm Sunday on purpose to comfort the terror-stricken population. Victor-Emmanuel even penetrated in his motor-car as far as Torre Annunziata, in spite of the fumes of sulphur and the many difficulties in proceeding along roads clogged deep with volcanic dust and ashes.   On another occasion the King and Queen paid a visit to the afflicted district of the slopes of Monte Somma, where Ottajano and San Giuseppe had been almost buried by the continuous falling of burning material from the crater.   In fact, these localities suffered even more severely than the towns on the seaward face of the Mountain (Bosco-Trecase excepted), and at Ottajano hardly a house in the place remained intact at the close of the eruption, whilst the loss of human life was probably higher here than elsewhere. The Duke and Duchess of Aosta—he the king's cousin, and she the popular Princess Hélène, daughter of the late Comte de Paris — were likewise inde-fatigable in their efforts to assist and reassure the demoralized population, and to make every possible arrangement for the feeding and housing · of the numberless refugees and the tending of the injured in the hospitals of Naples.   Equally valorous was the conduct of the great scientist, Professor Matteucci,

* *La Nazione,* April 24, 1906.

who remained together with a few Carabinieri throughout all phases of the eruption at the Vesuvian
Observatory, although in imminent peril of death
amidst a deadly atmosphere of heat and sulphureous
fumes.

It was on April 5th that the streams of burning
lava first burst from the riven crater and made their
way down the south-eastern slopes, destroying Bosco-
Trecase and reaching to the very suburbs of Torre
Annunziata. Pompeii itself was imperilled, and it is
always well to remember that during an eruption this
precious relic of antiquity may possibly be lost to the
world. Meanwhile the rain of ashes and mud—formed
by dust and hot water commingling—fell incessantly ;
150,000 inhabitants of the Vesuvian districts fled in
precipitate flight towards Naples, towards the shore,
towards the hill country beyond the Sarno. It was
truly a marvellous spectacle to observe the relentless
stream of burning lava crushing irresistibly every
opposing object in its fatal path. Onlookers at a
distance could perceive the walls of houses bulging
outward under pressure of the moving mass, until the
roof collapsed in an avalanche of tiles upon the ground,
whilst with a final crash the whole structure—cottage,
farm, church or stately villa—succumbed to the
overwhelming weight.

Many are the tales of courage and intrepidity; not
a few, alas! are the stories of folly and cowardice that
are related in connection with the eruption. It cannot
be said that the population of Naples, where everybody was perfectly safe even if the atmosphere was
unpleasant and the distant thunders of the Mountain
reverberated alarmingly, comported itself with dignity

or calm ; and this criticism applies in particular to
the hundreds of visitors—English, German, American
and other *forestieri*—who besieged the railway station
in frantic and indecent anxiety to remove themselves
with all speed from the city. Some excuse might
perhaps be found for the hysterical terror of the poor
inhabitants of the Mergellina or the Mercato, who
spent their time in wailing within the churches or in
screaming for the public exhibition of the venerated
relics of their patron Saint, which again on this occasion the Archbishop, *nolens volens*, was compelled by
the mob to produce. But for the great mass of
educated foreigners then filling the hotels and pensions
of the place, it cannot be said that their conduct was
edifying, particularly in face of the example set by the
King and Queen of Italy. To add to the general
panic prevailing in the city, the Neapolitans themselves
were not unnaturally greatly exasperated by the
serious accident which took place at the Central
Market Hall near Monte Oliveto in the heart of the
old town. Here, early one morning during the course
of the eruption, the great roof of corrugated iron
collapsed, killing many and frightening the whole of
the populace, already sufficiently unnerved by recent
events. That this catastrophe was due to the casual
methods, amounting in this case to criminal neglect of
plain duty, of the municipal authorities, who had
neglected to sweep the accumulation of heavy volcanic
ash from off the thin metal roof, none can deny ; and
this glaring example of public stupidity had of course
a bad effect on the demoralized multitude, which
threatened to grow unruly, as well as terrified. No,
the graceless stampede of educated foreigners to the

railway-station, the incompetence of the Municipality, and the behaviour of the Neapolitan crowd do not appear very creditable to the supposed enlightenment of the twentieth century. It had been confidently predicted that nearly fifty years of State education and liberal government would work wonders in dispelling the crass ignorance and the deep-seated superstition of the dwellers on the Bay of Naples. Yet, so far as can be judged from recent events, matters seem to have changed but little on these shores, for the mass of the population evidently preferred to pin its hope of safety to the miracle-working relics of San Gennaro, rather than to the reassuring messages of Professor Matteucci, sent from his post of undoubted peril on the mountain-side.

If the inhabitants of a great city, which was never seriously threatened with danger, should have acted thus, there is undoubtedly much excuse to be found for the Vesuviani themselves, whose houses and lives were certainly in danger from the devastating streams of lava. It was with a sigh and a smile that we learned how the good people of Portici attributed their escape from the fate of Bosco-Trecase to the direct interposition of a wonder-working Madonna enshrined in one of their own churches. For some days the town had been threatened, so that many were convinced of its impending doom, when happily at the last moment the expected fate was averted, as though by a miracle. And miracle it truly was in the eyes of the people of Portici, when it was observed that the snow-white hands of their popula⟍ Madonna had turned black in some mysterious manner during the night hours. What could be a simpler

o

or easier deduction from this circumstance, than that
Our Lady's Effigy, taking pity on its affrighted
suppliants, had with its own hands pushed back the
advancing mass of lava, and thus saved the town!
Great was the joy, and equally great the gratitude,
displayed by these poor souls at Portici, who at once
organised a triumphal procession in honour of their
prescient patroness "delle mani nere." Does not such
an incident, we ask, lend a touch of picturesque
medievalism to a modern scene of horror and darkness, exhibiting to us, as it does, the traits of a simple
touching faith and of genuine human thankfulness?

Well, the great eruption of 1906 is over, and the
inhabitants of the Vesuvian communes are once more
settling down in their ruined homes, or their damaged
farms and gardens. No doubt a new Bosco-Trecase
will arise on the shapeless ruins of the old site, for fear
of danger seems powerless to deter the outcast population from reoccupying its old haunts. Ottajano will
be rebuilt, not for the first time, and its citizens will
again trust to luck—and to St Januarius—for protection from the evil fate which has repeatedly
overtaken their town. The two Torres, Resina,
Portici, and the villages along the shore, have this
time contrived to escape the lava streams, and
though their buildings have been severely shaken, and
even wrecked in many instances, the people will
doubtless mend the cracks in their walls and place
fresh tiles on the injured roofs. They are wise in
their own generation, for the Mountain is not likely to
burst forth again for another quarter of a century at
least after so violent a fit, *salvo complicazioni*, of course,
as the more cautious Italians themselves say. But

another outburst is inevitable ; and whose turn to
suffer will it be then ?   Will it be Portici, or either of
the Torres ?   Who knows ?—and what dweller under
Vesuvius to-day cares at this moment ?   "Under
Vesuvius," but it is a new Vesuvius, for the tall cone
which was so conspicuous a feature of the Bay of
Naples has disappeared completely, and the summit
of the volcano has been once more reduced to the
level of Monte Somma. How many years, we
wonder, will be required for the Mountain to raise for
itself once more the tall pyre of ashes that it has
itself demolished and flung on all sides to the winds ?
At any rate let us now look for a period of rest, a
period of prosperity to recoup the disturbed denizens
of these *paesi già ridenti* for their heavy losses and
terrible experiences.   *Speriamo.*

CHAPTER V

THE CORNICHE ROAD FROM CASTELLAMARE
TO AMALFI

IT is without any feelings of regret that we learn of the non-existence of a railway line beyond Castellamare, so that our journey to Amalfi along the coast must be performed in the good old-fashioned manner of long-past *vetturino* days. Three skinny horses harnessed abreast are standing ready at the hotel door to draw our travelling chariot, each member of the team gorgeously decked with plumes of pheasant feathers in his head-gear and with many-coloured trappings, whilst on the harness itself appears in more than one place the little brazen hand, which is supposed to ensure the steed's safety from the dangers of any chance *jettatore*, the unlucky wight endowed with the Evil Eye. Nor is the swarthy picturesque ruffian who acts as our driver unprovided with a talisman in case of emergency, for we observe hanging from his heavy silver watch-chain the long twisted horn of pink coral, which is popularly supposed to catch the first baleful glance, and to act on the principle of a lightning-conductor, in deflecting the approaching danger from the prudent wearer of the coral trinket. Merrily to the sound of jingling bells and the deep-chested exhortations of our coachman do

POZZANO

we bowl along the excellent road in the freshness of the morning air and light " through varying scenes of beauty ever led," for the Corniche road towards Amalfi is admitted to be one of the finest in the world. Following the serpentine curves above the cliffs, we have on our right hand the dazzling Mediterranean with classic capes and islands all flushed in the early sunshine, whilst above us on the left rise the steep fertile slopes of the Lactarian Hills. Convent and villa, cottage and farmhouse, peep out of embowering verdure, whilst our road is shaded in many places by the overhanging boughs of blossoming almond and loquat trees. The whole region is in truth a veritable garden of the Hesperides, where in the mild equable climate fruit and flowers ripen and bloom without a break throughout the rolling year.

> " Tall thriving trees confess'd the fruitful mould ;
> The verdant apple ripens here to gold ;
> Here the blue fig with luscious juice o'erflows,
> With deepest red the full pomegranate glows,
> The branches bend beneath the weighty pear,
> And silver olives flourish all the year ;
> The balmy spirit of the western gale
> Eternal breathes on fruits untaught to fail.
> Each dropping pear another pear supplies,
> On apples apples, figs on figs arise ;
> The same mild season gives the blooms to blow,
> The buds to harden, and the fruits to grow."

A lovely and a fertile scene it is indeed, and thoroughly typical of the peculiar charm of Southern Italy, wherein the rich well-tilled lands appear in striking contrast with the near-lying stony fallows and scrub-covered wastes.

Beneath the picturesque pile of Santa Maria a

Pozzano, perched aloft above the roadway, we pass along the edge of the sea-girt precipice, rounding the Capo d'Orlando, until we reach the pretty little town of Vico Equense, with its churches and gay-coloured villas nestling amidst groves of olive and orange trees. Vico owes its prosperity in the first instance to the patronage of "Carlo il Zoppo," Charles the Dwarf, the lame son and heir of King Charles of Anjou, who founded a settlement and built a villa upon the site of the ancient Roman colony ; and it was in the old royal demesne of the Angevins that the hand of the deformed king's daughter, the Princess Clementia, was demanded formally in marriage by the French monarch, Philip the Bold, who sought to marry her to his third son, Charles of Valois. The match between the young prince of France and his cousin, the Neapolitan princess, appeared suitable to all concerned in every respect save one ; for it was well known that the King of Naples had been lame from his birth, and it could never be deemed fit for the expected heir of . France to marry any but a perfectly sound and healthy bride. Now the Queen of Naples was too proud to accede to the hints of the French ladies, who evidently were most anxious to acquaint themselves with the satisfactory condition of her daughter's "walking members," though she went so far as to allow the maiden to appear before them clad only in a flowing robe of gossamer silk. The possible danger of losing her opportunity to become Queen of France proved, however, beyond the ambitious young lady's powers of endurance, and to the horror of her haughty mother and the delight of the foreign emissaries, the Princess Clementia then and there doffed her silken

robes and appeared before all in the historic garb of
Lady Godiva. A glance at the princess's form *in
puris naturalibus* sufficed to convince the inquisitive
Frenchwomen that no hereditary taint from Il Zoppo
descended to his daughter; and accordingly the
betrothal of the two young people was celebrated that
very evening amidst the usual revels and feastings.

The clean cheerful town on the sheer limestone
crags boasts a cathedral, wherein, so the guide-book
informs us, we shall find the tomb of Filangieri, the
great Italian jurist. But the building contains in
reality far more stirring associations than those connected with a prominent lawyer. It is but a rococo
structure of the usual Italian type, and its painted
series of portraits of past bishops is by no means an
uncommon complement of cathedral churches in the
South. But here, amidst the long rows of indifferent
portraits, we note an omission, a space that is occupied, not by a likeness but by a medallion, which
represents a cherub with the forefinger of his right
hand laid as a seal of silence upon the lips. Here-
by indeed hangs a tale, obscure perhaps, but pathetic
and human to the last degree. We all remember the
broad frieze filled with Doges' faces which is carried
round the great hall of the ducal palace in Venice,
wherein the place assigned to the traitor, Marino
Faliero, contains a black veil instead of the usual
portrait. Here in little Vico Equense is to be found
a somewhat similar incident, but with this important
difference :—the bishop whose portrait is here omitted
was the most worthy of remembrance of all his peers.

The crime of Monsignore Michele Natale, Bishop
of Vico Equense, to which the silent cherub bears

everlasting witness, was that of being a patriot and a Liberal (in the truest sense of that term) during the anxious times of the ill-fated Parthenopean Republic, that short-lived period of aristocratic government which was set up in self-defence by certain Neapolitan nobles, prelates and men of science after the abrupt departure of their cowardly King and Queen to Palermo.   We all remember the terrible ending of that government : how the vile rabble-army of Cardinal Ruffo assaulted Naples ; how the city capitulated to the Cardinal on the express condition that all life and property should be spared ; and how Lord Nelson, refusing to recognise the terms that Ruffo himself had agreed to, and overruling the Cardinal's protests, treated the unhappy prisoners. The Bishop of Vico Equense was one of this band of martyrs, for he suffered death under circumstances of exceptional brutality on the morning of August 20th 1799, in the piazza in front of the church of the Carmine, together with two Neapolitans of noble rank, Giuliano Colonna and Gennaro Serra, and with the poetess, Eleonora Pimentel, a Portuguese by birth but the widow of a Neapolitan officer.   All went nobly to their doom amidst the execrations of the demoralised bloodthirsty mob of *lazzaroni*, yelling at and insulting the " Jacobins," and kept back with no little difficulty by the royal troops from mutilating the corpses of women, bishops and princes. Monsignore Natale himself was hanged, and in his case the public executioner—" Masto Donato " as he was nick-named by the populace — gave vent to many pleasantries concerning the episcopal rank of his victim.   Blindfolded and with the cord of infamy

depending from his neck, the Bishop was led up to the
fatal ladder amid deafening shouts of

"Viva la forca e Masto Donato ;
Sant' Antonio sia priato ! "

On reaching the top of the gallows, the hangman
made fast the rope to the cross-tree, and then an
assistant (*tirapiede*) from below adroitly pushed the
unseeing prisoner into space, catching on to his legs
meanwhile, whilst "Masto Donato" himself adroitly
leaped from the gallows - top upon the prelate's
shoulder.   With the hangman on his back, shouting
aloud how much he was enjoying his ride upon a
real bishop, and with the other ruffian clinging to his
heels, Monsignore Natale swayed backwards and forwards amidst yells of execration and gratified hate
on that hot August morning in front of the Church
of the Carmine little more than one hundred years
ago.   His body was left on the gallows to be insulted
by the mob throughout the long sweltering day, and
then, stripped of all its clothing, was finally flung
with other corpses of noble men and women into a
charnel-house at Sant' Alessio al Lavinaio.   Who it
was that placed this quaint little memorial to the
murdered prelate in his cathedral church we know
not ; but here the speechless yet eloquent cherub
tells Natale's sad story of brutality and injustice to
all who care to listen.   Happily the spell of silence
is at length broken, and the true history of that
hateful era of crime, cruelty, lying, and intrigue is
gradually being revealed ; and the enemies of the
Church in Italy learn with an astonishment, which
is perhaps feigned, that in that glorious army of

martyrs of 1799 more than one ecclesiastic of high rank suffered in the ill-starred and premature cause of Neapolitan liberty.

Crossing the little river Arco, we proceed uphill through the region of vines and olives, until we have passed the Punta di Scutolo, where begins our descent into that famous tract of country, the Piano di Sorrento, a plateau above the cliffs, some four miles in length by one in breadth.   Poets of antiquity and bards of the Middle Ages alike have sung the delights of the Sorrentine Plain, and have painted in glowing colours of inspired verse its race of happy peasants, its fruitful fields and orchards, its luscious vines, its excellent flocks.   Galen, the cunning old physician, recommended to his nervous patients what would now be termed a "rest cure" in these favoured regions ; whilst the grateful Bernardo Tasso, father of the immortal Torquato, speaks of the capital of this district as "l'Albergo della Cortesia," and in an ecstasy of delighted appreciation, goes on to add: "l'aere e si sereno, si temperato, si salutifero, si vitale, che gli uomini che senza provar altero cielo ci vivono sono quasi immortali."   And though praise from Torquato's courtly sire must not be taken too seriously, yet few will deny that the beautiful plain deserves many of the eulogies that have been showered upon it.   At the small town of Meta, the next place of importance after Sorrento itself, the road divides at the Church of the Madonna of the Laurel : our way to Amalfi leading southward over the opposing ridge—the "Sorrentini Colles" of Ovid—whilst the other traverses the length of the plain by way of Pozzopiano and Sant' Agnello, until it reaches Sorrento.

One prominent feature of this district has already
attracted our attention ; the number of deep ravines
with which the whole plain is intersected.   These
natural clefts are marvellously lovely in their rich
luxuriance of foliage, and with their precipitous sides
and verdure-clad depths will recall the wonderful
latomiè, the ancient stone-quarries of Syracuse.   Their
depths are filled with orange and lemon trees, mingled
with sable spires of cypress and the tall forms of bays,
which here bear jet-black berries, such as are rarely seen
in our northern clime ; whilst the edges of the cliffs
are clothed with a serried mass of wild flowers ; red
valerian, crimson snap-dragon, tall blue campanulas,
the dark green wild fennel, white-blossoming cistus,
and a hundred other plants, gay with colour and
strong with aromatic perfume.

> The quarry's edge is lined with many a plant,
> With many a flower distilling fragrant dew
> From brightly coloured petals. Almond trees
> Give snowy promise of sweet leaves and fruit ;
> Here all the scented tangle of the South
> Covers the boulders, calcined by the sun
> To pearly whiteness ; thorn or asphodel
> Sprout from each cranny of the topmost ledge
> To nod against the deep blue sky, or peer
> Into the verdure-clad abyss below.

It is not surprising to learn that these romantic glens,
filled with greenery, are reputed locally to be the haunts
of fairies, *Monacelli*, as the Sorrentine inhabitants
name them.   Like the " good folk " of certain country
districts in England, the pixies of Devonshire, and the
" Tylwyth Teg " of rural Wales, these elfin people of
the ravines are not malicious or unkindly in their nature,
but they are particular and somewhat exacting in

certain matters. They appreciate the attentions of
mortal men, and offerings of fresh milk or choice
fruit are not beneath the notice of the Monacelli.
Borrowing the idea from the votive offerings they
make in the churches to the Virgin and the Saints,
the peasants sometimes place little lamps in the fern-
draped grottoes of these gullies, and to such as
punctually perform these acts of courtesy, the
Monacelli frequently show signs of favour.   The
padrone of a local inn has assured us that he and
his wife stood very high in the good graces of the
little people, who had on one occasion actually
written them a letter, although as the characters
employed were unknown to any person in the
village, the object of their communication by this
means seems somewhat of a mystery.   Another and
a more practical instance of their patronage was
then related, for the favoured landlord assured us
that on one occasion, when he and his wife descended
downstairs in the morning, they found the house
cleared, the hearth ready swept, and all the contents
of last night's supper-table relaid on the brick floor,
but *d'un modo squisito*, such as no human hand could
ever have been deft enough to contrive. Just a simple
innocent trifle of Sorrentine folk-lore, but how closely
does it resemble the old-time gossip of rustic England,
of which the great poet has left us so charming
a picture !—

> " Tells how the drudging Goblin sweat
>   To earn his cream-bowl duly set,
>   When in one night, ere glimpse of morn,
>   His shadowy flail hath threshed the corn
>   That ten day labourers could not end."

For, as we have already said, the Monacelli show themselves grateful to those who anticipate their wants, and will serve their votaries with industry and fidelity. *Fuore avra il Monacello in casa*— perhaps he has had the Fairy in the house—has passed into a local phrase to designate a neighbour's unexplained prosperity. But, again, the lucky recipient of these favours must never blab or even hint at the origin of his good fortune, for all gossip is highly distasteful to the fairy folk; and that, we suppose, is the true reason why so little authentic information can be gleaned as to the methods of the Monacelli.

In direct contrast with the Monacelli of the ravines, who are, on the whole, well inclined towards mortals, are the Maghe, first cousins evidently to the terrible *ginns* of Arabian folk-lore; perhaps the Saracenic pirates themselves may have introduced their oriental sprites to the Neapolitan shores. In the popular mind the Maghe are supposed to possess vast treasures hidden in caves by the seashore, or on the bleak mountain side, and it was doubtless concerning these spirits that the guide's tale, given in a previous chapter, relates. The most celebrated Maga of all is the demon who haunts a certain underground corridor near Pozzuoli, containing an immense hoard of gold and jewels, which he is willing to present to anybody that is ready to give in exchange a new-born baby, presumably for purposes of devouring. Nor was the general belief in the cave-dwelling monster at Pozzuoli limited to the poor peasants and fisher-folk, for rumour persistently asserted that King Francis of Naples, father of Bomba of impious memory, more than once attempted to negotiate with the guardian of this buried treasure; but the Maga's terms, it seems, were too bloodthirsty and extravagant even for a Neapolitan Bourbon to comply with, and in that case they must indeed have been pretty startling. Malignant fairies are, in short, quite common upon the Sorrentine plain, where exasperated mothers are sometimes in the habit of frightening their squalling children into silence by threatening to introduce them to *Mammone*—perhaps a corruption of the old Greek word *mormo*—a terrible ghost, that must be a near relation to the " Big Black Man " of English nurseries, who is ever ready to carry off naughty boys and girls in his sack.

But the whole of the Sorrentine Peninsula is full of local superstitions, the vast majority of which can easily be traced to the influence of Catholicism, whilst comparatively few seem to be the legacy of ancient Greek or Roman mythology. Belief in witchcraft is universal in these parts, but the witch herself (*strega*) is regarded somewhat in the light of a beneficent " wise woman," who can arrest the far more dreaded spell of the Evil Eye, rather than as the malevolent old hag of bucolic England in the past. Certainly there has never been recorded in Southern Italy any such popular persecution of poor harmless old crones as once disgraced English countrysides; nor has any Italian jurist, like the erudite Sir Matthew Hale, ever condescended to supply legal information concerning the peculiarities of witches, and the best methods of prosecuting and burning them. But the *strega*, though not as a rule dangerous to mankind, provided she be not disturbed or insulted, has the same supernatural power of transit on a broomstick that is possessed by her northern sister. On many a dark night have the peasants crossed themselves with fear on hearing the witches flying through the storm-vexed air to keep their unholy tryst beside the famous walnut tree of Benevento, which has been described for us by the learned Pietro Piperno in his mysterious treatise, entitled *De Nuce Beneventana*. Even snatches of the witches' song can sometimes be distinguished above the howling of the gale—

> " Sott' aero e sopra vento,
> Sotto la Nuce di Benevento ! "

Perhaps it may afford some consolation to those who have a dread of witches that the word " Sabato," solemnly pronounced on these awful occasions, is of real service to the utterer ; whilst such as have had the good fortune to be born on a Friday in March are permanently placed outside the evil power of their spells, since our Saviour was crucified on a Friday in that month.

But at length we have finished the ascent of the ridge, and our driver halts for a moment at the inn of the " Due Golfi." A smiling damsel, dressed in the picturesque native costume, advances to offer us the national drink of Italy, sweet vermouth that is frothed up with a little fizzing water in a narrow tumbler ; and though carriage exercise is not liable to produce thirst, yet we cannot be so churlish as to refuse the draught, especially as the delay allows us to take our farewell look at the Bay of Naples. For here we have reached the peak of the rocky saddle that divides the two famous gulfs ; and before us we now behold the wide crescent of the Bay of Salerno with its sunburnt vineyards and its precipitous cliffs. To

our right we perceive the craggy headlands stretching
southward till they culminate in the Cape of Minerva:—
how much more attractive sounds the good old classical
name than the new-fangled Punta della Campanella,
so called from the alarm bell which used to be tolled
in the ruined fortress at the approach of the Moslem
pirate galleys I   Vastly different is the aspect on this
side of the peninsula to that which we have just left
behind us.   There is the plain below us, thickly dotted
with farms and villas set amidst crops and orchards, a
fertile scene of industry and population ; here on the
Salerno side are wild stony tracts affording only pas-
turage for a few sheep and goats, and covered for
miles with broom, cytizus, coronella, myrtle, and numberless fragrant weeds, all struggling fiercely for existence on the dry barren soil, and filling the clear air
with an incense-like perfume.   Such is our first acquaintance with the Costiera d'Amalfi, that wonderful
stretch of indented rocky coast-line once containing
the Republic of Amalfi, which was the forerunner of
the glorious Commonwealths of Florence and Venice.
From the grey cliffs of Capri to the west, as far as the
headland beside Salerno, stretched this diminutive
state, composed of a confederacy of sister-cities, whereof
Amalfi herself was the queen and metropolis.   Its
glories have long vanished, but the Costiera d'Amalfi
remains an enchanted land, not only on account of its
natural beauties, but also by reason of its historical
associations which give an additional charm to every
breezy headland and every little town upon this
wonderful shore.

Below us, as we rapidly descend the slopes by the
curves of the Corniche road, lies the little beach known

as Lo Scaricotojo, whence in the days previous to the
construction of this splendid highway all visitors were
wont to embark for Amalfi ;—that is, unless they
attempted the expedition by way of the mountain
roads leading thither from Castellamare or La Cava.
It raises a smile in these days of swift and luxurious
travelling to learn from an early Victorian guide-book
that " the most elegible mode of going from Sorrento
to Amalfi is either to ride or to be carried in a *chaise
à porteurs* to that part of the Colli where begins a
rapid descent, and thence descending on foot to the
Marinella of the Scaricotojo on the Gulf of Salerno.
. . . The ride occupies about an hour and a quarter,
and the descent which, though steep, is not dangerous,
occupies about an hour."   *Nous avons changé tout ça ;*
yet there are still living amongst us those who lament
the passing away of the old-fashioned days of Italian
travel, when inns were bad but picturesque, and expeditions to such remote places as Amalfi were not
only difficult but even dangerous ; since in compensation for slow progress and risk of brigands every town
owned a primitive charm which is now rapidly disappearing before the modern irruption of locust-like
swarms of tourists with their motor cars, their luncheon
baskets, and their kodaks.   Well, to the majority of
travellers the value of natural scenery is not a little
enhanced by the sense of comfort, and here on the
Costiera d'Amalfi the most particular can have no
cause to complain, since it is one of the few lovely
spots of Southern Europe that has not yet been in-
vaded by the dividend-paying railway.   No, the old
Republic retains to a great extent its ancient atmosphere of unspoiled beauty and remoteness from the

H

bustling world. It is still a stretch of glorious and historic country wherein one can obtain a pleasant and valued respite for a time from the overpowering improvements of an industrial age.

As we look southward across the breadth of the Bay, our eye is at once caught by the group of the Isles of the Sirens, which, though in reality fully a mile distant from the nearest point of the coast, seem in this clear atmosphere as though they were lying within a stone's throw of the beach. Around these bare bluffs of rock, seemingly flung by the hand of Nature in a sportive mood into the blue waves, lingers one of the most insidious of all the old Greek legends, for it was past these lonely cliffs that the cunning Ulysses sailed during his long career of mazy wanderings in search of his island home and his faithful Penelope. In those days, so the Greek bard tells us, there dwelt upon these islets strange sea-witches with the faces and forms of most beautiful maidens, although their lower limbs had the resemblance of eagles' feet and talons. Two sirens only, says Homer, dwelt upon these coasts, although later poets have increased the number of the fatal sisters to three or even four. Singing the most enchanting songs to the sound of tortoise-shell lyres, there used to bask in the sunlight beside the gentle ripple the Sirens, their nether limbs well hidden from the gaze of passing seamen, who, attracted by the tuneful notes, hastened hither to discover the whereabouts of the musicians. Innocent eyes, angelic faces, flowing golden locks and white beckoning hands had every power to draw the curious mariner nearer and nearer, until he came within reach of the fell en-

chantresses.   For the Sirens loved the flesh of
mortals, and bleached skulls and bones of digested
victims lay in heaps upon the sandy floor of their
azure-hued caverns.   Gold and jewels, too, the spoils
of many a brave galley that had been lured to destruction by these charmers, likewise littered their
retreat, and perhaps it was as much the glittering of
this gold as their own lovely features that in certain
cases enticed the wary merchant into this fatal trap.
Gold and a pretty face : what male heart could be
proof against the double temptation the Isles of the
Sirens offered to the navigator in the days of the
Odyssey !   Only one sailor over these seas proved
himself a match for the wiles of the cruel goddesses
of the Amalfitan coast ; for Ulysses, as we know,
stopped the ears of his companions with wax on
their approach towards this dangerous spot, whilst he
himself, always eager to hear and see everything yet
perfectly well aware of the Sirens' magnetic power,
had himself tightly bound by cords to the mast.   So
whilst the deaf rowers stolidly tugged at their oars,
oblivious of the weird unearthly melody around them,
the clever King of Ithaca gained the honour of be-
becoming the only mortal who had listened to that
subtle song without paying the penalty of a hideous
and ignoble death.

It is strangely disappointing to find that no recollection of Sirens or of Ulysses lingers in the lore
of the present dwellers upon these coasts.   They
have no more notion of the aspect of a Siren than
they have of a pleisosaurus, and, as a modern writer
naïvely complains, they are not sharp-witted enough
to invent fanciful tales to please the enquiring foreigner.

Nor is this lack of intelligence to be wondered at, when we recall to mind the clean sweep of all classical learning and tradition which that period of time, truly known as the Dark Ages, made throughout Italy ; if Petrarch found it necessary to explain to King Robert the Wise with the greatest tact and delicacy that Vergil was a poet and not a wizard, what must have been the appalling ignorance prevailing amongst the peasant and the fisherman ? And yet these barren rocks were known as the Isles of the Sirens centuries before the verses of the Aeneid immortalized the mythic voyage of the Trojan adventurer, who passed along this iron-bound coast on his way towards the mouth of Tiber. Their modern, or rather medieval name of I Galli is somewhat of a puzzle. Erudite scholars affect to derive it from Guallo, a fortress captured during a war between King Roger and the Republic of Amalfi, but this explanation, we confess, does not sound very reasonable. Others prefer to imagine that the word Gallo (a cock) contains an allusion to the claws and feathers of the Sirens themselves, for certain of the ancient writers endowed these dire Virgins of the Rocks with the wings as well as the claws of birds ; —in fact, they represented them as Harpies, those horrible fowls with women's faces that appeared upon the scene at Prospero's bidding to spoil the bad king's supper party. But why, if the Sirens were female,—and on this point all their critics agree with an unanimity that is wonderful—should their ancient haunts be called " The Cocks ? " The untutored natives themselves, understanding nothing of Sirens or of Odysseys, hold their own theory with regard

to the disputed name, which they connect with the
construction of a harbour at distant Salerno, and
though this legend sounds foolish enough, it is
scarcely less flimsy than the notions already quoted.
A certain enchanter, one Pietro Bajalardo, undertook
—in modern parlance, contracted—to build in a
single night the much needed breakwater at Salerno
on the strange condition that all cocks in the
neighbourhood should first be killed ; for the wizard,
so the story runs, had a special aversion to Chanti-
cleer on account of his having caused the repentance
of St Peter by his crowing.   In any case, the reigning
Prince of Salerno gladly complied with the eccentric
request, and at his command every cock in or near
the place was accordingly slaughtered, with the
solitary exception of one old rooster, who, being very
dear to the heart of his aged mistress, was kept concealed beneath a tub and thus escaped the general
holocaust.   Throughout the livelong night Bajalardo
was busily engaged in superintending the work of
building the harbour, whilst the fiends who carried
out his behest were actively conveying huge blocks
of broken cliff from the Cape of Minerva to place in
the waters of Salerno.   But at daybreak the cock
imprisoned beneath the tub, the sole survivor of his
race, according to natural custom announced the dawn,
to the despair of Bajalardo and the terror of his attendant fiends, who in their precipitate flight dropped
into the sea near the Punta Sant' Elia the huge masses
of stone they were then carrying ; and these rocks
are called by men I Galli in consequence to this day.
     But, to be strictly impartial, it was not the Sirens
alone who were responsible for all the victims who

perished on these arid rocks. *Homo homini lupus ;* man is always ready to prey upon man, and many of the dark tales concerning the Galli go to prove the truth of the terrible old adage. At what period the Sirens abandoned their ancient retreat and swam or flew away to more congenial haunts is unknown to history ; but certain it is that the rulers of proud Amalfi committed many a cruel deed of murder or torture upon their deserted islets. For here, many a hapless political prisoner languished for years in abject misery, a prey to the heat and glare of summer and to the fierce gales of bitter winter nights. Rock-cut steps and ruined towers still remain as mementoes of those dark days, when callous human gaolers worthily filled the places of the absent Sirens. It was in a chamber of yonder turret, still standing, that the Doge Mansone II., blinded by a brother's vengeance, dragged out years of utter misery in pain and darkness, until the Emperor of the East, suzerain of Amalfi, at last took compassion upon the prisoner's wretched plight and allowed him to be removed into honourable con- finement at Byzantium. For many hundreds of years the Isles of the Sirens have lain untenanted, nor are they visited nowadays save by a few inquisitive travellers or by the fishermen of the Scaricotojo, who find safe shelter under their lee during the sudden squalls of the Mediterranean. For, strange to relate, there are no dangerous currents, no treacherous whirl- pools close to these rocky islets, such as we might expect to give some natural interpretation to the ancient myth, the origin of which remains unexplained and constitutes a very pretty mystery as it stands.

We bid farewell to the group of ill-omened rocks,

as we proceed rapidly under the rocky slopes of the
Monte di Chiosse towards Positano, which extends in
a long curving line of cheerful-tinted flat-roofed houses
from the summit of its protecting cliff to the strand
below, sprinkled with boats and nets and cloths with
heaps of grain a-drying. The descent to the lower
portion of the little town is singularly charming with
its varied scenery of rocks and hanging woods above
us, with the tiled domes of churches outlined against
the deep blue waters, and with the whole scene
dominated by the pierced crag of Montapertuso,
beyond which thrusts up into the cloudless sky the
triple peak of the giant Sant' Angelo.   Positano is a
thriving as well as an ancient place, and of its dense
population we have abundant evidence in the swarms
of children that pursue our carriage, brown-skinned
picturesque little nuisances, shrilly and incessantly
crying out for *soldi*.   Most of these infants wear
bright coloured rags, but not a few are dressed in
garments that at once recall the ginger-coloured robes
of the Capuchin friars, for the brothers of the Order
of St Francis are popularly reputed to be especially
competent in keeping aloof evil spells from young
persons entrusted to their charge ; and of course,
argue the doting parents, it is only natural that the
spirits of darkness should not dare to molest the little
ones tricked out in robes similar to those worn by
these holy men.

From the point of view of history the chief interest
of Positano centres in the time-honoured tradition
that Flavio Gioja, the original inventor of the compass,
was a native of this town, once a flourishing and
important member of the group of cities which com-

prised the Amalfitan Republic in its palmy days.
But Clio, the Muse of History, is an inexorable
mistress, and she will not rest content with mere
hearsay, however venerable, and as a result of careful
investigation it would seem that Flavio Gioja, who for
centuries has been generally credited with this marvellous
discovery, must himself have been a personage almost
as mythic as the Sirens of this shore, for his very
name is spelled in a variety of ways that is hopelessly
confusing.   Nor has the question of his place of birth
ever been satisfactorily settled, for both Positano and
Amalfi claim this hero of science for a son, although
only in Amalfitan annals can the disputed name
be detected.   Be this as it may, it was a citizen of
this Costiera who has ever been acknowledged as
the inventor of the compass, though concerning both
himself and his alleged discovery there is a complete absence of any contemporary record.   Later
writers have, it is true, always admitted the honour on
behalf of the Republic, and Pontano goes so far as to
call Amalfi *magnetica* in compliment thereof, whilst
during the later crusades the Amalfitani, who were
evidently convinced of the genuine nature of Gioja's
claim, had an heraldic figure of the mariner's compass
emblazoned on their banners.   It seems a thousand
pities to throw doubt upon so picturesque a tradition,
for the date of the invention of the compass has been
fixed as 1302, two years only after the holding of the
famous Papal Jubilee in Rome which Dante's verse
has described for us.   Nor can the ingenious theory
be upheld that the fleur-de-lys, the emblem of the
French kings of Naples, which still decorates the dial
of the compass in almost all lands, is in any wise

connected with Carlo il Zoppo, the monarch to whom
Gioja is said to have dedicated his ingenious discovery.
No, we have little doubt that the compass, like so
many of the scientific wonders that crept into Europe
before and during the time of the Renaissance, was
originally brought from the far East, a farther East
than the argosies of Amalfi had ever penetrated. The
little magic box with its moving needle was first used,
it is now admitted, by the cunning merchants of
Cathay during their trading expeditions across the
stony monotonous plains of Central Asia that lay
between the Flowery Land and the civilization of
Persia. From Cathay the use of the magnetic needle
was introduced to the Arab mathematicians of Baghdad
and Cairo, and through them the secret of the lode-
stone of China was conveyed to the coast towns of the
Levant. At Aleppo or Alexandria some astute trader
of Amalfi—perhaps his name really was Flavio Gioja
—contrived to learn the new method of steering from
some Moslem or Jewish merchant, and he in his turn
brought this novel and precious piece of information
back to the Italian shores. If, then, a native of
Amalfi did not evolve the idea of the compass out of
his own brain, at least it was the old Republic which
first impressed the Western world with its immense
value, and this, too, at a far earlier period than the
date usually assigned to Gioja's "discovery." For a
Christian bishop of Jerusalem a hundred years before
Gioja's day makes mention of the compass as being in
common use amongst the Saracens of Palestine, whilst
its existence was certainly known to Brunetto Latini,
the tutor of Dante, whom for certain moral failings
upon earth his brilliant pupil somewhat harshly places

in the infernal regions. History has, in short, long deprived poor disconsolate Positano of its vaunted glory in the production of a medieval scientist whose very existence has now become a matter of speculation.

As we thread our way along the road that curves round headland after headland, and is carried over sheer precipices whose base is lapped by the cool jade-green water, we begin to realize the essential difference between the Sorrentine shores we have left behind us, and the marvellous Costiera d'Amalfi we are now passing. Ever green and smiling are the favoured districts that stretch from Castellamare to Massa Lubrense, with the mountain tops acting as screens to protect the groves and crops from the sun's ardent rays and with the fresh reviving breezes from the Abruzzi ever breathing upon them. But here we seem to be under the very eyes of the Sun-God, who stares fixedly from rising to setting upon the Amalfitan coast. Welcome enough is this continuous basking in his smiles during the short winter days; but oh! the long, long summer hours wherein King Helios relentlessly pours down his burning glances upon the shallow soil that covers the rocky face of the Costiera! We who visit the territories of the old Republic in winter or early spring only perceive one aspect of the picture. We rejoice in the gladdening warmth afforded by unbroken sunshine and by the complete absence of cutting winds which Monte Sant' Angelo's towering form excludes from these shores; we note with delight the premature unfolding of buds and blossoms, and we marvel at the young fruit of the dark-leaved loquat trees—the *nespoli* of the South—turning to pale yellow even in

February. But we cannot realise the blinding glare and the torrid heat of a July or August, making a perfect furnace of this sheltered corner, where the thin layer of cultivated soil, that has been scraped together painfully by human hands, becomes baked through and through, when the water-tanks are exhausted, and when the clouds of thick dust hang like a pall of white smoke for miles above the sinuous course of the Corniche road. How close and sweltering must be the atmosphere of these populous coves, when the very waves are flung luke-warm upon the hot sand! How must the inhabitants sigh for a breath of cool air from the Abruzzi, for the zephyr that tempers the heat on the Sorrentine plain! *Carpe diem;* let us enjoy the Costiera d'Amalfi in the freshness of early spring-time, before the oranges and lemons have been stripped from the leafy groves and before the sun has had time to scorch up the vegetation that now gives colour to every cleft and crevice of the rocky coast-line.

As we advance eastward from Positano we obtain glimpses from time to time of mountain valleys thickly clothed with brushwood, and far above our heads we perceive Agerola perched aloft under the shadow of the topmost crag of Monte Sant' Angelo—Agerola, where wolves still haunt the dim recesses of the chestnut woods, and where the charcoal burners can tell us of the great grey Were-Wolf that prowls round the village on stormy nights. Passing the torrent of the Arriengo and the Punta di San Pietro with its lonely chapel looking out to sea; glancing down upon the deep set strand and gloomy caverns of Furore, and rounding Cape Sottile, we find ourselves at Prajano, one of the prettiest spots to be found on all this wonderful coast. Here we stop to visit the church of San Luca, which stands on a little grassy platform overhanging the sea and commanding a superb view of the Bay of Salerno. It is a baroque structure of the type common everywhere in Italy, which travellers are apt to despise without acknowledging how picturesque this decadent style of architecture can appear. At Prajano the wooden doors of green faded to the hue of ancient bronze, the yellow-washed plaster façade and the lichen-covered tiles of the roof and tower make up a charming mass of varied colouring when viewed against the broad blue band of sea and sky beyond. Within, the church is mean and tawdry, just a

> Sad charnel-house of humble hopes and crimes,
> Long dead and buried in obscurity ;

but the afternoon sun struggling through the curtains that cover its fantastic windows allows a mellow light to fill the expanse of the building. A toothless old woman and a young girl, both of them thinly and poorly clad, are the sole occupants of the church, and they are evidently too much absorbed in prayer to notice our presence. They have placed beside the Madonna's altar lighted tapers which glimmer feebly in a shaft of strong sunlight that falls through a rent in the curtain overhead. For what purpose, we wonder, have these candles been bought out of a scanty store! Are they burning on behalf of some sailor-boy now being tossed upon the ocean? Or are they offered to obtain some boon more selfish and less pathetic? At any rate, this pair of intent worshippers,

EVENING AT AMALFI

representing fresh Southern youth and crabbed age, make up a pretty picture as they kneel together on the pavement of tiles ornamented in bright rococo patterns to represent the coat-of-arms of some forgotten noble benefactor : it is too simple and every-day a sight in Italy to offer a theme for verse, too sacred a subject for an idle photograph. We leave the church on tip-toe, and return to the terrace with its low marble seats and its stunted acacia trees to sit a few moments before re-entering the carriage.

Skirting the Capo di Conca we obtain our first sight of proud Amalfi, and we realize that our drive, long in distance perhaps, but all too short with its varied beauties and interests, is drawing to a close. Nearer and nearer do we approach our goal, the shining turrets of the Cathedral tower acting as our beacon, until at length our chariot clatters beneath the echoing tunnel hewn in the cliff that leads into the town itself.

CHAPTER VI

AMALFI AND THE FESTIVAL OF ST ANDREW

THE traveller's first impressions of Amalfi, which is essentially the beauty-spot of the Riviera of Naples, are usually associated with the old Capuchin convent, long since turned into a hotel and now the bourne of most visitors to this coast. Its arcaded façade and its terraced garden stand on a plateau seemingly cut out of the sheer face of the cliff, whilst high above the town the lofty barren rocks enfold the Convent and its verdant demesne within a natural amphitheatre and protect this sunny paradise from the keen blasts of winter. A flight of steps zigzagging up the rocky hill-side connects the building with the high road below; whilst a narrow pathway, leading between stone walls and now passing beneath dark mysterious archways, wherein the lamps burning before the Madonna's shrines afford a welcome light even at midday, descends by steep gradients from the garden above into the main piazza of the little city. Built by the celebrated Cardinal Pietro Capuano nearly seven hundred years ago for Cistercian monks, the monastery in the sixteenth century came into the possession of the Capuchin Friars, those brown-robed figures that with their bare feet and girdles of knotted white cord are such familiar and picturesque objects in the daily crowds of every Italian town. But the friars have been forced to abandon their airy retreat ever since the suppression of the religious houses, which succeeded the union of the old Neapolitan kingdom with young Italy, and their convent has long been put to secular uses. Yet the old monastic church still exists, and superstitious people declare that the spectral forms of ejected Capuchins are sometimes to be seen advancing slowly up the rocky ascent in order to revisit the sacred building that is now closed for worship. Nevertheless the church is cared for by the members of the Vozzi family, its present owners, who every Christmas-tide still prepare the popular *presepio*, that curious representation of the scene in the stable at Bethlehem, wherein a score of gaily dressed figures of painted wood represent the Holy Family and the worshipping peasants. Little in fact has been changed within the building itself, and the exquisite cloistered court with its slender intertwining Saracenic columns still remains to delight alike the artist and the antiquary. We say "still remains" advisedly ; for beyond the tiny quadrangle our eyes at once light upon a scene of hideous devastation.

Doubtless many persons will recall the great land-slip of December 1899, when almost without warning the whole face of the rocky headland that shelters Amalfi on the west tore itself loose and slid with a crash like thunder into the sea below, overwhelming in its fall the little inn known as the " Santa Caterina " and burying in its ruins two English ladies and several fishermen. The sinister scar still continues as a blot upon the lovely landscape, speaking only too eloquently to all of sudden death and destruction amidst the

surrounding scenes of life and beauty.   The older
portion of the Capuchin convent, by a miracle as it
were, escaped the on-rush of the land-slide, but its
famous " Calvary," the large group of the Crucifixion
that appears prominently in so many pictures of
Amalfi, was completely swept away, so that the boat-
men from the sands below can no longer behold the
immense vivid representation of the Last Agony which
was wont to greet their upturned eyes.   Already
Time's kindly hand has begun to drape the scene of
the catastrophe with a decent mourning veil of grey
and green, for the hardy succulent plants that can with-
stand the sun's fierce rays and can thrive despite the
boisterous salt sea-winds are already sprouting from
every crack and cranny of the riven earth.   Perhaps
it is as well for us selfish and self-satisfied mortals to
possess a *momento mori* close at hand in a spot so
teeming with the joy of life ; yet somehow the first
sight of that mass of broken headland and the dark
ominous fissure in the hill-side, flung across the sunlit
scene, is apt to send a slight shiver through the frame
of the beholder.

   There are three indisputable advantages to be gained
by turning a suppressed religious house into a modern
hotel, so a cunning old Italian inn-keeper once confided
to us ; that is, of course, provided one is not afraid of the
proverbial curse that clings to the buying of any of the
Church's sequestrated property.   These three things are
good air, good water, and lovely views ; benefits that
a layman is fully as competent to understand as
any cloistered ecclesiastic.   And certainly the worthy
Vozzi are fully justified in offering these privileges
to their guests at the Albergo Cappuccini.   Signor

Vozzi! How many travellers in the South recall with infinite pleasure their host's tall commanding figure, his snowy drooping whiskers, the sun-shade that was rarely out of his hand, his old-fashioned courteous manners, and his famous family of cats, whereof the coal-black Nerone was the prime favourite, a feline monster almost as tyrannical as his Imperial namesake of evil reputation. Signor Vozzi's striking personality, the sable fur of agate-eyed Nerone, the eternal sunshine, and the wide all-embracing views over sea and land, are somehow all jumbled together in our perplexed mind, as it recurs to the many days spent beneath the convent roof. Nay, not beneath the roof! For we were wont to pass the whole day, even the short December day, in basking on the warm sheltered terrace and peering over the busy beach and the dazzling waters below, whereon the tale of Amalfitan fisher-life could be read as it were from the pages of a book.

Somehow the old monastic buildings appear marvellously well adapted to modern needs. The former inmates' cells, wherein the brown-robed brethren of the Order of St Francis until lately were wont to pass their placid uneventful lives, afford comfortable if somewhat limited accommodation ; whilst the covered *loggia* that runs the whole length of the cells has been turned into a series of delightful little sitting-rooms, their broad arc-shaped windows facing full south, a boon that only a winter resident in Italy can properly appreciate. *Dove non entra il sole, entra il medico*, is a hackneyed but well-proven adage ; consequently here in the old Capuchin convent the services of the local medicine-man ought rarely to be required.

I

Signor Vozzi's guests partake of their meals in the ancient refectory, a large bare echoing chamber with a vaulted ceiling, which still contains the old stone pulpit from which in more pious days a grave brother was wont to read aloud choice passages from the works of the early Fathers of the Church or of St Bonaventura, the Seraphic Doctor of the Franciscans, during the hours allotted to the frugal repasts of the friars.   But the public rooms and the cool white-washed corridors do not present such attractions as the glorious garden with its famous *pergola* and its views of the Bay. Here even in Christmas week we found quantities of plants in full bloom : the delicate yellow blossoms of the Soffrana rose ; trailing ivy-leaved geraniums with gay heads of carmine flowers ; the honey-scented budleia with its little globes of dark yellow flowerets : clumps of gorgeous scarlet salvia ; and straggling masses of the pretty cosmia, red, pink and white. Humming-bird hawk-moths darted hither and thither in the sunshine, restless little creatures whose wings are never for a moment still, as they poise gracefully over each separate blossom in turn.   The *pergola* itself, which every artist at Amalfi paints as a matter of course, generally with a Capuchin friar—at least a friar *pro hac vice*—or a pretty dark-eyed damsel in the native costume, sitting in the foreground, was certainly bare of foliage, we admit, for even in the soft warm air of the Bay of Salerno the grape-vine wisely refuses to burst into leaf at Yuletide, no matter how enticing the warmth.   But the thick white pillars and their wooden cross-beams, around which are entwined the leafless coiling limbs of the sleeping vine, throw dark blue patterns of chequered shadow upon the sunlit ground.

Above the terraced garden rises the orangery, well watered by many artificial rillets, and from the midst of the orange and lemon trees there emerges a path leading to the entrancing *bosco*, or grove, that fills the deep hollow space formed by the sheltering cliffs behind. It was mid-winter, as we have said, yet pink cyclamens and strong-scented double narcissi were blooming freely, whilst from the dark boughs of the ilex trees overhead there fell upon the ear the pleasant twittering of innumerable birds, for happily the cruel snare and the gun are strictly forbidden in this sacred spot, so that his " little sisters, the birds," that the gentle Saint of Assisi loved so tenderly, can still sing their songs of innocence and build their nests in peace amidst the trees that no longer remain the property of the great humanitarian Order. At nightfall this garden is almost equally beautiful beneath a star-lit sky and with the many lamps of the town below throwing long bars of yellow light upon the placid waters of the Bay. As we pace the long terrace, wrapped in the glory of a million stars and revelling in the exalted yet fairy-like loveliness of the scene around us, we perceive the mellow night air to be redolent of a strange but fascinating perfume. It is the *olea fragrans*, the humble inconspicuous oriental shrub that from its clusters of tiny white flowers is thus giving out its secret soul at the falling of the night dews, and permeating the whole garden with its marvellous floral incense. But if the star-lit, flower-scented nights of Amalfi are to be accounted as exquisite memories, how much more glorious and exhilarating is the rising of the sun, as he appears in full majesty of crimson and gold above the classic hills

that overlook Paestum to the east ! Leaning at early
dawn from the windows of the Cappuccini, we have
watched the sky flush at the first caress of " rosy-
fingered Eôs " and seen the fragment of the waning
moon turn to silver at the approach of the burning
God of Day, still tarrying behind the lofty barrier of
the capes and mountains of the Lucanian shore.

> Slowly beyond the headlands comes the day,
> Though moon and planet on a sky of gold,
> Chequered with orange and vermilion-stoled,
> Have floated long before the sun's first ray
> Has shot across the waters to display
> Amalfi in her dotage ; as of old
> His beams lit up her splendours manifold,
> Her quays and palaces that fringed the bay.
> His smile makes every barren hill-side blush
> In rose and purple for the glories fled,
> As early watchers note th' encroaching flush
> From proud Ravello to Atrani spread,
> And curse the cruel arm that once did crush
> This sea-sprung Niobe, and leave her dead.

Dead, alas !   For the old liberties of the great
Republic of Amalfi have been extinct for more than
half a thousand years, and it is in consequence difficult
for us to realise that the quaint noisy squalid
picturesque little city by the sea-shore, huddled into
the narrow gorge of the Canneto, is that self-same
Amalfi whose navies rode triumphant over the
Mediterranean before the days of the Early Crusades.
Yet Amalfi, which may be reckoned amongst the
first-born of that fair family of medieval cities that
their prolific parent the land of Italy brought forth in
an age of darkness, was also the foremost to droop and
die, her glories scattered and passed before Florence had

AMALFI

ceased to be an obscure country town. In this case History presents to us a most forcible, not to say an unique example of the origin, rise and decline of a power, all occurring within a short space of time. Amalfi springs, as it were, out of the void as a city of importance, for no Roman colony occupied its site in antique times. Its very nomenclature is a puzzle to scholars, and the usual statement that it owed its name to Byzantine settlers coming hither from the ancient town of Melfi in the Basilicata does not sound very convincing, though for want of a better theory it must suffice. Why, when, and by whom the city was in reality founded remains an enigma, yet we learn from a passage in one of the letters of St Gregory the Great that the place was of sufficient size to be governed by a bishop in the sixth century. By the tenth we find the Republic of Amalfi already risen to a position of commanding importance, and holding its own against the rival states between which its territories were wedged ; the dukedom of Naples to the west and the principality of Salerno to eastward. Dexterously playing on the greed and prejudices of the various tyrants who ruled Naples and Salerno, and occasionally allying itself with them in order to repel the fierce attacks of their common enemy, the Saracenic hordes who were then harrying the Lucanian coast, Amalfi continued to uphold its political freedom and dignity in the face of immense difficulties. And in gratitude for the vigour with which the Amalfitani had waged war against the infidel invaders, Pope Leo IV. in course of time conferred upon the Duke or Doge, the chief magistrate of the Republic, the title of " Defender of the Faith." Nominally under the suzerainty of the Greek Emperor at Constantinople, Amalfi was practically independent; its system of government was conducted on lines somewhat akin to those of aristocratic Venice; its population is said to have exceeded fifty thousand in the capital city alone; its boundaries extended from the Promontory of Minerva on the west to the town of Cetara upon the confines of Salerno; whilst many daughter-towns of wealth and importance, such as Scala and Ravello, sprang into being within the narrow limits of the sea-girt republic. Owning a small and by no means fertile extent of land, the inhabitants of Amalfi from its earliest days were forced to become merchants and sailors; to use a modern phrase, the Amalfitani came to possess a complete monopoly of trade with Eastern lands, both Christian and Mahommedan. It was the ships of the Republic that alone brought to the shores of Italy the rich stuffs, the gold and silver embroideries, the dried fruits and the strange birds and beasts of Asia Minor and Arabia, and in exchange for their oriental merchandise obtained an abundance of corn, wine, oil, meat and other commodities of life that their beautiful but somewhat sterile dominions were unable to supply to an ever increasing population. But it was not only the material products of the East that the sailors of Amalfi conveyed to Europe in their home-bound argosies; for they brought back with them the rudiments of arts and sciences that distracted Italy had well-nigh forgotten during the period of the barbarian invasions. Through the merchant princes of Amalfi, the secrets of astronomy, of mathematics and of scientific navigation were reintroduced into the land that had almost lost its old Roman civilization. A priceless manuscript of that great code of laws, the Pandects, which a Byzantine Emperor, the famous Justinian, had caused to be compiled with such skill and labour, putting into concise and accurate form the collected wisdom of generations of Roman jurists, was included amongst the treasures of the East that were borne back to Italy in the Republic's vessels. And in addition to restoring the old Roman jurisprudence to its original home, the city of Amalfi had the honour of promulgating the celebrated *Tabula Amalphitana*, the new maritime laws that were henceforth destined to regulate the whole commercial system of the western world. No marvel then that the poet William of Apulia should praise in unmeasured terms the glories of the new-sprung city, whose trade extended to the shores of India and whose merchants possessed independent settlements in every great city of the Levant.

> "Nulla magis civitas argento, vestibus, auro
> Partibus innumeris ; hac plurimus urbe moratur
> Nauta marit coelique vias aperiri peritus.
> Huc et Alexandri diversa feruntur ab urbe
> Regia et Antiochi.   Zeus haec freta plurima transit
> His Arabes, Indi, Siculi nascuntur et Afri.
> Haec genus est totum prope nobilitata per orbem,
> Et mercanda ferens, et amans mercata referre.

> (No city richer in its store of gold,
> Of precious stones and silks doth Europe hold ;
> Her skilful mariners o'er treacherous seas
> With aid of compass sail where'er they please.
> From Egypt and from Antioch they land,
> Their precious cargoes on th' Italian strand.

Scathless Amalfi's navies penetrate
The distant ports of every Paynim state.
Match me throughout the circuit of this earth
Another race so full of zeal and worth.)

A small state on a barren shore, yet the holder
of the balance between East and West by means of
its wide-spread commerce, such was Amalfi during
the tenth and eleventh centuries. In some respects
this Republic of the Middle Ages appears as the
prototype of the Venice of the Renaissance, for there
is not a little in common between the city that was
built upon the marshy islets of the Adriatic lagoons,
and the city that was erected at the base of the
treacherous cliffs of the Tyrrhene Sea. Solely by
means of commerce both foundations rose from
nothingness to splendour and power: both held the
gorgeous East in fee; and both fell lamentably from
their high estate. The chief point of difference in
this comparison of their careers is obvious; Amalfi
collapsed suddenly and utterly, whilst the Queen or
the Adriatic has sunk gradually to decay until she
has become the interesting monument of a vanished
magnificence which we admire to-day.

It was the rising naval power of Pisa that finally
crushed the greatness of Amalfi, although the Republic
had already entered into its days of decline when
Robert Guiscard at the time of the First Crusade had
temporarily annexed its dominions to his new principality. Some thirty years later King Roger of
Naples forcibly seized the whole of the Costiera
d'Amalfi, allowing the citizens to retain their own form
of government. Four years after this, the Pisan fleet,
coming to aid the people of Naples against King

Roger, utterly destroyed the once vaunted navy of Amalfi, and sacked both the city itself and the two hill-set towns of Scala and Ravello. Its political liberty had already been crushed by the Normans, and now its ships and its wealth were dissipated by the Pisans; it was a double measure of ignominy and disaster from which Amalfi never recovered. Amidst its humiliations and sorrows, the stricken city had also to mourn the loss of its greatest treasure, its secular *palladium*, that most precious copy of the Pandects of Justinian, which the Pisan marauders seized and carried back with them to their city on the Arno. Here in Pisa the famous volume remained in safe keeping for some three hundred years, and then, as Time's round brought its inevitable vengeance on the plunderers of Amalfi, it was removed by the victorious Florentines to their own city. So intense a veneration for the book itself now manifested itself amongst the scholars and students of Florence, that at one period offerings of incense were often made to the inscribed wisdom of past ages as to a most holy relic of some Saint, and the clerk or jurist about to peruse its faded characters was wont, first of all, to breathe a prayer of genuine gratitude on his knees for the preservation of this ancient book. Amalfi, Pisa, Florence, each in its turn has owned the guardianship of this most famous literary jewel, which is to-day jealously guarded as the chief treasure of the world-renowned Laurentian Library.

It is true that the prosperity of Amalfi did not disappear immediately after the inroad of the Pisans, for Boccaccio, writing in the fourteenth century, still speaks of the ancient territory of the destroyed

Republic as "a rocky ridge beside a smiling sea, which its inhabitants call the Costa d'Amalfi ; full of little cities, of gardens, of fountains, and of rich and enterprising merchants." It was in fact reserved for relentless Nature herself to complete the work of destruction that Norman armies and Pisan fleets had more than half accomplished. We have already spoken of the terrible land-slips to which this beautiful shore is eminently subject, even at the present day, as the mass of wreckage outside the old Capuchin convent only too clearly testifies. In the year 1343, during the progress of a storm of exceptional fury, of which the poet Petrarch has left us a vivid account in one of his letters, the greater part of the devoted city was swept away by a tidal wave. The whole line of quays stretching from the headland by the Cappuccini to the point of Atrani on the east, together with churches, palaces, and warehouses, was now swallowed up by the surging waters and engulfed for ever in the depths of the sea ; and thus the very element that had brought wealth, power, and prosperity to Amalfi in the past now proved the direct cause of her final calamity. With this fearful cataclysm of Nature following upon the heels of its political extinction, we can hardly wonder at the rapid decline of this "Athens of the Middle Ages," whose population has now sunk to about one seventh part of the 50,000 citizens it once boasted in the far distant days of her maritime supremacy.

Reflecting upon the famous past of this ancient city, let us descend the steep pathway from the terrace of the Cappuccini to visit the crowded beach below. Here we find ourselves in the midst of a cheerful animated throng, engaged in mending nets, in painting boats, and in other occupations connected with a seafaring life. The tall fantastic houses with balconied windows that line the curve of the sea-shore, the glistening sands and the brown-legged, gay-capped fishermen, combine to present a charming picture of southern Italian life, so that we could gladly linger in observing the ever-changing scenes of life and industry. But we cannot tarry long, for the ubiquitous beggars who have begun to pester us ever since we passed the hotel gates have meantime dogged our descending footsteps, and their forces have been recruited on the way hither by many willing assistants. No doubt the vast majority of the Amalfitani are hard working and self-respecting, for the little town possesses maccaroni factories and old-established paper mills of no small importance, yet it is obvious that a considerable portion of the total population and at least one-half of all the children spend their whole time in demanding alms of strangers. Before, behind, and from a distance arises the ceaseless cry of "*Qual co', signor' ! Fame ! Fame !*" in hateful tones of make-belief misery, and these whining appeals are aided by all the expressive pantomimic gestures of the South. You are placed on the horns of a dilemma : give, and the report that a generous and fabulously wealthy Signore has arrived in Amalfi will run like wild-fire through the whole place, and your life in consequence will become an absolute burden for the remainder of your sojourn in this spot. Refuse, and the wretches who have hitherto been wheedling and cringing at your heels, will at once grow insolent and threatening, especially in the case of unprotected

ladies.   It is in fact a choice of two evils, and the
only remedy that we ourselves can suggest is for the
persecuted traveller to select a good stout larrikin and
pay him freely to keep at arm's length his detestable
brothers and sisters in professional beggary.   But the
uninitiated usually endure these odious importunities
for a certain length of time, and then, exasperated by
the unchecked mendicancy of the place, at last fly
precipitately from this beautiful shore, to seek comparative peace and freedom elsewhere.   For it is
useless to argue ; it is foolish, even dangerous to
grow angry.   "Why should we give to you?" we
asked one day in desperation of a particularly persistent woman.   "Because," was the unabashed and
impudent but unanswerable reply, "you have much,
and I have nothing!"   Driven by these human pests
from the sunlit strand, we make our way through the
busy piazza, where peasant women with piles of fruit
and vegetables make a glowing mass of colour around
the central fountain below St Andrew's statue, and
proceed towards the Valley of the Mills.   A different
phase of Amalfitan life now greets us, for here are to
be found the hard-working bees of this human hive,
and it must be confessed their ways make an agreeable
change from the habits of the pestering drones that
infest the beach and the neighbourhood of the hotels.
The whole of the steep rocky gorge of that tiny
torrent the Canneto is full of mills, each emitting a
whirring sound which mingles with the continual
plash of the water as it descends in miniature
cascades the full length of the ravine, providing in its
headlong course towards the sea the motive power
required to turn all this quantity of machinery.

IN THE VALLEY OF THE MILLS, AMALFI

Bridges span the Canneto at several points, whilst
either bank is occupied by tiny factories of paper or
soap, and by winding stone stair-ways that lead upward to terraces contrived to catch the sunshine for
the purpose of drying the goods. The whole valley,
with its strong contrasting effects of sun and shade
and its varied atmosphere of intense heat and of
chilly dampness, is full of seething picturesque
humanity. The combined sounds of creaking wheels,
of falling water and of human chattering are almost
deafening within this narrow echo-filled gorge, above
which in the far distance we catch a glimpse of rocky
heights with the town of Scala perched eyrie-like
against the deep blue of the sky overhead. Pretty
laughing girls, bare-footed and with marvellously
white teeth, emerge from the open door-ways to
smile pleasantly at us, for the workers of the Valle
de' Molini are thoroughly accustomed to the presence
of strangers in their midst. Half-naked men, who
have stepped for a moment out of the hot rooms of
the maccaroni factories in order to breathe the fresh
air, regard us with calm disdain and without any
seeming interest. Our presence is tolerated, even if
our reception excites no feelings of surprise or
cordiality, so that we are allowed to pursue our walk
up the ever-narrowing valley in peace and comfort
and to admire at our leisure the wonderfully
beautiful effects of colouring produced by the
cascades of purple-stained water, the graceful forms
and gay dresses of the girls, and the peeps of fruit-
laden orange trees above fern-clad walls. And how
dark the people are! For though black eyes and
hair are commonly associated with the Italian race,

yet in the North we find abundant evidence of the admixture of Teutonic blood, whilst in the South the fair-haired Norman settlers have left indelible marks of their conquest of Naples and Sicily in many blue-eyed and white-skinned descendants ; but here in Amalfi a blonde complexion seems to be absolutely unknown. " *Com' è bianco ! Com' è bianco !* " called out one of a party of girls with swarthy skin and ebon hair and tresses, who languidly came out to stare at us, as we wended our way slowly up the Valley of the Mills.

But the chief pride of Amalfi, and indeed its sole surviving fragment of departed magnificence, is the Cathedral, dedicated to St Andrew the Apostle, who is patron of the city. A broad flight of steps, flanked on either side by the Archbishop's Palace and the residence of the Canons, leads to a platform covered by a most beautiful Gothic *loggia* set with richly traceried windows and upheld by antique marble columns. At its northernmost angle we see springing into the blue aether the tall graceful red-and-white striped campanile, surmounted by its barbaric-looking green-tiled cupola and pinnacles. Facing the top of the steps are the two magnificent doors, specially designed in distant Byzantium to embellish this church more than eight hundred years ago, and cast by the famous artist in bronze, Staurachios. Two Latin inscriptions, incised in letters of silver upon the baser metal, relate to the world that one Pantaleone, son of Maurice, caused this work to be under-taken in honour of the holy Apostle Andrew, in order that he might obtain pardon for the sins he had committed whilst upon earth. These glorious

gates were the gifts to their native city of members
of the family of Pantaleone of Amalfi, merchant
princes who had amassed an immense fortune by
trade in the Levant. They are splendid specimens of
niello work, which consisted in ornamenting a surface
of bronze by engraving upon it lines that were
subsequently filled in with coloured enamel or with
some precious metal. These portals of Amalfi,
perhaps the earliest example in Southern Italy of
this rare form of art, are divided into panels adorned
with Scriptural subjects simply and quaintly treated,
wherein the stiff attitudes of the figures and the
many long straight lines introduced testify plainly
enough to their Byzantine origin and workmanship.
As we enter the cool dark incense-scented building,
we note that though cruelly maltreated by the
baroque enthusiasts of the eighteenth century, the
general effect of the interior is still impressive with
its rows of ancient pillars and its richly decorated
roof. On all sides marble fragments with exquisite
reliefs meet the eye, spoils evidently filched from the
abandoned city of Paestum across the Salernian Bay
and presented to the church by the Norman conquerors
of Amalfi. After inspecting the classical bas-reliefs,
we descend into the ancient crypt, which well-meaning
artists have completely encased with a covering of
precious marbles and garish frescoes of the Neapolitan
school. It is a place of more than local sanctity,
this modernized crypt, for the possession of the relics
of the Apostle which Cardinal Capuano proudly
brought hither after the sack of Constantinople in the
early years of the thirteenth century, was considered
by many to constitute a sufficient recompense to

Amalfi for her lost independence. Popes and sovereigns were in the habit of approaching the shrine, and the number of these illustrious visitors includes the names of St Francis of Assisi, Pope Urban IV., the holy St Bridget of Sweden, and the notorious Queen Joanna II. of Naples. Aeneas Silvius Piccolomini, afterwards Pope Pius II., however, seems to have thought Amalfi, ever dwindling in size and importance, too mean a place to own so great a treasure, and he accordingly transported the head of the Saint to Rome, where it is now accounted amongst the four chief relics of St Peter's. Perhaps it was to counterbalance the loss of so important a member of the Saint's anatomy, that in the succeeding century there arose a report which spoke of the rescue of certain relics of the Apostle Andrew during the headlong course of the Reformation in Scotland. The most precious objects preserved in the Cathedral of St Andrew's, says this legend, were secretly saved from the expected fury of Knox's partisans and brought to Amalfi, where they were reverently added to the store of remains that had survived the plundering of Pius II. Whether or no there be any truth in this somewhat fantastic theory, it is enough to state that St Andrew continues to be patron Saint of this maritime city, for which office the character of the Galilean fisherman who was called to be a fisher of men seems specially appropriate. Nevertheless, despite the valuable additions made in Reformation days, the sanctity of the shrine is not held so high as it used to be. No longer do the venerated bones ooze with the sweet-scented moisture that in medieval days was piously collected to be used for purposes so

varied as the curing of warts, or the scattering of
Paynim fleets! Yet so late as the days of Tasso,
the great Apostle himself was evidently connected in
the popular mind with the performance of so bizarre
a miracle :—

> " Vide in sembianza placida e tranquilla
> Il Divo, che di manna Amalfi instilla."

But although the present times are too sinful to
allow of the distillation of the fragrant dew of Amalfi,
we observe the kneeling forms of not a few intent
worshippers within the dimly-lighted crypt, in the
midst of which the Spaniard Naccarino's bronze figure
of the Apostle uprises with dignified mien and life-like
attitude.   Sant' Andrea is still " Il Divo," the tutelary
god of the Amalfitani ; he remains in the estimation
of these simple ignorant folk the special protector of
the community.   Times and ideas change, but not the
old deep-rooted feeling of a personal tie between the
Saint and his favoured people.

We were lucky in happening upon the great popular
festival of Sant' Andrea during our visit to Amalfi,
and consequently were enabled not only to witness a
picturesque scene of considerable splendour, but also
to observe how strong a devotion the Amalfitani still
manifest towards their own especial Saint.   With the
first flush of early dawn, discharges of mortars from
the beach and the neighbouring hills began to arouse
the echoes and to remind the still slumbering population that once more the great anniversary had arrived.
The world was quickly astir to do honour to the great
St Andrew, and from a very early hour an interminable
stream of peasants and villagers, young and old, male

K

and female, began to enter the town from all quarters, and to congregate in the piazza where stands the large fountain crowned by the Saint's own effigy. Here with exemplary patience the throng waited until the hour of the ceremony in the Cathedral drew nigh. Within the huge building priests and lay-helpers were actively employed in preparing for the event, and by their exertions the whole interior had been transformed into what may be best described as a magnificent ball-room, for every blank wall had been covered with draperies of rich crimson damask and the very pillars had been swathed from base to capital in the same gorgeous material. Innumerable old cut-glass chandeliers, that had reposed since the last *festa di Sant' Andrea* in huge round boxes in some secluded vault, had been slung by means of cords from the ceiling and the arches of the nave, whilst a large number of mirrors set in carved gilt frames had been affixed to various points of the walls and columns. The fine marble pavement lay thickly strewn with bay and myrtle leaves, emitting a pleasant wholesome scent when crushed under foot by the picturesque but somewhat malodorous crowd of fisher-folk and peasants. On entering the church, at the first sound of the bells booming over head, we found ourselves heavily pressed by the surging throng of worshippers, and it was only with difficulty we could obtain a sight of the ceremonies at the high altar, prominent upon which stood the silver bust of the Apostle containing the precious relics. It was a typical Italian *festa*. The chanting was harsh and discordant ; the antiquated inharmonious organ emitted unexpected squeals, as if in positive pain ; there was, it is needless to add, a complete absence of that "churchy" demeanour which passes for reverence in the North ; yet withal, despite the shrill discordant music, the tawdry embellishments of the grand old building and the absence of propriety of the crowd, there was perceptible some mysterious underlying force that compelled us to note the extra-ordinary hold the Church has upon the people of Southern Italy.   For all this throng of persons had assembled that day with one definite purpose : to see their universal friend and patron, their Saint and their worker of domestic miracles ; they had come to pay their homage to a celestial acquaintance, with whom, thanks to the Church's teaching, they had all been intimate from their cradles.   They had not thus assembled at an early hour, deserting their mills and their shops, their boats and their nets, renouncing their chances of gain, to hear a preacher's eloquence or to listen to fine music, but merely to pay their annual visit of respect to their Spiritual Master.   Why should we aliens intrude upon so private a gathering ?   In any case, we have grown weary of standing in the close sickly atmosphere, wherein the fragrance of the crushed bay-leaves, the fumes of incense and the strange smell of garlic-eating humanity blend in an oppressive manner.   We push our way through the eager and intent congregation, and gaining the door-way step with a sigh of relief into the sunshine that is flooding the *loggia*.   But it is too hot to remain here, and we descend the great stair-case in order to take up a post of vantage in the shade on the opposite side of the piazza ; having gained our desired position we expect in patience the arrival of the procession.   Nor have we very long to wait.   The officials of the town suddenly dart forward to clear the steps of their crowd of ragged children, and almost simultaneously the great bronze doors of Pantaleone are flung open to the sweet air and the sunshine.   It was a wonderful and deeply interesting experience to watch the glittering train slowly emerge from the darkness of the church into the glare of day, and then descend that stately flight of marble stairs to the sound of joy-bells and to the accompaniment of explosions of fireworks.   First came the leading members of the various Confra-ternities of the little city, all bearing tapers whose tongues of flame shone feebly in the fierce contemptuous sunlight, and all wearing snow-white smocks and coloured scarves.   Red, green, blue, white, purple, yellow, gleamed the huge banners of these different societies, each borne by a tall *vessillifero*, or standard bearer, assisted by quaint solemn little figures who acted as pages.   Then followed the body of the clergy in copes of white and gold, with eyes downcast as they chaunted in loud nasal tones from books in their hands ; next came the Canons of the Cathedral in fine old festal vestments reserved for such occasions and with mitres on their heads, for Amalfi clings to the ancient ecclesiastical privileges that were granted in distant days when Florence and Venice were little more than villages.   Last of all walked the Archbishop, an aged tottering figure, weighed down by his cope of cloth of gold and seemingly crushed beneath his immense jewelled mitre.   Two lackeys, almost as infirm as their venerable master, and clad in thread-bare liveries edged with armorial braid, were in close attendance, whilst behind the Archbishop, beneath a gorgeous canopy of state upheld by six white-robed

AMALFI: PIAZZA AND DUOMO

assistants, was borne the great silver bust of St Andrew. The appearance of the Image of " Il Divo," upon which the sunbeams were playing in dazzling coruscations of light, was greeted with a murmur of applause and satisfaction from the expectant crowd in the open. Hats were doffed ; knees were bent ; prayers were muttered, as with slow and cautious steps the bearers of the Image and its canopy began to descend. Having gained the lower ground in safety, a momentary halt was made, during which we were able to note the mass of votive offerings—jewels, chains, rings, watches, seals—suspended round the Saint's neck, amongst them being many silver fishes, doubtless the gifts of grateful mariners. And at this point we were spectators of a pretty incident. A little girl with black ringlets and eager eyes was dexterously lifted on to her father's shoulder, in order that she might present "Il Divo" with a golden chain, which the tiny fingers deftly clasped round the bejewelled neck of the silver bust. The crowd saw and applauded ; it was a moment of triumph for the dark-eyed child, for the Church, and for the approving throng. With the new addition of the child's necklet to the treasury of the Saint, the procession pursued its way through the square towards the Valley of the Mills, with banners waving, with priests chaunting in harsh monotonous tones, and with clouds of incense rising into the sun-kissed air. It was truly a beautiful and curious sight, this festival of the Church amidst people so devout and surroundings so appropriate.

On his safe return to his now brilliantly lighted Cathedral, the Saint was welcomed with indescribable enthusiasm. The crazy old organ was made to pro duce the loudest and liveliest of music ; the uniformed municipal band awoke the echoes of the venerable but bedizened fabric with its complimentary braying ; and urchins were even permitted to scatter fire-crackers upon the floor in honour of the event. It was a real ecclesiastical Saturnalia of a most innocent and joyous description.   All Amalfi spent the remaining hours of day-light in feasting, dancing and singing, and when at last darkness fell upon the merry scene, rockets and Roman candles were seen to spring into the night air from many points in the landscape, illumining the sea with quickly dying trails of coloured light. Watching the bonfires and the fireworks, and listening to the sounds of revelry and song arising from the town below, we pondered over our experiences of the day as we paced our airy terrace of the Cappuccini. Surely the South has remained immutable for centuries in its deeply rooted love of religious festivals.   The forefathers of these devotees of Andrew the Fisherman were equally enthusiastic worshippers of Poseidon or of Apollo.   The Church has not in reality altered the outer attributes ; it has but added a special moral significance to the old pagan gatherings.   The ancient gods of Greece and Rome are dethroned, and their very names forgotten by the populace ; but their cult survives, for it has been adapted to the glorification of Christian Saints.   True it is that the milk-white sacrificial oxen and the gay garlands of antiquity have been omitted ; nevertheless, there remain the music, the incense and the unrestrained jollity of the people.   Much that is beautiful and suggestive has perished, yet there survives enough of the old classical ritual for us to see that the true spirit of antiquity has never wholly died out amongst these sunburnt children of Magna Graecia.

> See the long stair with colour all ablaze,
> With banners swaying in pellucid air,
> As mitred priests with cautious footsteps bear
> The silver Image, flashing back the rays
> Of jealous Phoebus—Ah ! the altered days
> When these Lucanians with wind-lifted hair,
> Blossom-bedecked, with limbs and bosoms bare,
> Sang to Apollo psalms of love and praise !
> With bells and salvoes all the hills resound,
> And incense mingles with the atmosphere,
> As still this Southern race, ill-clothed, uncrowned,
> Retains the memory of the Pagan year,
> When changed, yet all unchanged, Time's round
> Makes the Jew Fisherman a god appear.

CHAPTER VII

RAVELLO AND THE RUFOLI

NO visit to Amalfi can be considered complete without ascending to the decayed town of Ravello, that crowns the rocky heights to the north-east of the parent city by the sea-shore. The road thither leads along the beach, passing between the picturesque old convent that is now the Hotel Luna, beloved of artists, and the solitary watch tower on the precipice which stands sentinel above the waters on our right hand. At this point we turn the corner, and find ourselves in Atrani, lying in the deep gorge of the Dragone and joining its buildings to those of Amalfi on the road above the beach. Prominent upon the steep ridge that separates the two cities stands the ruined keep of Pontone, the last relic of the town of Scaletta that was a flourishing place in days of the Republic. A tall belfry of peculiar and striking architecture which dominates Atrani is usually attributed to the art of the Saracens, whom King Manfred called in to garrison this place during his wars with Pope Innocent IV. Atrani, which is but a suburb of Amalfi, suffered equally with the Capital during the great upheaval of Nature that desolated this coast in the fourteenth century, so that little of interest remains except the quaint church of San

Salvatore a Bireta, wherein the Doges of Amalfi were once elected and crowned. This ancient building lies hidden in a sandy cove beneath the roadway, and those who care to run the gauntlet of beggars and descend to the beach below, can examine its beautiful bronze doors, which the generous citizen Pantaleone gave *pro mercede animae suae et merito S. Sebastiani Martyris*. But there is very little else to inspect, for the interior has been hopelessly modernized.

Soon after passing Atrani we turn sharply up hill to the left, and begin our ascent towards Ravello. The dusty white road winds upwards through a region of carefully cultivated terraces filled with olives and vines, intermingled here and there with orange, lemon, fig, and pomegranate trees. As we gain higher ground, our horizon tends ever to widen, and we behold the expanse of sea and sky melting in the far distance into "some shade of blue unnameable," whilst the mountain-fringed ring of the Bay of Salerno becomes vividly mapped out to our eyes from the Cape of Minerva to the Punta di Licosia. On our left we peer down into the depths of the dark ravine of the Dragone, whose black shadows are popularly supposed to give its name of Atrani to the cheerful little town we have left behind. Let us thank Heaven that we are at last out of reach of the beggars, and that the only human beings to be encountered upon the road are a few peasants with loads of fruit or vegetables, and an occasional charcoal-burner bearing his grimy burden to the town below. The *carbonaio* with his blackened face and queer outlandish garments is a familiar figure throughout all parts of Southern Italy. He belongs to a race apart, that dwells in the belt of forest land clothing the higher hills, and he only descends to the cities of the shore and the plain in order to sell his goods.   He is despised by the sharper-witted townsman, who beats down his prices for the combustibles he has borne with such fatigue from his distant mountain home.   Sometimes the old people are despatched to do the money bargaining, the selling and buying.   Look at the old couple at this moment passing us ; an aged man and woman that Theocritus might have known in earlier days when the world was less civilized and less greedy of gain.   With bare travel-stained feet, with feeble frames supported by long staves and with the heavy sacks of charcoal on their bent backs, the modern Baucis and Philemon crawl along the white road beneath a broiling sun, patient and uncomplaining, and apparently with no feelings of envy as they cast one careless glance at our carriage.   Weary and foot-sore, they will only obtain a few *quattrini* in the town for all their toil and trouble, and then they must retrace every step up the long hill-side, with their little stock of provisions to help eke out a miserable existence.   Yet can any life in such a climate and amid such surroundings be truly accounted miserable, we ask, no matter how humble the dwelling or frugal the fare ?

As our carriage creeps slowly upward, we find the land less cultivated, and now and again we pass tracts of woodland whence little purling streams fall over rocky ledges on to the roadway.   We catch sight of small clumps of cyclamen, and in the shady hollows we detect tufts of the maiden-hair fern—*Capilli di Venere*, " Venus' tresses," as the Italians sometimes call this graceful little plant. At a curve of the road we are confronted by a smiling old peasant with gold rings in his ears, who in the expectation of *forestieri* coming this way has been patiently sitting for hours on a boulder. Doffing his battered hat and putting a sunburnt hand to his mouth, the old fellow in a deep musical bass wakens all the sleeping echoes that lie in the many folds of the valley, so that we hear the words of welcome repeated again and again, growing fainter and fainter as the sound of the voice travels from cliff to cliff. The performer is delighted with a few *soldi*, and the jaded scarecrow of a horse seems pleased with his momentary halt. *Iterum altiora petimus ;* by degrees we reach the airy platform upon which Ravello stands, and finally alight at the comfortable old inn so long associated with the excellent family of Palumbo.

Ravello undoubtedly owes its early foundation to certain patrician families of Amalfi, which after securing their fortunes decided to leave the hot close city beside the shore, and to seek new homes in the bracing air of the hill-top above. Placing itself under the protection of the powerful Robert Guiscard, Ravello became faithfully attached to the Norman interest, and in 1086, at the suggestion of the great Count Roger, who cherished a deep regard for the Rufolo family, the town was created a bishopric by Pope Victor III. As a subject city of the Norman princes, Ravello was during this period at the zenith of its fame and importance. Its actual population is unknown at this distant day, but we learn that under Count Roger the large area of the city was entirely girdled by strong walls set with towers ; that it contained thirteen churches, four monasteries, many public buildings, and

a large number of private palaces.   Its cathedral was
founded in honour of Saint Pantaleone by Niccolò
Rufolo, Duke of Sora and Grand Admiral of Sicily,
the head of the powerful family whose name is still
gratefully remembered in this half-deserted town.   In
1156 Ravello was honoured by a state visit from Pope
Adrian IV.—the English monk, Nicholas Breakspear,
the only Briton who ever succeeded in gaining the
papal tiara and who gave the lordship of Ireland to
Henry Plantagenet—and during his stay the Pontiff
was entertained as the guest of the all-powerful Rufoli.
Born of humble parents in the village of Bensington,
near Oxford, Nicholas Breakspear became a monk at
St Alban's, and having once entered the religious life,
he rose by sheer force of intellect and an iron strength
of will to the attainment of the highest honour the
Church could bestow.   It was in the hey-day of his
power that the English pope entered Ravello and sang
Mass in the Cathedral in the presence of all the noble
citizens of the place, for in the previous year he had
crushed for ever the dangerous heresy of Arnold of
Brescia, by boldly sentencing that ardent reformer to
be burnt at the stake in Rome and his ashes cast into
the Tiber.   The Pontiff during his visit sojourned in
the Palazzo Rufolo, the beautiful Saracenic building
that is still standing intact after so many centuries,
and by a curious coincidence is now the property of
the well-known English family of Reid.   Nor was Pope
Adrian the only sovereign who honoured Ravello by his
presence, for Charles of Anjou, brother of St Louis of
France and the murderer of poor Conradin, and King
Robert the Wise also received the hospitality of the
Rufolo family within these walls.   The whole existing

RAVELLO : IL DUOMO

town in fact is eloquent of the long extinct but by no means forgotten Rufoli, who may fairly be reckoned among the more enlightened of the petty tyrants of medieval Italy. That their name was still familiar in Italian society in the fourteenth century is evident from the circumstances that Boccaccio puts a story, no doubt founded on fact, into the mouth of the fair Lauretta, which deals with the adventures of one Landolfo Rufolo of Ravello, "who, not content with his great store, but anxious to make it double, was near losing all he had, and his life also." The novel proceeds to relate how this member of a wealthy and respected family turned corsair, after losing all his capital in a mercantile speculation in Cyprus ; how he, in his turn, was robbed of his ill-gotten gains on the high seas by some thievish merchants of Genoa ; and how Landolfo, after passing through a variety of more or less improbable adventures, was finally rescued from drowning off the coast of Corfù by a servant-maid who, whilst washing dishes by the sea-shore, chanced to espy the unconscious merchant drifting towards the beach with his arms clasped round a small wooden chest, which kept him afloat. " Moved by compassion," says the relator of the tale, " she stepped a little way into the sea, which was now calm, and seizing the half-drowned wretch by the hair of his head, drew both him and the chest to land, where with much trouble she unfolded his arms from the chest, which she set upon the head of her daughter who was with her. She herself carried Landolfo like a little child to the town, put him on a stove, and chafed and washed him with warm water, by which means the vital heat began to return, and his strength partially revived. In due

time she took him from the stove, comforted him with
wine and good cordials, and kept him some days till
he knew where he was ; she then restored him his
chest, and told him he might now provide for his
departure." *   Of course the little chest that Landolfo
had clutched by chance in his agony of drowning
eventually turned out to be filled with precious stones,
which by a miracle—and miracles were common
enough in the days of the *Decameron*—not only floated
of itself but also supported the weight of Master
Landolfo.   In any case, the rescued merchant, with
the greed and ingratitude which are often accounted
for sharpness and wit, presented his kind hostess with
the empty trunk, whilst he concealed the gems in a
belt upon his own person.   Equipped with these
jewels, he made his way across the Adriatic to the
Apulian coast, and thence reached Ravello with
greater wealth than he had ever hoped to obtain with
his original capital at the time he set sail for Cyprus.

Fortunately Ravello, though shrunk to such modest
proportions nowadays, still possesses many memorials
of its glorious past.   Travellers will of course turn
their steps towards the Duomo, with its yellow
baroque façade abutting on the little piazza that,
with its daisy-starred turf and old acacia trees, forms
so pleasant a play-ground for the merry dark-eyed
children of the place.   The cathedral of St Pantaleone
is—or rather was—one of the most interesting and
richly decorated churches erected in Southern Italy
under the combined influence of Norman and Saracenic
art at a time when cunning workmen were able to
blend together the styles of East and West, and to

* The Decameron. *Novel IV. of the Second Day.*

produce that rich harmonious architecture of which the splendid churches of Monreale and Palermo present to us the happiest examples. There still exist intact the magnificent bronze doors with their fifty-four panels of sculpture in relief, the gift of Sergio Muscettola and his wife, Sigilgaita Rufolo, and the work of the Italian artist Barisanus of Trani, who likewise designed and cast the portals of the cathedrals of his native town and of Monreale. But alas! the interior of the building, that was once rich with mosiac and fresco and fanciful carving, has been converted into one of those dull soulless caverns of stucco that the wanderer in all parts of Italy meets with only too frequently. This deplorable act of vandalism at Ravello dates of course from the eighteenth century, and appears to have been the work of a bishop named Tafuri, who in his frenzied eagerness to possess a cathedral worthy of comparison with the fashionable atrocities in plaster then being erected at Naples, did not hesitate to destroy whole-sale almost all the ancient and elaborate ornamentation of his Duomo. His architect—perhaps the miserable Fuga, who ruined the interior of the Cathedral at Palermo, who knows?—dug up the fine old pavement, tore out the mosaics and had them carted away, effaced the frescoes, and at last transformed the venerable building with its memories of popes and princes into a commonplace white-washed chamber. Why this wretched prelate stayed his hand at the pulpit, it is difficult to say: perhaps he was meanwhile translated for his private virtues, perhaps Death overtook him in the work of destruction; at any rate, the famous pulpit of Ravello mercifully escaped the general onslaught, though it must have been by fortunate accident and not by design that Monsignore Tafuri omitted to remove this unique specimen of a style of architecture, which doubtless he considered barbaric and un-Christian in its character. For this pulpit is one of the finest examples of the ornate, if somewhat bizarre art of the thirteenth century, and belongs to a type of work that is not unfrequently met with throughout Italy. Six spiral columns, springing from the backs of crouched lions, support the rostrum of marble inlaid with beautiful mosaics ; whilst above the arch of the stair-way of ascent stands the famous portrait, usually called that of Sigilgaita Rufolo, wife of the founder of the Cathedral. The striking face, which is surmounted by an elaborate diadem with two pendent lappets, is evidently an excellent likeness of the original ; yet there can be no doubt that this interesting bust has been wrongly named, since the pulpit itself, as a Latin inscription duly records, was erected in the year 1272 by Niccolò Rufolo, a descendant of the famous Grand Admiral, so that we may fairly conclude that the portrait represents the wife, or perhaps sister or daughter, of the donor. But popular tradition dies hard ; and the name of Sigilgaita will probably cling for ever to the female face which has for over six centuries looked calmly down upon generation after generation of worshippers. Perhaps those severe proud features may have impressed the ignorant Vandal-Bishop as that of some unknown Saint, whom it might be dangerous to offend, and may thereby have saved the pulpit of Niccolò Rufolo from the destruction that must have seemed inevitable. Be that as it may, the bust has survived uninjured, which, apart from the feeling of sentiment, is particularly fortunate, for it belongs to a small class of artistic work, of which existing specimens are rare and highly prized. For there must have been a local and premature Renaissance in this part of Italy during the thirteenth century, otherwise a statue so imbued with true classical feeling and so correct in technical finish as that of Sigilgaita in Ravello Cathedral could never have been produced; yet the names of the artist or artists who thus anticipated the great plastic revival remain undiscovered. Portrait-busts, similar in treatment and idea to that of the so-called Sigilgaita, are to be found here and there in museums, but this effigy in remote Ravello remains unique amidst its original surroundings.

Turning aside from Sigilgaita's steady gaze and making the round of the bleak white-washed building, our eyes are suddenly attracted by a fine picture, in the manner of Domenichino, representing the martyrdom of Pantaleone, the popular Amalfitan Saint to whom this church was dedicated by the Rufolo family.

The cult of this Asiatic martyr in Amalfi is of course another legacy of the Republic's close connection with the Levant, whence some relic-hunting admiral or merchant of the state reverently brought Pantaleone's bones to the Italian coast. As the veneration of this Saint still exists so deep-seated that his Hellenic name is frequently bestowed on children at baptism, it may not be deemed amiss to give a very brief account of this eastern Martyr, who

L

is so closely associated with Amalfitan, and later with Venetian life.   Pantaleone was born at Nicomedia, in Bithynia, the son of a Pagan father and a Christian mother.   Well educated by his parents, he became a physician, and on account of his skill, his learning, his graceful manners and his handsome face, was finally selected to attend the person of the Emperor Maximian.   At the Imperial Court the young doctor, who had meantime neglected the faith of his mother, was recalled to a true sense of Christian duty by the precepts of an old priest named Hermolaus. Pantaleone now began to heal the sick and to preach the Gospel, and even at times to perform miracles. Information as to his conduct having reached the Emperor's ears, Maximian gave the young physician the choice of renouncing Christianity or of suffering death, whereat Pantaleone boldly declared he would rather die than apostatize.   Thereupon the Saint, together with the Christian priest Hermolaus, was bound to an olive tree and beheaded with a sword. The story of his martyrdom has been frequently treated in Venetian art, for as an eastern Saint Pantaleone has a church dedicated to him in Venice, wherein the brush of Paul Veronese has painted in glowing colours the chief incidents of his life and death.   As in the case of other physician-saints of the Roman Church— St Roch, St Cosmo and St Damiano—Pantaleone was especially besought in cases of the plague, which owing to the intercommunication between Amalfi and the Orient, frequently ravaged the towns of this coast.

From the Cathedral we proceeded to visit the quaint little church of Santa Maria del Gradillo, that with its

A STREET IN RAVELLO

oriental-looking towers and cupolas affords a pleasing
example of the mixed Lombard and Saracenic style
which was in vogue in the years when the house of
Hohenstaufen were masters of Southern Italy. We
found little that was worth seeing inside the building, except the pretty black-eyed daughter of the
toothless tottering old sacristan, who slunk off grum-
bling on his child's appearance, leaving her to do the
honours of the place. Her merry face with its wel-
coming smile and her modest loquacity excited our
interest, and in answer to our questions we gathered
that she was twenty years old, and was still unmarried,
not for lack of opportunity, she naïvely told us, but
because she was unwilling to leave her old parents,
who had no one in the world but herself to attend to
them. Coming to the door of the church, Angela
(for that was her name) pointed out her home, a
little white-washed cottage with a heavily barred
window over-hanging the grass-grown lane. We
wished our pleasant companion a warm good-bye,
or rather *a riverderla*, at the entrance of the dwelling, where through the open doorway we could espy a
small sun-smitten courtyard tenanted by a wizened
old woman sitting in the shade of an orange tree, by
three cats, and by a large family of skinny hens. On
a low wall we noted some shallow earthenware pans
filled with carnation plants, whose red and yellow
heads were clearly silhouetted against the blue sky
over head. Perhaps Angela's life, we thought, is after
all happier thus spent in the tending of her parents,
her poultry and her garden, than if joined to that of
some swarthy rascal of the beach below or dull
peasant of the hillside. Long may the old people

survive to keep their guardian Angel from the mingled
sorrows and joys of matrimony !

> "Tenete l'uocchie de miricula nere ;
> Che ffa la vostra matre che n'n de' marite?
> La vostra matre n'a de' marito' apposte
> Pe' ne' lleva' son fior, a la fenestre."

> (" Your eyes are marvellously black and bright !
> How is it that your mother does not wed you ?
> She will not wed you, not to lose her light—
> Not to remove the flower that decks her window ! ")

.   .   .   .

The well-known hotel kept by Madame Palumbo,
who is thoroughly conversant with English ways and
requirements, occupies a delightful position in the old
aristocratic quarter of Ravello known as " Il Toro,"
the name of which is still retained in the interesting
little church of San Giovanni del Toro close by.
This comfortable hostelry has been constructed out of
the *Vescovado*, the ancient episcopal residence, and it
still retains many curious and attractive features of
the original building, notably the quaint little stair-
way that descends from the bishop's private chamber
into the chapel, which is now the *salon* of the hotel.
With its magnificent views, its interesting buildings
and its pure exhilarating air, Ravello would seem to
be an ideal spot wherein to linger, and it affords
a most agreeable change in the later Spring months
from the close atmosphere and enervating heat of
Amalfi or the coast towns.   Perched on this breezy
hill-top, from the terrace of the hotel can be observed
the whole circuit of the Bay of Salerno, whilst behind
to the north and east the ring of enclosing mountains
rises sharp and distinct against the sky.   From this
point we are presented with a complete view of

the territories of the ancient Republic, spread out like a map beneath our feet and stretching from the Punta della Campanella to the heights above Vietri, and backed by the arid grey mountain peaks. If the garden of the Hotel Palumbo seems a fitting place wherein to idle or to dream, might not it also appeal to some historian, not tied to time nor to the hard necessity of money-making, as a suitable spot for the conception of a history of the origin, rise, decline and fall of the great maritime Republic, whose dominions, still smiling and populous, surround Ravello on all sides? Gibbon found the first suggestion for his Roman History whilst musing upon the ruins of the Capitol, and he finished his great work in a Swiss garden amidst the scent of acacia bloom ; might not the annals of the Amalfitan Republic likewise spring from reflections made upon this terrace, where the memories of a former greatness still beautiful in its decay must operate so powerfully? Well, perhaps some future Gibbon—or more probably some budding Mommsen —may in time present the world with a true impartial and erudite history of the Costiera d'Amalfi.

We bask lazily in the afternoon sunshine, to the soft, rather soporific cooing of some caged doves, that live in the back-ground out of sight behind a screen of lemon trees in huge red jars, such as Morgiana must have been familiar with. Beyond the terrace wall we note the carefully tended vines, precious plants, for their grapes produce the delicate *Episcopio* wine, perhaps the choicest vintage to be obtained around Naples, and boasting a flavour and bouquet that are rarely to be encountered except in the products of the most celebrated vineyards of France or Germany.

"O quam placens in colore,
O quam fragrans in odore,
O quam sapidum in ore,
    Dolce linguae vinculum.

"Felix venter quem intrabis,
Felix guttur quod rigabis,
Felix os quod tu lavabis;
    Et beata labia!"

Below the vinery we catch glimpses of the dancing waters of the Bay and of the little towns of Minori and Majori, seen through a screen of olive and almond trees that are gently swayed by the south wind. Opposite to us towers the huge form of the mountain of the Avvocata, upon whose slopes centuries ago the Madonna herself appeared in a flood of glory to an ignorant but pious shepherd lad, promising the startled youth to become his mediator, the *avvocata* of his simple prayers. The story must be true, say the peasants, for there on the hillside can still be seen the ruins of the shrine that the wondering and grateful villagers raised upon the very site of the apparition in honour of their celestial visitor. But the whole country-side teems with interesting and often beautiful legends and traditions, handed down by generations of the simple hardy folk who toil for their daily bread amidst the vineyards and olive groves that clothe the sun-baked slopes descending to the shore.

The intervening distance is not great between Ravello and La Scala, which surmounts the opposite ridge of the valley of the Dragone, whence good walkers can easily descend by the ancient mule track that leads down direct to Amalfi by way of Scaletta. Like its neighbour and historic rival across

the valley, the annals and fortunes of Scala are closely
interwoven with those of Amalfi ; and it was during
the palmy days of the Republic that this daughter-
town reached its height of prosperity. Although the
tradition that once Scala possessed a hundred towers
upon its walls and a hundred and thirty churches is
obviously exaggerated, yet it must have been a place
of importance even as early as 987, when Pope John
XVI. raised it to the rank of a bishopric, an honour
which did not fall to Ravello until many years later.
Early in the twelfth century Scala was pillaged by the
Pisans, but some years afterwards, when the mother
city tamely submitted to the demands of these Tuscan
invaders without the smallest effort at self-defence, the
higher-spirited mountaineers of La Scala manned their
walls with skill and vigour, though without avail.
The hill-set city was ultimately carried by storm, and
so thoroughly did the enraged Pisans wreak their
vengeance upon the place that Scala never again rose
to fame or eminence, but henceforward dwindled in
wealth and size until it finally sank to the condition of
a large village, whilst Clement VIII. offered an
additional indignity to the city in its dotage by depriv-
ing it of episcopal rank. But though the citizens of
modern Scala no longer possess a bishop in their
midst, they are still the proud possessors and jealous
guardians of the magnificent mitre presented by Charles
of Anjou, who was greatly pleased by the men and
money that this ancient town sent to aid his brother,
St Louis of France, in his Crusade. Some sculptured
tombs, one of them a monument in honour of Marinella
Rufolo of Ravello, who was married to a Coppola of
Scala, remain in the churches to interest the curious

traveller, but most visitors will find the principal charm
of this dilapidated little city in its lofty striking situation beneath the frowning mass of Monte Cerrato.

But the sunset has come and gone, and the last
tints of its rose-pink glow are rapidly disappearing from
the serrated line of mountain tops against their background of daffodil sky. Stars are beginning to peep
in the firmament, and yellow lights, the stars of earth,
are springing up fast in the town below, and even
appearing at rare intervals of space amongst the
cottages of the woody hillside, or upon the fishing
boats that lie on the bosom of the Bay, now turning
to a deep purple under the advancing shadows of
night. A cheerful concert of unseen insects greets
our ears as we descend rapidly towards Atrani, whilst
the goatbells amid the distant pastures tinkle pleasantly
from time to time. We soon exchange the dewy
freshness of evening in the country for the heavy air,
thick with dust, that hangs over the coast road, and
in a few moments more find ourselves at the foot of
the rock-cut staircase that leads to our convent inn.

.   .   .   .   .   .

But our days upon the beautiful Costiera d'Amalfi
are at an end, and the moment has at last come
for us to bid farewell to these enchanted scenes and to
the ancient city slumbering peacefully in its rocky
valley by the shore. Our rows upon the glassy waters
of the Bay, our scrambles up the wild scrub-covered
hillsides above the town, our evening walks along the
broad high-road to catch the fleeting glories of the
sun-set,—all are ended ; the day, the hour of departure
has actually arrived.

Casting a longing look behind we quit Amalfi in

the cool of the evening, in order to cover the eight
intervening miles of coast road that lie between us and
Salerno. We pass Atrani, with its tall parti-coloured
tower, and proceed towards our destination with the
smooth plain of waters below us and the fertile slopes
above our heads, and thus we quickly gain Minori,
another of the busy little settlements that once helped
to make up the collected might of the old Republic.
We meet with bare-footed sun-embrowned peasants,
in their suits of blue linen and broad shady straw
hats ; lean sinewy figures, returning from a long day's
work in the fragrant orange groves by which the town
is surrounded. We meet also, alas! with the usual
crowd of beggars, the halt, the maimed, and the
pseudo-blind, who are quickly left behind ; nevertheless the naughty picturesque half-naked children,
loudly screaming for *soldi*, caper in the dust alongside our carriage, until these little pests are out-
stripped, but only to give way to other imps, equally
naughty and unclothed, from Majori. Majori, nestling
by the seashore amidst the enfolding mountains, appears
to us a second Amalfi, with its crowded beach and
brightly coloured boats, with its paper and maccaroni
mills, huddled into the narrow ravine of the Senna,
which cuts the town in half ere it empties itself into
the Bay. Overhead the huge ruined castle of San
Niccolò looms distinct against the rose-flushed evening
sky, crouching like some decrepit old giant above the
little city which he so oppressed in the bad old days
when Sanseverini and Colonna carried on a perpetual
selfish strife that allowed their humble neighbours no
repose. Beautiful as is Majori, it is no lovelier than
many another spot upon this exquisite coast ; it is but

as one pearl in a well-matched necklace, for the country that lies between Amalfi and Salerno is fully as rich in historical interest and natural charm as is the western portion that we have just traversed.   Behind Majori we behold Monte Falerio, with its rocky summit tipped with the glow of evening and its base in purple shadow, descending abruptly into the darkening waters of the Bay.   Slanting down to the surf-fringed beach, the great mountain seem to bar our further progress, but with a guttural imprecation and a loud cracking of the whip, our coachman deftly guides his half-starved but cunning little horses round the sharp corner of the mountain spur known as the Capo del' Orso, and in a trice Amalfi, whither we have been straining our eyes, is snatched from our vision ; a few minutes later, and we have rounded the Capo del Tumulo, with its memories of the great Genoese admiral, Filippino Doria, who in the treacherous currents that circle round this Cape, destroyed the Spanish fleet of the Emperor Charles V.   Already the sun has dipped below the horizon, and the calm expanse of the Tyrrhene has lost the last reflected ray ; forward our driver urges his horses in the fast-fading light.   The Angelus rings out from half a score of belfries beside the seashore and on the hillside, breaking the stillness of the gloaming with musical reverberations.   Sunset and evening star, twilight and evening bell ; how exquisite is the fall of night upon the shores of the Bay of Salerno !   We pass the fishing village of Cetara, and in so doing we pass by the willing strength of imagination out of the dominion of the ancient Republic of Amalfi into the Principality of Salerno.   Onward we press, and it is not long

MINORI AT SUNSET

before a shrill familiar sound bursts upon our ears,
a sound that quickly tears the gossamer threads of a
fancy revelling in the thoughts of long-extinct princi-
palities and powers.   It is the whistle of a railway-
engine descending the slope from Vietri above us
down to Salerno ; it is the neighing of the iron horse
that has not yet pranced along the unconquered
Costiera d'Amalfi, nor befouled its crystal-clear air
with his smoky breath.   For at Vietri we re-enter the
every-day world, and leave behind us the sea-girt fairy-
land ; Vietri, not Cetara, is the true frontier town to-
day.   But the lights of Salerno are drawing nearer
and nearer, and in a few moments of time we are
tearing along the broad lamp-lit Marina of the town,
in the middle of which our driver pulls up suddenly
at the entrance of that old-fashioned comfortable inn,
the Albergo d'Inghilterra :

> "Another day has told its feverish story,
> Another night has brought its promised rest."

CHAPTER VIII

SALERNO AND THE HOUSE OF HAUTEVILLE

BACKED by gentle slopes well wooded and well tilled, and screened from the northern blasts by its guarding amphitheatre of grey crags, Salerno occupies a delightful position upon the Bay to which it gives its own name. The long stretch of its Marina, tolerably clean to the eye if not at all points agreeable to the nostrils, follows the broad curve of the strand, and an idle hour or so may pleasantly be whiled away in watching the fishing craft moored beside the mole and the attendant sailors. At the northern end of this promenade, in what constitutes the most fashionable quarter of the place, is a tiny garden with palms and daturas, whilst hard by stands a large theatre, evidences of the gentility of modern Salerno. But the whole town appears sleepy and dead-alive to a stranger, though at the sunset hour a band occasionally plays in this open space, the music attracting hither a crowd composed of all the divers elements of society in the quiet old city. Yet though not possessing any great attractions for a sojourn in itself, Salerno makes an excellent centre whence to explore the neighbourhood, for it lies within easy reach of the great Benedictine Abbey of Santa Trinità; of beautiful La Cava, "that Alpine valley under an Italian sky"; of

Nocera, with its ancient cathedral that was once a pagan temple ; and last, but very far from least, of that glorious group of temples at Paestum. It has tolerable hotels, and if only their *padroni* could be brought to realise that a flavouring of rosemary and garlic in every dish is not appreciated by the palates of the *forestieri*, the fare provided would be excellent. As in all Italian cities, northern or southern, however, the nocturnal noise is prodigious. Shouting and shrieking, quarrelling and yelling rend the air at all hours, whilst the practice of serenading, more agreeable in romantic poetry than in everyday life, is here carried to excess, and the twanging of the mandoline and the throaty voices of ardent lovers are rarely silent o' nights in the dark narrow streets of Salerno.

> "A lu scur' vagi cercann'
> La bella mia addo è ?
> Mo m'annascunn' po' fann' dispera',
> I mor', I mor' pe' te,
> Ripos' cchiù ne ho ! "

> (" In favouring dusk I wandering go,
> My fair, where shall I find her?
> Now she attracts, now drives me wild ;
> I die, I die for her ;
> Repose no more have I.")

Behind the long line of lofty well-built houses facing the Bay, the streets are gloomy, narrow and crooked, a labyrinth of dark mysterious lanes that contain no palaces or churches of note, and but few artistic " bits " to catch the eye and delight the soul of a painter. As in the case of Amalfi, the Cathedral of San Matteo at Salerno is almost the sole monument left standing of a past that is peculiarly rich in historical associations.

Ever since the accession of the Angevin kings Salerno
has remained a quiet provincial town, neither rich nor
poor, but stagnant and without commerce. Into its
harbour, which Norman and Suabian princes attempted
to improve, the sand has long since silted, and Naples
for many centuries past has been able to regard with
serene contempt the city that it was once intended to
make her commercial rival :

> "Se Salerno avesse un porto,
> Napoli sarebbe morto."

Well, Naples owns an excellent harbour, and has
in consequence grown into one of the largest sea-ports
on the shores of the Mediterranean, whilst little Salerno
can only afford anchorage for fishing boats.

The chief interest of the place centres in its close
connection with the great Norman house of Hauteville,
and especially with Robert Guiscard, Duke of Apulia
and Calabria, who after a fierce struggle managed to
capture this city from the Lombard princes. Sprung
from a hardy race of *valvassors* or *bannerets* in Normandy, Duke Robert was one of the twelve sons of
Tancred of Hauteville in the bishopric of Coutances.
Joining his elder half-brother William Bras-de-Fer in
Italy, Robert at once began to make a remarkable
display of soldierly and statesman-like qualities. An
adventurer pure and simple in an alien land, this
sharp-witted Norman in course of time obtained the
nick-name of Guiscard, or the Wiseacre, and on the
death of his elder brother he was nominated Count of
Apulia by acclamation of the Norman followers, to the
exclusion of his helpless young nephews. Robert
Guiscard's appearance and character have been sketched

for us with loving care by one of the most famous of
the world's historians, who was fully able to appreciate
the mingled force and cunning, the *suaviter in modo*
and the *fortiter in re*, of this leader of a handful
of Normans in a hostile and distant country. Let
Gibbon's stately prose therefore present to us a
word-painting of the Great Adventurer himself :—

" His lofty stature surpassed the tallest of his army ;
his limbs were cast in the true proportion of strength
and gracefulness ; and to the decline of life he maintained the patent vigour of health and the commanding dignity of his form. His complexion was ruddy,
his shoulders were broad, his hair and beard were long
and of a flaxen colour, his eyes sparkled with fire, and
his voice, like that of Achilles, could impress obedience
and terror amidst the tumult of battle. In the ruder
ages of chivalry, such qualifications are not below the
notice of the poet or historian ; they may observe that
Robert at once and with equal dexterity could wield
in the right hand his sword, his lance in the left ; that
in the battle of Civitella he was thrice unhorsed, and
that on the close of that memorable day he was ad-
judged to have borne away the prize of valour from
the warriors of the two armies. His boundless ambition was founded on the consciousness of superior
worth : in the pursuit of greatness he was never
arrested by the scruples of justice, and seldom moved
by the feelings of humanity : though not insensible of
fame, the choice of open or clandestine means was
determined only by his present advantage. The
surname of *Guiscard* was applied to this master of
political wisdom, which is too often confounded with
the practice of dissimulation and deceit ; and Robert

is praised by the Apulian poet for excelling the
cunning of Ulysses and the eloquence of Cicero.   Yet
these arts were disguised by an appearance of military
frankness : in his highest fortune he was accessible and
courteous to his fellow soldiers, and while he indulged
the prejudices of his new subjects, he affected in his
dress and manners to maintain the ancient fashion
of his country.   He grasped with a rapacious, that he
might distribute with a liberal hand ; his primitive
indigence had taught the habits of frugality ; the gain
of a merchant was not below his attention ; and his
prisoners were tortured with slow and unfeeling cruelty
to force a discovery of their secret treasure.   According
to the Greeks, he departed from Normandy with only
five followers on horse-back, and thirty on foot ; yet
even this allowance appears too bountiful ;—the sixth
son of Tancred of Hauteville passed the Alps as a
pilgrim, and his first military band was levied among
the adventurers of Italy."

Gaining over the Pope Nicholas II. to his interests,
the new Count was able to exact an oath of fealty in
1060 from the Italian barons, hitherto his equals, to
recognise him as " Duke of Apulia, Calabria, and here-
after of Sicily, by the grace of God and of St Peter,"
although it took many years of hard fighting before
these lands, thus proudly claimed, could be subdued.
Beginning with the conquest of the Duchy of Benevento, Guiscard at once laid siege to Salerno, taking it
after an obstinate resistance lasting over eight months,
during which he was himself severely wounded by a
splinter from one of his own engines of war.   The
city captured with such difficulty now became the
victor's favourite residence and the recipient of his

bounty and enlightened rule, so that Salerno quickly rose to the rank of one of the most illustrious towns in Europe, supplanting even its magnificent neighbour Amalfi in popular esteem.

> Urbs Latii non est hâc delitiosior urbe,
> Frugibus arboribus vino redundat ; et unde
> Non tibi poma nuces, non pulchra palatia desunt,
> Non species muliebris abest probitasque virorum.

> (All Latium shows no more delightful place,
> Whose sunny slopes the vine and almond grace ;
> 'Midst fruitful groves her palaces uprear,
> Her men are virtuous, and her women fair.)

It was under the Guiscard's auspices that the famous school of Medicine that had long been seated at Salerno rose to its highest point of excellence. " Paris for learning, Bologna for law, Orleans for poetry, and Salerno for Medicine" ;—such was the verdict of the age. With the somewhat grudging consent of the clergy, the hygienic skill of the dreaded Arabs was in this city permitted to temper the crass ignorance of medieval Italy, and at Salerno alone were the works of the infidel Avicenna and of the pagans Galen and Hippocrates openly studied. The result was that the fame of the doctors of this *Fons Medicinae* spread over all Western Europe, so that distinguished patients either came hither to be treated in person or else sent emissaries to explain their symptoms and to obtain advice. Nor were the professors of the healing art at Salerno tied down by a strict adherence to drugs and boluses, for they fully realised that the height of all human ambition, the *mens sana in corpore sano*, is in any case more easily to be obtained by self-control than by all the in-

M

gredients of the pharmacopoeia. They were warm believers apparently in the doctrine of moderation in all things, which after all is one of the most valuable prescriptions of modern hygiene :

> Curas tolle graves, irasci crede profanum,
> Parce mero, cœnato parum, non sit tibi vanum,
> Surgere post epulas, somnum fuge meridianum.

> (Throw off dull care ; thine angry moods restrain ;
> Eschew the wine-cup ; lightly eat, nor vain
> Deem our advice to make Enough thy feast.
> Take exercise, and shun the noon-day rest.)

Such was the oracular reply of the Salernitan sages to Robert, Duke of Normandy, and no one can dispute the sound common sense of the prescription given, nor doubt that it is applicable to half the patients who to-day throng the consulting rooms of fashionable London physicians.

But to return to Robert Guiscard, who shares the historical honours of the place, together with the great Pope Gregory VII., of whom we shall speak presently. After subduing the southern half of Italy and the island of Sicily, the great Duke next turned his victorious arms against the Eastern Empire, with the secret intention, it was suspected, of ascending the throne of Constantine. With the pseudo-Emperor Michael in his train, the Great Adventurer in 1081 assembled a vast army at Otranto, consisting of 30,000 Italian subjects and of 1300 Norman knights, with the object of crossing over to Epirus. Durazzo on the opposite Albanian coast, the Dyrrachium of the ancients, a city that was henceforth destined to be closely associated with succeeding dynasties of South Italy, was the objective of this gigantic expedition, for it was commonly reported to be the key of the Eastern Empire. Thither the flotilla set sail, but before reaching the Greek shore, an unexpected and unseasonable tempest scattered Guiscard's argosy, destroying many of the ships and drowning many crews. Nevertheless, the undaunted spirit and endless resources of the Norman Duke rose superior to all misfortunes. Landing with the remnant of his army he at once laid siege to Durazzo, despite the fact that the Emperor Alexius was marching to its relief, and that the Venetian fleet was already anchored in its harbour. In spite of overwhelming odds, Guiscard utterly routed the Byzantine army. With his heir Bohemond and his wife Sigilgaita beside him, the Duke watched the progress of the battle, and at its most critical juncture, at a moment when it appeared inevitable that the hard-pressed Italian army must yield to the sheer numbers of the foe, the deep voice of the leader could be heard booming like a deep-toned bell over the battlefield, as he addressed his wavering troops. "Whither do ye fly? Your enemy is implacable, and death is less grievous than slavery!" Joined with the hoarse voice of Guiscard, the Norman warriors could distinguish the exhortations of the Amazon-like Sigilgaita, "a second Pallas, less skilful in arts, but no less terrible in arms than the Athenian goddess." Rallying at the words of their master and shamed by the martial ardour of the Duchess, the invading troops made one last desperate effort, whereby the Imperial army was driven back and scattered, so that Alexius barely escaped with his life. Having routed the Emperor in fair fight, Guiscard now made use of his unparalleled cunning by bribing the treacherous Venetians, who eventually assisted the Italian forces to enter the city gates, and thus Durazzo was gained at the point of the sword after one of the fiercest sieges known to history. Scarcely had the beleaguered town been reduced, than the indomitable Guiscard found himself compelled to return to Italy, where the Emperor of the West, the unhappy Henry IV., vainly endeavouring to wipe out the humiliation of Canossa, had seized Rome and was actually besieging the great Hildebrand in the Castle of Sant' Angelo. Leaving his son Bohemond in command of the army in Macedonia, Robert recrossed the sea, and hastened with a handful of men towards Rome. But so intense a fear did the victor of Durazzo inspire, that the terrified Emperor without waiting to give combat fled headlong together with his anti-pope from the Holy City, where Guiscard was received with acclamation. " Thus, in less than three years," remarks Gibbon, " the son of Tancred of Hauteville enjoyed the glory of delivering the Pope, and of compelling the two Emperors of the East and West to fly before his victorious arms." Guiscard's triumphal entry into Rome was however marred by scenes of violence and scandal, due to the conduct of the Saracen troops which his brother, the great Count Roger of Sicily, had brought to assist the enterprise. So infuriated were the Romans by the behaviour of the infidels, that the prudent Gregory deemed it wiser to return to Salerno together with his deliverer, and it was in Guiscard's palace that the famous " Caesar of spiritual conquest " expired three years later. As to the Great Adventurer himself, he died in the island of Cephalonia in the very year of the Pope's death at Salerno (1085) and was buried beside his first wife, the gentle Alberada, at Venosa in Apulia, though the city which he had always loved and favoured would seem to have offered a more appropriate spot for his interment.

But although the mortal remains of the Great Adventurer do not rest within the precincts of his beloved city, an undying monument of his glorious but turbulent reign is to be found in the Cathedral, which despite the neglect and alterations of eight centuries may still be ranked as one of the most interesting buildings in Southern Italy. Standing in a secluded part of the town, this magnificent church gains nothing from its position, for it can only be reached by means of tortuous dingy lanes, and even on a near approach the effect produced on the visitor is not impressive. "The Cathedral-church of San Matteo," says the Scotch traveller, Joseph Forsyth, in quaint pedantic language, " is a pile so antique and so modern, so repaired and rhapsodic, that it exhibits patches of every style, and is of no style itself." But is not this quality, we ask, exactly what a great historic building, such as Guiscard's church, truly demands? Ought not it to bear the impress of the various ages it has survived, and of the many famous persons who have contributed to its embellishment? From Duke Robert's day to the present time, the Cathedral is an epitome of the history of Salerno, a sermon in stones concerning the great past and the inglorious present of the city.

In the year preceding his own death and that of the great Pontiff, who was tarrying at Salerno as his not over-willing guest, Duke Robert erected this Cathedral, obtaining the chief ornaments for his new structure and also its most important relic, the supposed body of the Apostle St Matthew, from the lately deserted city of Paestum across the bay.   The church is approached by means of a quadrangular fore-court, a cloister supported on antique columns, such as can still be observed in a few of the old Roman churches, so that we venture to think that this idea at Salerno was suggested by the great Pope himself.   A number of sculptured sarcophagi, which, like the pillars, were the spoils of Paestum, are ranged alongside the entrance walls ; and once upon a time there stood in the centre of the courtyard the huge granite basin that all visitors to Naples will recall as set in the middle of the Villa Reale, where it performs the humble office of decorating a miniature pond, wherein lily-white ducks quack and gobble at the bread crumbs thrown to them by children and their nurses.   Fancy the irate disgust of Duke Robert at waking to learn that the antique fountain for his new Cathedral, brought with such care and toil from distant Poseidonia, should have been transported to the rival city and turned to such base uses !   Above the splendid bronze doors, the gift of Landolfo Butomilea and his wife shortly after Guiscard's death, we perceive the dedication of the church to the Apostle Matthew by the proud conqueror of the Two Sicilies and the protector of Hildebrand.

"A Duce Roberto donaris Apostole templo :
Pro meritis regno donetur ipse superno."

The donor, we note, is confident that the Apostle, in return for so glorious a fabric, will undertake to obtain the Kingdom of Heaven for this generous client upon earth.

The interior, which is sadly marred by white-wash

and gaudy decoration, is a perfect treasure-house of works of art—antique, medieval, Renaissance—of which the guide-book will give a detailed list. Succeeding generations have put to strange uses some of the fine marble reliefs that Guiscard transported hither from Paestum, and we note that one archbishop has gone so far as to filch a sarcophagus carved with a Bacchanal procession to serve for his own tomb. We might perhaps infer that the deceased prelate was addicted to the wine-flask, and to have been a firm believer in and follower of one of the rules of the medical school of his own diocese :

> "Si nocturna tibi noceat potatio vini,
> Hoc ter mane libas iterum, et fuerit medicina.

> (If a carouse at night do make thee ill,
> For morning medicine drink of wine thy fill.)

Let us hope that this extraordinary receipt for " hot coppers " was intended satirically, or else given seriously as the only advice that a confirmed toper was likely to follow in any case. But the use of classical adjuncts to adorn Christian tombs, which to-day appears so incongruous to us, was popular enough at the time of the Renaissance, and readers of Robert Browning's poetry will call to mind the story of the dying Bishop's injunction to his heirs concerning his tomb in St Praxed's church at Rome :

> The bas-relief in bronze ye promised me,
> Those Pans and Nymphs ye wot of, and perchance
> Some tripod thyrsus with a vase or so,
> The Saviour at His sermon on the mount,
> Saint Praxed in a glory, and one Pan
> Ready to twitch the Nymph's last garment off,
> And Moses with the tables. . . .

But it is necessary to shake off the spirit of Renaissance dilettantism before we venture to approach the chapel of John of Procida to the right of the high altar, where stands the stern figure of the greatest of the medieval Pontiffs. Above the marble statue of the Caesar of the Papacy, that was tardily erected to his memory by the unfortunate Pio Nono, appear the glittering mosaics of the apse of the chapel, from which look down the figures of John of Procida and of King Manfred, the last sovereign prince of the hated Suabian line that Gregory twice anathematized. Beneath the cold forbidding eye of the last of the Hohenstaufen and his friend and avenger here rest, strangely enough, the ashes of that "great and inflexible asserter of the supremacy of the sacerdotal order: the monk Hildebrand, afterwards Pope Gregory the Seventh." Born the son of a poor carpenter in the Tuscan village of Soana, this extraordinary man rose to eminence as a monk of Cluny, where he became famous for his extreme asceticism of life in an age of undisguised clerical corruption and luxury, when simony, lay investiture and priestly marriages were the rule rather than the exception on all sides, so that but few Churchmen were able to rise above their surrounding temptations. Such few as could resist the world, the flesh and the devil were accounted, and not unfrequently were in reality, ignorant crazy fanatics, half-pitied and half-despised. Between these two extremes of worldly indulgence and of unreasoning severity of life, Hildebrand ever pursued a middle course, for whilst on the one hand he eschewed the vanities of life around him, on the other he never sank into the self-effacement of a hermit. His acknowledged purity and zeal soon won for him from the laity a respect mingled with awe, whilst his natural talents, his indomitable will, and his genuine piety in course of time brought all Churchmen who had any regard for their holy office to fix their hopes upon this Clugniac monk, now a Cardinal. For some years before his actual election to the Papal throne in 1079, Hildebrand had begun to exercise an immense control over the councils of the Church, and he was personally responsible for the epoch-making resolution under Nicholas II., which declared that the choice of a new Pontiff was vested in the College of Cardinals alone. His own election, under the terms of this new and drastic arrangement, became the signal for the fierce struggles, equally of the battlefield and the council-chamber, that were destined to distract Italy for generations to come. For, as might have been expected, the Emperor Henry IV., King of the Romans, was not long in protesting against so decided an infringement of his secular claims. From the synods of Worms and Piacenza came the Imperial decree of deposition against Gregory, which was addressed by "Henry, not by usurpation but by God's holy ordination, King, to Hildebrand, no longer Pope, but false monk." Gregory, strong alike in virtue and in resolve, and aided by the might of the Countess Matilda of Tuscany and of Robert Guiscard, answered by pronouncing a solemn anathema upon his secular adversary. In awe-struck silence the Council of the Lateran listened to the Pope's final excommunication of the King, and of all those who dared to associate themselves with him. " I absolve," said Gregory, "all Christians from the oaths

which they have taken or may take to him ; and
I decree that no one shall obey him as king ; for it
is fitting that he, who has endeavoured to diminish
the honour of the Church, should himself lose that
honour which he seems to have." We all know
the final act of that terrible unequal struggle, the
duel of brute force against spiritual terrors in a rude
age of violence and superstition, which took place
in the courtyard of the Castle of Canossa, the
Countess Matilda's fortress in the Apennines.

"On a dreary winter morning, with the ground
deep in snow, the King, the heir of a long line
of Emperors, was permitted to enter within the
two outer of the three walls which girded the Castle
of Canossa. He had laid aside every mark of
royalty or of distinguished station ; he was clad
only in the thin white linen dress of the penitent,
and there, fasting, he awaited in humble patience
the pleasure of the Pope. But the gates did not
unclose. A second day he stood, cold, hungry and
mocked by vain hopes. And yet a third day dragged
on from morning till evening over the unsheltered
head of the discrowned King. Every heart was moved
save that of the representative of Jesus Christ."

Can we wonder then that the phrase "to go to
Canossa" (*gehen nach Canossa*) has become ingrafted
on to the German language, or that so significant an
expression was openly used by Prince Bismarck
during the fierce religious struggles in the days of
the "Kultur-kampf" between the newly-formed
Empire and the direct successor of the spiritual Caesar
who had thus humbled a former Emperor of Germany ?
It was in vain that Henry afterwards endeavoured,

ON THE ROAD TO RAVELLO

by making war upon his oppressor, to undo the evil effects of his public recantation at Canossa; the act of humiliation was too marked ever to be wiped out either by himself or by his descendants. For good or for bad, Gregory had succeeded in rendering the Papacy free from lay control; he had gained for ever for the Church one of her most cherished tenets, the absolute independence of the Pope's election by the College of Cardinals; and he had even partially reduced the Western Empire into a fief of the Church itself. The former of Gregory's great objects, the freedom of election, still remains intact after an interval of more than eight hundred years; the latter attempt, though long struggled for and apparently with success at times, has, we know, ultimately failed.

Having accomplished so much during his reign, it is strange to think that Gregory's last days should have been passed in a form of exile away from the Eternal City which he claimed as the metropolis of the Universal Church. There is pathos to be found in the Pope dying at Salerno, far removed from the scene of his ambition and success. With the bitter feeling that his name was execrated in Rome after Guiscard's sack, and that his host was bent upon obtaining the imperial title from his reluctant guest, Gregory's declining days were spent in melancholy reflections. To the last he spoke confidently of the righteousness of his cause, and whilst making his peace with all mankind in anticipation of his approaching end, he deliberately excepted from his own and God's mercy the names of his arch-enemy Henry and the anti-pope Guibert, together with all their followers. Thus the aged Pontiff languished to his end within

the walls of the Castle of Salerno, encircled by flatter-
ing Churchmen who did their utmost to cheer their
dying champion. " I have loved justice and hated
iniquity, and therefore I die in exile," are the
famous words recorded of Hildebrand in the face of
the King of Terrors. " In exile thou canst not die ! "
eagerly responded an attendant priest. " Vicar of
Christ and His Apostles, thou hast received the
nations for thine inheritance, and the uttermost parts
of the earth for thy possession."

Perhaps the expiring Pope was cheered by these
words—who can tell ? In any case they were prophetic, for the present world-wide character of the
Roman Church, which embraces in its fold all nation-
alities and holds its members together all the globe
over in one indissoluble bond of a spiritual empire,
is largely due to the trials and exertions of one man :
the monk Hildebrand, Pope Gregory the Seventh.

Here then he sleeps his last sleep, the friend of Matilda,
the mortal foe of King Henry, the patron of William
the Conqueror, the guest of Robert Guiscard :—what
a galaxy of illustrious names shines upon that dim
silent chapel in the Cathedral of Salerno ! Here
stands in unchanging benediction his gleaming marble
effigy, calmly surveyed by King Manfred near at
hand in imperial robes, the last prince of the hated
and twice banned Suabian House, whose bones were
destined to bleach in the sun and rattle in the wind
by the bridge of Benevento under a Papal curse.

Before we quit the Cathedral in order to enjoy the
evening sunshine, which is filling the interior with
its roseate glow, let us return for one brief moment
to the northern aisle, to glance at the grave of the

Duchess who fought so boldly by her husband's side
at Durazzo. It is easy to find, for her simple tomb
stands not far from the beautiful and elaborate
monument of Margaret of Durazzo (strange coincidence!) wife of King Charles of Naples, wherein
the sculptor has portrayed angels drawing aside a
curtain so as to display the sleeping form of the dead
Queen within. Close to this monument of a not
unusual Renaissance type, we discover the last resting
place of Robert Guiscard's second wife, the Duchess
Sigilgaita, their son Roger Bursa and their grandson
William, in whom the direct line of the Great Adventurer became extinct. Many stories are told by
the old chroniclers of this bold intrepid princess (not
always to her credit)—daughter of the last Lombard
prince Gisulf of Salerno and wife of her father's
supplanter, whose humble Norman ancestry she affected
to despise. But despite her reputation for cruelty
and even for murder, Sigilgaita was a faithful wife
and a brave woman, with a character not unlike that
of our own Queen Margaret of Anjou; and it seems
strange that so devoted and well mated a pair as
herself and Robert Guiscard should be separated in
death, he at Venosa and she in the cathedral of
her husband's foundation.

Passing out of the silent church into the warm
light of eventide, by steep alleys and by stony
footpaths we gradually mount upwards towards the
ruined castle that commands a lofty position with an all-
embracing view of the bay and its encircling mountains.
The crumbling fragment of the old palace of Salerno
differs but little in appearance from any one of those
innumerable dilapidated piles of the Middle Ages with

which Southern Italy is so thickly studded, yet
coming fresh from visiting Guiscard's cathedral and
Hildebrand's last resting-place, we find it comparatively easy to conjure up some recollections of its
past, so as to invest its crumbling red-hued walls
with a spell of interest. These broken apertures
were surely once the windows through which the
dying Pope must have wearily glanced upon the
sun-smitten waves and violet-shadowed hills that we
behold to-day ; here in this embrasure, long despoiled
of its marble seat, must have brooded the fierce and
unscrupulous Sigilgaita, thinking of how best to rid
herself of her step-son Bohemond, in order that her
own children might inherit their father's realms.
The ghosts of princes and popes are around us, yet
the only living inhabitant of the roofless castle is
the ragged little goat-herd, whose unsavoury charges
are cropping the short grass that covers the site of
the banqueting hall, where Norman knights and
Italian barons once caroused in the crusading days
of long ago. We seat ourselves on the dry sward
in a sun-warmed angle of the ruins, where an almond
tree that has sprouted from the rubble sends down
from time to time upon our heads a tiny shower of
pale pink blossoms at the bidding of the soft evening
breeze. At our feet are masses of the dark shiny leaves
of the wild arum, and rank grass which is plentifully
starred with tall-stemmed crimson-petalled daisies
and the mauve wind-flowers that are drowsily closing
their cups at the approach of night. The little goat-
herd eyes us solemnly, but—strange and welcome to
relate—shows no inclination to pester the *signori*.
The soft murmuring of the distant sea, the subdued

hum of the city far below us and the drowsy buzzing
of the bees in the almond and ivy bloom close at
hand combine to strengthen the golden chain of
imagination. As we sit basking in the peaceful
beauty of the scene around us and serenely conscious
of its glorious past, one of our party suddenly remem-
bers in a welcome flash of inspiration that this deserted
courtyard has been made the scene of one of
Boccaccio's most famous tales. It is a story that
many writers of succeeding ages have endeavoured
to imitate in prose or verse, but this fictitious love-
tragedy between a princess and a page at Salerno has
a simple charm and dignity in its original setting
that only the master-hand of the Tuscan author
could impart. The scene of the novel of Guiscard
and Ghismonda is laid, as we have said, at this very
spot, and as the hero, the heroine and the villain of
the tale have Norman names, we may be allowed
to conjecture that this graceful story, which Boccaccio
puts into the mouth of the lady Fiammetta, was
founded upon some actual but half-forgotten family
scandal in the annals of the mighty but self-made
House of Hauteville.

Once upon a time there reigned in Salerno the
Prince Tancred, who was a widower, and the father
of an only daughter, Ghismonda, Duchess of Capua.
The Duchess, who was considered one of the most
beautiful, accomplished and virtuous princesses of
her day, had been early married to the Duke of
Capua, but on his death after a very few years
of matrimony had been left a childless widow.
Being still very young, the Princess Ghismonda was

now taken back to his court by her father, who jealously guarded her and seemed unwilling for her to be remarried.   Living in rooms that over-looked the courtyard of the palace, the Duchess, who found time hang on her hands somewhat heavily, used to spend hours daily in watching the lords and pages of her father's household passing and repassing the quadrangle below, and amongst the many well-favoured youths a certain page named Guiscard found most favour in her sight.   Now Guiscard, who had thus all unwittingly attracted Ghismonda's attention and finally won her heart, was a young Norman of no great lineage and of small means, but being discreet, upright and sensible-minded, had obtained a high place in Prince Tancred's estimation.   Skilfully questioning her maids of honour without exciting their suspicions, the Princess gained all she wished to know concerning Guiscard's position and attainments, and it was not long before she found means of conveying the secret of her affection to the youth, who in fact had already fallen head over ears in love with the beautiful Duchess who so often leaned from the casement above.   She now sent him a letter hidden in a pair of bellows, wherein she explained to him the existence of a secret passage, long disused, that led from a hollow in the hillside below the castle walls up to her own apartment. Over-joyed at receiving this missive, the infatuated page took the first occasion, as we may well imagine, to make use of this friendly clue, and before many hours had passed after receiving the letter, the young man, flushed and triumphant, was standing in the chamber of his beloved mistress, who had meanwhile

taken every necessary preparation for receiving her
lover in secret. Many a time were the pair able to
meet thus without awakening the least suspicion in
the minds of Prince Tancred or of the maids of
honour, and all would doubtless have gone well for
an indefinite period of time, but for a most unforeseen
accident. It appears that one morning the old Prince
of Salerno, wishing to confer with his daughter on
some matter of state, came to her private apartment,
and on learning that she had gone out riding settled
himself upon a couch that stood within a curtained
alcove, and whilst waiting for her return fell sound
asleep. After some hours of repose the prince was
suddenly roused from his heavy slumber by the sound
of two voices in the room, that of his daughter and of
a strange man. Peeping stealthily through the folds
of the draperies, he now beheld to his fury and
amazement the Duchess alone with his page Guiscard.
But the descendant of Robert the Wiseacre well knew
how to temper vengeance with dissimulation. Dread-
ing the scandal that would follow an open exposure,
the Prince, in spite of his years and the stiffness of
his joints, contrived to quit the chamber unperceived
by means of a convenient window. That very night
the unsuspecting Guiscard was seized by his sovereign's
orders and thrust into a foul dungeon of the palace,
whither Tancred himself descended to question his
prisoner and to reprove him violently for his base
ingratitude. But the unhappy page could only make
repeated answer: "Sire, love hath greater powers
than you or I!" On the following morning Tancred
proceeded to visit the Duchess, still ignorant of her
paramour's fate, and in a voice strangled with the

N

conflicting emotions of paternal love and desired vengeance bitterly upbraided his erring child. "Daughter, I had such an opinion of your modesty and virtue, that I could never have believed, had I not seen it with mine own eyes, that you would have violated either, even so much as in thought. The recollection of this will make the pittance of life that is left very grievous to me. As you were determined to act in that manner, would to Heaven you had made choice of a person more suitable to your own quality; but this Guiscard is one of the meanest persons about my court. This gives me such concern, that I scarce know what to do. As for him, he was secured by my order last night, and his fate is determined. But with regard to yourself, I am influenced by two different motives: on one side, the tenderest regard that a father can have for a child ; and on the other, the justest vengeance for the great folly you have committed. One pleads strongly in your behalf; and the other would excite me to do an act contrary to my nature. But before I come to a resolution, I would fain hear what you have to say for yourself."

Seeing clearly from her father's words that her secret had been discovered and that her lover was in prison, the intrepid Ghismonda, a true daughter of the high-spirited House of Hauteville, assuming a composure she was very far from feeling, made a dignified appeal on behalf of Guiscard and herself.

"Father, it is not my purpose either to deny or to entreat ; for as the one can avail me nothing, so I intend the other shall be of little service. I will by no means bespeak your love and tenderness towards me ; but shall first, by an open confession, endeavour to vindicate myself, and thus do what the greatness of my soul prompts me to. It is most true that I have loved, and do still love Guiscard ; and whilst I live, which will not be long, shall continue to love him ; and if such a thing as love be after death, I shall never cease to love him. . . . It appears from what you say, that you would have been less incensed if I had made choice of a nobleman, and you bitterly reproach me for having condescended to a man of low condition. In this you speak according to vulgar prejudice, and not according to truth ; nor do you perceive that the fault you blame is not mine, but Fortune's, who often exalts the unworthy, and leaves the worthiest in low estate. But, not to dwell on such considerations, look a little into first principles, and you will see that we are all formed of the same material and by the same hand. The first difference amongst mankind, who are all born equal, was made by virtue ; they who were virtuous were deemed noble, and the rest were all accounted otherwise. Though this law, therefore, may have been obscured by contrary custom, yet is it discarded neither by nature nor good manners. If you regard only the worth and virtue of your courtiers, and consider that of Guiscard, you will find him the only noble person, and these others a set of poltroons. With regard to his worth and valour, I appeal to yourself. Who ever commended man more for anything that was praise-worthy than you have commended him ? And deservedly, in my judgment ; but if I was deceived, it was by following your opinion. If you say, then, that I have had an affair with a person base and ignoble, I deny it ; if with a poor one, it is to your shame to have let such merit go unrewarded. Now concerning your last doubt, namely how you are to deal with me: use your pleasure. If you are disposed to commit an act of cruelty, I shall say nothing to prevent such a resolution. But this I must apprise you of; that unless you do the same to me, which you either have done, or mean to do to Guiscard, mine own hands shall do it for you. If you mean to act with severity, cut us off both together, if it appear to you that we have deserved it."

The Duchess' able defence of her choice of Guiscard and her democratic views of society were hardly likely to influence the proud tyrant of Salerno, although his house was sprung from a plebeian stock of Normandy. Ignoring her plea and arguments, Tancred left his daughter alone with her grief, and proceeded to the cells below to give the order for Guiscard's immediate death by strangling. But Tancred's fury was by no means appeased by the page's death, for tearing the unhappy youth's heart from the warm and still quivering body, the brutal prince had the bleeding flesh placed in a golden covered cup, which he bade his chamberlain deliver to Ghismonda, with these cruel words: "Your father sends this present to comfort you with what was most dear to you; even as he was comforted by you in what was most dear to him." With a calm countenance and with a gracious word of thanks, the Princess accepted the gift, and on removing the cover and realising the contents of the cup, said with meaning to the bearer of this gruesome present: "My father has done very wisely; such a heart as this requires no worse a sepulchre than one of gold."

Then after lamenting for a while over her lover's fate, Ghismonda filled the goblet with a draught of poison that she had already prepared in anticipation of her father's vengeance, and quaffed its contents. After this she lay down upon her bed, clasping the cup to her bosom, whereupon her maids, all ignorant of the cause of their mistress' conduct, ran terrified to call Prince Tancred, who arrived in time to witness his unhappy daughter's death agony. Now that it was too late, the Prince was stricken with remorse and began loudly to bewail the violence of his late anger. "Sire," said the dying Princess, "save those tears against worse fortune that may happen, for I want them not. Who but yourself would mourn for a thing of your own doing?" Then dropping her tone of irony, she made one last request of her weeping and repentant father, that her own and Guiscard's bodies might be honourably interred within the same tomb. Thus perished by her own hand the beautiful Princess Ghismonda of Salerno, Duchess of Capua, urged to the fell deed by a parent's inexorable cruelty. And it is some slight consolation to the sad ending of the story to learn that Tancred did at least carry out his daughter's dying entreaty, for the bodies of Ghismonda and Guiscard were duly laid in one grave amidst the pomp of religion and the cold comfort of a public mourning.*

But the sun has long since sunk below the horizon, and the chill dews of night are falling round us. Hastily we leave the old palace of the princes of Salerno to the solitary occupation of the bats and owls, to seek warmth and cheerfulness in our inn upon the Marina.

* *The Decameron*—Novel I, of the Fourth Day.

CHAPTER IX

PAESTUM AND THE GLORY THAT WAS GREECE

IN these days of easy travelling there lies a choice
of two routes to Paestum and its temples : one
by driving thither direct from La Cava or Salerno,
in the mode of our forefathers ; and the other by
taking the train to the little junction of Battipaglia,
and thence proceeding southward by the coast line
to the station of Pesto itself, that stands almost
within a stone's throw of the chief gate of Poseidonia.
A third, and perhaps a preferable way, consists in
using the railway beyond Battipaglia to Eboli, a
town of no little interest in the upper valley of the
Silarus, and thence driving along the base of the
rocky hills that enclose the maritime plain and through
the oak wood of Persano that was brigand-haunted
within living memory.   But though the scenery
between Eboli and Paestum undoubtedly owns more
charm and variety than the marshy flats can boast,
yet the strange loneliness of the sea-girt level has
a fascination of its own, which will appeal strongly
to all lovers of pristine undisturbed nature.   For
the larger portion of these Lucanian plains still
remains uncultivated, so that thickets of fragrant
wild myrtle and lentisk, of coronella and of white-
blossomed laurustinus, stud the landscape ; whilst

the open ground is thickly covered with masses of hardy but gay flowering weeds. The great star-thistles run to seed unchecked by the scythe, and the belled cerinthia and the glaucous-leaved tall yellow mulleins seem to thrive heartily on the barren soil. Boggy ground alternates with patches of dry stony earth, and in early summer every little pool of water affords sustenance to coarse-scented white water-lilies, and clumps of the yellow iris that are over-shadowed by masses of tall graceful reeds. These *arundini*, which are to be found near every water-course or pool throughout Italy, are characteristic of the country with their broad grey leaves, their heads of pink feathery bloom, and their mournful whispering answers to the question of every passing breeze; elegant in their growth, they are also beloved by the practical peasant who utilizes their long slender stems for a variety of purposes in his domestic economy. For the reeds, stripped of their foliage, support his tender young vines and make good frame-work whereon to train his peas and tomatoes; the longest canes of all, moreover, serve well as handles for the long feather brushes which are used so extensively in all Italian households. Other floral denizens of the plain are the great rank *porri*, or wild leeks, con-spicuous with their bright green curling leaves issuing from globe-like roots above the ground, and of course, the asphodel, the plant of Death. For the asphodel is pre-eminently the flower of Southern Italy and of Sicily, since it presents a fit emblem of a departed grandeur that is still impressive in its decay. How beautiful to the eye appear the dark grey-green sword-like leaves from the centre of which up-shoots the tall branching stem with its clusters of delicate pink-striped blossoms, that show so lovely yet smell so vile! Apart from its fetid odour, the asphodel is a thing of intense beauty, so that a long line of these plants in full bloom, covering some ridge of orange-coloured tufa or the velvety-grey crest of some ancient wall, with their spikes of starry flowers standing out distinct like floral candelabra against the clear blue of a southern sky, makes an impression upon the beholder that will ever be gratefully remembered.

But flowers and shrubs are not the only occupants of the Poseidonian plain, for as we proceed on our way towards the Temples, we notice in the drier pastures large herds of the long-horned dove-coloured cattle of the country, whilst in marshy places our interest is aroused by the sight of great shaggy buffaloes of sinister mien. The buffalo has long been acclimatized in Italy, though its original home seems to have been the trackless marshes of the Tigris and Euphrates. The conquering Arabs first introduced these uncouth Eastern cattle into Sicily, whence they were imported into Italy by the Norman kings of Naples. In spite of its malevolent nature and the poor quality of its flesh and hide, the buffalo came to be extensively bred in the Pontine and Lucanian marshes, where the moisture of the soil and the unwholesome air always affected the native herds unfavourably. For hours together these fierce untameable beasts love to lie amidst the swampy reed-beds, wallowing up to their flanks in slimy malodorous mud and seemingly impervious to the ceaseless attacks of the local wasps and gad-flies, which try in vain to penetrate with their barbed stings the thick hairy covering of defence.

Perchance between Battipaglia and Paestum we may
encounter a herd of these shaggy beeves being driven
by a peasant on horse-back, with his *pungolo* or small
lance in hand : a human being that in his goat-skin
breeches and with his luxuriant untrimmed locks,
seems to our eyes only one degree less savage and
unkempt than the fierce beasts he guides. As cultivation has made progress of recent years and the
unhealthy marshes of the coast line are being gradually
drained, the numbers of buffalo tend to decrease, whilst
the native Italian oxen are being introduced once
more into the newly reclaimed pastures. That former
arch-enemy of the cattle in the days of Vergil seems
to have disappeared : that "flying pest," the *asilo* of
the Romans and the *aestrum* of the Greeks, which in
antique times was wont to drive the grazing herds
frantic with terror and pain, until the valley of the
Tanager and the Alburnian woods re-echoed with the
agonised lowing of the poor tortured creatures. And
speaking of noxious insects, a general belief prevails
in Italy that their bite—as well as that of snakes and
scorpions—becomes more acute and dangerous when
the sun enters into the sign of Lion, so that human
beings, as well as defenceless cattle, must carefully
avoid all chances of being bitten during the months of
July and August.

Before our goal can be reached it is necessary for
us to cross the broad willow-fringed stream of the Sele,
the Silarus of antiquity, which according to the testimony of Silius Italicus once possessed the property of
petrifying wood. In the distant days of the eighteenth
century, the traveller to Paestum had to endure amidst
other difficulties and dangers of the road the disagree-

able business of being ferried across the Sele, which was then bridgeless.   Owing to the malaria and the loneliness of the spot, the acting of ferryman over this river was not an agreeable post, and Count Stolberg, a German dilettante who has left some memories of his Italian wanderings, relates how a feeble dismal soured old man, a veritable Charon of the upper air, had great difficulty in conveying himself, his horse and his servant across the swollen stream.   The old man's age and misery aroused the Count's compassion, so that he asked him why he continued thus to perform a task at once so arduous and so distasteful. "Sir," replied the boatman, "I would gladly be excused, but that my master compels me to undertake this work."   "And who, pray, is this tyrant of a master of yours?" indignantly enquired the Count. "Sir, it is my Lord Poverty!" grimly answered the old ferryman, as he pocketed the Teuton's fee.   Times have changed with regard to the necessity of a ferry over the Sele, but to judge from the appearance of the people and from the accounts in the journals, we much doubt if my Lord Poverty's sway has been much weakened in these parts.

At length we reach the tiny hamlet and station of Pesto, surrounded by its groves of mournful eucalyptus trees, and if we visit the station itself, we cannot help noticing the fine gauze net-work over every window and door, also the veiled faces and be-gloved hands of the station-master and his *facchini*.   It is not difficult to gauge the reason of the eucalyptus trees at Pesto, an alien importation like the buffalo, for these native trees of Australia have been planted here with the avowed object of reducing the malaria, for which the place is only too renowned. Scientists have positively declared that the mosquitoes which rise in clouds from the poisonous swamps at sunset are directly responsible for this terrible form of ague, and a paternal Government has accordingly introduced gum-trees to improve the quality of the air, and has presented gloves, veils and fine lattice work to its servants in the hope of protecting them from the bites of these tiny pestilence-bearing insects. We do not wish to dispute the wisdom of modern bacteriologists, but somehow we have no great faith in this elaborate scheme for battling with Nature; and indeed not a few persons who have studied the matter declare that though the reeking marshes are certainly productive of malaria in themselves (so much so that it is dangerous to linger amidst the ruined temples of an evening), yet these spiteful little creatures are at least innocent of innoculating humanity with this particular disease. Moreover, a plausible idea that is now largely held insists that the recent spread of cultivation over the Lucanian Plain is itself largely responsible for the increase of malaria ; it is the up-turning of the germ-impregnated earth that has lain fallow for centuries, say the supporters of this theory, which awakens and sets free the slumbering demon of fever in the soil, so that the speeding of the plough on the Neapolitan coast must inevitably mean also the spreading of this fell and mysterious sickness. Let us therefore give the devil his due : the mosquito is a hateful and persistent foe, and his sting is both painful and dis-figuring, but do not let us accuse him of carrying malaria until the case can be better proved against him. But enough of fevers and doctors' saws ! Let

us turn our willing eyes towards the three great
temples that confront us close at hand. Before however proceeding to inspect these great monuments of
Grecian art and civilization, which rank amongst the
most venerable as well as the most beautiful relics of
antiquity, it is only meet that we should carry with
us into their ruined halls a few grains of historical
knowledge, whereby our sense of reality and our
appreciation of their greatness and splendour may be
increased.

Although we do not possess a definite history of
Paestum, similar to that of Rome or of Athens, yet
from the many allusions to be found scattered throughout the pages of classical historians, as well as from
the various inscriptions and devices found upon ancient
coins of this city, it is not a difficult task to piece
together the main features of Poseidonian annals.
From a very remote period of antiquity there was
undoubtedly a settlement on or near the coast to the
south of the river Silarus, whilst it is commonly held
that this spot was called Peste—a name almost
identical with the modern Italian appellation—many
hundreds of years before the arrival of Doric settlers
on the shores of the Tyrrhene Sea. Late in the
seventh century before Christ, the Greek colony of
Poseidonia, the city of the Sea God, was founded on
or near the site of Italian Peste by certain Hellenic
adventurers from Trœzen, who were amongst the inhabitants of Sybaris, at that time one of the most
flourishing of the famous cities of Magna Graecia:
and this new colony of Trœzenians henceforward was
accounted one of the twenty-five subject-towns that
recognised Sybaris for their metropolis, or mother and

THE TEMPLE OF NEPTUNE, PAESTUM

suzerain city. We have no details of its early history, but it is quite certain that under the protection of Sybaris the new city of Poseidonia rose by degrees to such wealth and importance that in course of time it gave its own name to the whole Bay of Salerno, which henceforth became known to the Greeks as the Poseidonian Gulf and later, to the Romans, as the Bay of Paestum. With the fall of the mother city, this flourishing colony was left alone to face the attacks of the Samnites, the native barbarians who peopled the dense forests and the barren mountains of Lucania ; yet it somehow contrived to retain its independence until the close of the fourth century B.C., when the Samnite hordes, forcing the fortified line of the Silarus, made themselves masters of Poseidonia, and put an end, practically for ever, to its existence as a purely Hellenic city. From its Lucanian masters the captured town received the name of Paestum, and its inhabitants were at once deprived of their independence, were forbidden to carry arms, and were probably in many instances reduced to the level of serfs. A large number of Samnites also settled within the walls of the town, and compelled the former owners to surrender to them the larger and richer portion of the public and private lands upon the maritime plain. The use of the Hellenic language and public worship was however permitted, and, strange to relate, no interference was made with a solemn annual festival, which the depressed and enslaved population now inaugurated with the confessed object of remembering for ever their Greek origin and their former greatness. For once a year at a fixed date all Greeks were wont to gather together and to bewail in public, outside the great temple of Poseidon, their lost liberty and their vanished power.   It is evident that the Lucanians did not fear the tears and lamentations of this unhappy subject state, for this custom continued to be observed throughout the whole period of Samnite oppression, and survived even till Roman times—perhaps to the very end of the city's existence,—although in the course of passing generations there could have been but few persons of pure Greek descent left in the place.

With the advent of Alexander of Epirus, who had been called into Italy by the Greeks of Tarentum in order to assist the sorely-pressed colonies of Magna Graecia, Epirot troops were landed at the mouth of the Silarus.   Under the very walls of Pæstum there now took place a stubborn fight wherein the army of the Samnites was completely routed, and its survivors driven in confusion from the coast into the wild woods and rocky valleys of the Lucanian hills.   For a brief interval of years Poseidonia regained its lost liberty and its Hellenic name, but with the overthrow and death of Alexander of Epirus, the scattered hordes pressed down once more from their mountain fastnesses upon the rich plain, and the city was for the second time enslaved by the ruder conquering race. Forty years later, after the Pyrrhine war, all Lucania fell under the rising power of Rome, a change that was by no means unacceptable to the Greek cities, which were groaning under the rude tyranny of the Samnites.   A Latin colony was now planted at Pæstum, to form a convenient centre whence the neighbouring district could be kept in order and peaceably developed according to Roman ideas. These Roman colonists, although they did not restore the lands and buildings held by the expelled Samnites to their rightful owners, yet lived on terms of amity with the Greek population, with whom they must have freely intermarried. The original Hellenic inhabitants, relieved of the bonds of servitude, were now placed on an equal footing with the new colonists, partaking of political rights in the city thus freshly re-created under the supremacy of Rome, and soon they grew to imitate the speech and manners of their new masters, so that as an immediate result of the expulsion of the barbaric Samnites and the entry of the progressive Romans, Paestum began to recover a considerable portion of its ancient splendour.

During the course of the second Punic War the name of Paestum is not unfrequently mentioned in Roman annals, and owing its revived prosperity to its annexation by Rome, it is not surprising to find the existence of a strong feeling of gratitude amongst the inhabitants. At the date of fatal Cannæ this faithful Greek city sent assurances of unswerving allegiance to the Senate, and also more substantial help in the form of all the golden vessels from its temples. It was Paestum also that early in the third century B.C. supplied part of the ill-fated fleet of Decius Quinctius, that was raised to run the blockade of Tarentum. But even the loss of its ships and men did not deter this loyal city from coming forward a second time with expressions of fealty and promise of further aid to the great suzerain city in this dark hour of its difficulties. From this point onward till the close of the Republic, History is almost silent with regard to Paestum ; but its numerous coins go far to attest its continued welfare, for it now shared, together with

Venusia, Brundusium and Vibo Valentia, a special right to strike money in its own name and with its own devices. Under the Empire, Paestum managed to uphold its size and importance, so that it became the capital of one of the eight Prefectures into which the district of Lucania had been divided. At this period, there can be no doubt, the surrounding plain was in the highest state of cultivation, whilst its prolific rose-gardens—*biferi rosaria Paesti*—have supplied the theme of every Roman poet from Vergil to Ausonius. Yet in spite of its apparent prosperity, the seeds of coming decline had already been sown. Strabo tells us that even in early Imperial days the city was obtaining an unenviable reputation for malaria : a circumstance that was due to the over-flowing of the unwholesome streamlet, the Salso, whose reeking and fever-bearing waters began to impregnate the earth. Engineering works on a large scale were planned to remedy this drawback, but these were never executed, and in consequence the unhealthiness of the place increased. With the decline of the Roman power the population and prosperity of Paestum likewise tended to lessen, so that its citizens were placed in a worse position than before with regard to the carrying out of this vast but necessary scheme of sanitation.

In a spot so accessible to external influence, it is easy to understand that Christianity early took root in Paestum, which in the fifth century of our own era had already become a bishopric. The story of the growth of the Faith in Lucania is closely connected with a legend that centres round a native of the place, a certain Gavinius, a general in the army of the Emperor Valentinian, who whilst serving in Britain against the Picts by some means succeeded in obtaining a valuable relic, supposed to be nothing less than the body of the Apostle Matthew, which he brought back with him to his native place. Early in the ninth century there appeared a fresh cause of alarm, more serious and far-reaching even than the dreaded malaria, for plundering Saracens, foes alike to the old Roman civilisation and to the new Christian creed, now began to harass the Tyrrhenian shores. Settling at Agropoli to the south of the Bay, these Oriental freebooters found little difficulty in effecting a landing on the Poseidonian beach, and in raiding the weakened and almost defenceless city. Able-bodied men and young maidens were forcibly carried off to the pirates' nest at Agropoli, or perhaps even to the distant coast of Barbary, to be sold into perpetual slavery. Alarmed beyond measure by this raid, the remaining inhabitants of the place, at the advice and under the guidance of their bishop, now decided—wisely, for they had to choose between immediate flight or gradual extermination by disease, slavery and the sword—to remove themselves to the barren mountains in their rear, once the haunts of the Samnites, and to build a new Paestum on a site at once more healthy and better protected by Nature against the raids of infidel corsairs. In a body therefore the remaining citizens amid deep wailing left for ever the ancient city with its glorious temples, and retired to a strong position to the east. The spot chosen for the new residence of these exiles lay close to the source that supplied with pure water their ancient aqueduct, known for this reason as Caputaqueum, now corrupted into Capaccio. A link with the

o

old city, that lay deserted in the plain below, was still
retained by the bishop of the newly founded town in
the mountains, who continued to be known as *Epis-
copus Paestanus*. In the eleventh century Robert
Guiscard systematically plundered the ruins of Paestum
in order to erect or embellish the churches and palaces
of Salerno and Amalfi. Every remaining piece of
sculpture and of marble was removed, and it was only
the vast size of the pillars of the three great temples,
and the consequent difficulty attending their transport
by boat across the bay or along the marshy ground
of the coast line, that saved from destruction these
magnificent relics of "the glory that was Greece."
But even humble Capaccio did not afford a final
resting-place to the harried Paestani, for in the year
1245 the great Emperor Frederick II., who had been
defied by the feudal Counts of Capaccio, besieged and
utterly destroyed this stronghold of the mountains
that had been the child of Poseidonia of the sea-girt
plains. Another and a yet loftier retreat had to be
sought by the survivors of the Imperial vengeance, so
that the ruined Capaccio the Old was abandoned for
another settlement, which still exists as a miserable
village amidst those barren hills that had ever looked
down with jealous envy upon the proud city with its
pillared temples. One curious circumstance with
regard to Paestum must finally be mentioned, in that
the existence of its ruins, the grandest and most
ancient group of monuments on the mainland of Italy,
remained unknown to the learned world until comparatively modern times. Only the local peasants
and the inhabitants of the poverty-stricken towns in
the Lucanian hills seem to have been aware of the

presence of the gigantic temples standing in lonely majesty by the shore, and as the superstitious nature of these ignorant people attributed these structures to the work of a magician—perhaps to the great wizard Vergil himself—they were shunned both by night and by day as the haunt of malignant spirits. Poor fisher-folk and buffalo-drivers, who had of necessity to pass near the ruined fanes, were wont to slink by in fear and trembling, and doubtless they brought back strange stories of its ghostly occupants with which they regaled their friends or families by the fire-side of a winter's evening. Yet it is most strange that during the period of the Renaissance, at a time when enthusiastic research was being made into the neglected antiquities of Italy, this unique group of Doric temples should have escaped notice. For neither Cyriaco of Ancona nor Leandro Alberti, who visited Lucania ostensibly for the sake of recording its classical remains, make mention of "the ruined majesty of Paestum," and it was reserved for a certain Count Gazola (whose name is certainly worthy of being recorded), an officer in the service of the Neapolitan King, to present to the notice of scholars and archaeologists towards the middle of the eighteenth century the first known description of what is perhaps Italy's chief existing treasure of antiquity. From Gazola's day onward the beauty and interest of Paestum have been appraised at their true worth, and number-less artists and writers of almost every nationality have sketched or described its marvellous temples.

With this brief introduction to the history of a city, whose chief building is still standing almost intact after a lapse of 2500 years, let us take a rapid survey of Poseidonia as it exists to-day.　Its walls, of Greek construction but probably built or restored as late as the time of Alexander of Epirus, who gave the captured town a fleeting spell of liberty, form an irregular pentagon about three miles in circumference, wheron the remains of eight towers can be observed, whilst the four gates, placed at the four cardinal points of the compass, are clearly traceable.　We enter this *città morta* by the so-called Porta della Sirena, the eastern gate that faces the hostile Samnite Hills and (oh, the prosaic touch !) the modern railway-station.　This gate remains in a tolerable state of preservation, and draws its name from the key-stone of its arch, which bears in low relief a much defaced design of a mermaid or siren, its counterpart on the inner keystone being a dolphin : two devices very appropriate to the entrance of a city dedicated to the Lord of Ocean.　Passing the picturesque yellow-washed Villa Salati, with its high walls and iron-barred windows testifying only too plainly to the lawlessness that once reigned in this district, we find ourselves face to face with the great temple of Neptune or Poseidon, and its companion-fane, the so-called Basilica.　The Temple of Neptune (for in this instance at least the popular appellation chances to be the correct one), in all probability co-eval with the first Greek foundation of the city, formed the central point of the life of Poseidonia during the 1400 years of its existence as a Hellenic, a Samnite, and finally a Roman city.　In its simple grandeur and its perfect proportions this wonderful temple possesses only one rival outside Greece itself : the Temple of Concord at Girgenti, which the poet Goethe compared to a god, after designating the building before us as a giant. Superiority in grace is therefore a disputed point between the two great structures of Poseidonia and Agrigentum, yet in every other respect the temple of the Lucanian Plain surpasses its Sicilian rival.

To-day, after more than a score of centuries of exposure to the salt winds and to the burning sunshine of the south, the walls and pillars of these great buildings have been calcined to a glorious shade of tawny yellow, fit to delight the soul of every artist, whether he views their Titanic but graceful forms outlined against the deep blue of sky and sea on the western horizon, or against the equally lovely background of grey and violet mountains to the east. But it was not always thus. The porous local travertine that gave their building material to the Greeks of the sixth century before Christ was once carefully stuccoed, and, in the manner of Hellenic art, painted in the most brilliant hues of azure and vermilion, so that it becomes hard for us to realise the original effect of such gorgeous masses standing erect in a landscape that is itself fraught with glowing colour. But better to appreciate the magnificence before us, let us give a brief technical description of the greatest of the temples in the choice words of an eminent French antiquary.

"The largest and most elegant, and likewise the oldest of the Temples of Paestum, is that commonly known by the name of the Temple of Neptune. This building shares, together with the Temple of Theseus at Athens, the honour of being the best preserved monument of the Doric order in existence, and the impression of grandeur that it gives to the spectator rivals even the first sight of the Parthenon itself. In front of the building is a platform in the midst of which can be seen the hollow space that formerly held the altar of sacrifice, for according to the practice of the Greek religion, these rites of blood-shedding took place in the open air and outside the temple. With a length of 190 feet and a breadth of 84 feet, this building is hypoethral, which means that the *cella*, or sanctuary that held the statue of the deity, was constructed open to the sky. It is peripteral, and presents a row of six pillars fluted at base and top, with twelve on each side, making thirty-six in all. The *cella* itself in the interior is upheld by sixteen columns about six feet in diameter, which in their turn are surmounted by two rows of smaller pillars above that support the roof. With the exception of one side of the upper stage of the interior every column of the temple remains intact, as do likewise the entablature and pediments. Only the wall of the *cella* has been pulled down ; doubtless to supply material for building." *

Having quoted Monsieur Lenormant's careful description of the chief pride of Poseidonia, we shall confine ourselves to as few remarks as possible concerning the two remaining temples. The Basilica, a misnomer of which the veriest amateur must at once perceive the absurdity, is inferior both in size and in beauty of proportion to its close neighbour of Neptune. Its chief peculiarity from an architectural point of view will be at once remarked, for it has its two façades composed of seven—an odd number—of columns, so that its interior easily divides itself into two narrow chambers of equal length, affording ample ground for the theory, now generally held, that this building was not a hall of Justice, or *Basilica*, but a temple intended

* F. Lenormant : *A travers l'Apulie et la Lucanie.*

expressly for the worship of dual divinities. Almost
without a doubt it was erected—probably not long after
the Temple of Poseidon—in honour of Demeter (Ceres)
and of her only child Persephone (Proserpine), who
was seized from her mother's care by the amorous god
of the Infernal Regions, as she was plucking anemones
in the verdant meadows of Enna. We all know "the
old sweet mythos"; we all understand its hidden
allegory with regard to the sowing, the up-springing
and the garnering of the yellow corn, that spends
half the year in the embraces of the earth, the
palace of Pluto, and half the year on the broad
loving bosom of Mother Demeter. Here then within
these bare and ruined walls were mother and daughter
worshipped by the people of Poseidonia, who reason-
ably considered that the two goddesses of the Earth
should have their habitation as near as possible to the
Sanctuary of the Sovereign of Ocean.

Much smaller than either of these immense temples
is the third remaining Greek building of Paestum,
which lies a good quarter of a mile to the north, not
far from the Golden Gate, the Porta Aurea, that leads
northward in the direction of Salerno. Like that of
Neptune, this temple is hexastyle, with six columns on
each of its façades and twelve on either flank, but as it
is little more than half the size of its grander and older
brethren, it is now frequently known as "Il Piccolo
Tempio," although its former incorrect ascription to
Ceres still clings to it in popular parlance. It is from
this building, which stands on slightly rising ground,
that the best impression of the whole city and of its
wondrous setting between the savage Lucanian hills
and the blue Mediterranean can be obtained.

Between the mountains and the tideless sea
Stretches a plain where silence reigns supreme ;
A land of asphodel and weeds that teem
Where once a city's life ran joyfully.
'Vanity ! Vanity ! All Vanity !'
Whisper the winds to Sele's murmuring stream ;
Whilst the vast temples preach th' eternal theme,
How pass the glories and their memory.
Think what these ruins saw ! what songs and cries
Once through these roofless colonnades did ring !
What crowds here gathered, where the all-seeing skies
For centuries have watched the daisies spring !
Dead all within this crumbling circle lies :
Dead as the roses Roman bards did sing.

Beautiful as Paestum presents itself in the bright noontide of a Spring day, beneath a cloudless sky and with the blue waters of the Mediterranean lapping the distant yellow sands, there appears something incongruous in the sharp contrast between this joyfulness of vigorous life and the solemn atmosphere of the deserted city.   The noisy twittering of multitudes of ubiquitous sparrows, equally at home in Doric temples as amongst the sooty chimney stacks of London ; the twinklings and rustlings of the lizards in the young leaves and grass ; the polyglot babble of excursionists from Naples or La Cava that a warm day in Spring invariably attracts to Paestum :—these are not sounds that blend well with the solemn spirit of the place.   We long to cross the intervening ages so as to throw ourselves, if only for one short hour, outside the cares and interests of to-day into the heart of that refined civilisation which is gone for ever ;— with the cheerful sunlight around us, and with our fellow-mortals on pleasure bent close at hand, we find it difficult to forget the present.   Would it be possible, we ask ourselves, to spend a nocturnal vigil within the hall of the great temple of the Sea God, so as to behold, like that undaunted traveller, Crawford Ramage, the shafts of crystalline moonlight shed through the aperture of the roof leap from pillar to pillar, making bars of brilliant light amidst the surrounding blackness ! O to sit and meditate thus engrossed with the memory of the past, and with no other sounds around us than the sad cry of the *asiola*, the little downy owl that Shelley so loved ! But the gaunt spectre of Fever ever haunts this spot, and after sunset his power is supreme ; so that he would be a bold man indeed who in an age of luxury and selfish comfort would carry out an idea at once so romantic and so perilous.

We ourselves were especially fortunate on the occasion of our last visit to Poseidonia on a mild day in December, a month which on the Lucanian shore somewhat resembles a northern October. A soft luminous haze hung over the landscape and over the Bay of Salerno itself, rendering the classic mountains at once indistinct in outline and unnaturally lofty to the eye. More grandiose and mysterious than under the fierce light of a sunny noontide appeared that day the three giant pillared forms, as we entered the precincts of the ruined city by the Siren's Gate, and made our way through the thick herbage still pearled with dew, since there was neither sunshine nor sirocco to dry "the tears of mournful Eve" off the clumps of silver-glinted acanthus, or the tall grasses bending with the moisture. In the warm humid air we seated ourselves on the plinth of a column, and gazing around allowed the influence of this marvellous spot to sink deep into the soul. No tourists with unseemly or unnecessary chatter arrived that day to share our selfish delight or to break the all-pervading spell of solitude ; all lay peaceful and deserted. All was silent too save for the low monotonous sobbing of the sea on the unseen beach near at hand, the historic beach on which at various times throughout the roll of past ages Doric colonists, Epirot warriors, Roman legionaries and fierce Moham- medan pirates had disembarked, all with the same object :—to seize the proud city that had now for the last thousand years lain uninhabited, save for the owls and the bats. It was too cloudy a day for sun-loving creatures such as lizards or serpents to emerge and rustle amongst the broken stones and leaves, over all of which during the silent hours of the past night Arachne had been employed in weaving her softest and whitest textures, that the windless morning had allowed to remain intact. The only sign of animate life was visible in a pair of lively gold- finches, which with merry notes were fluttering from thistle to thistle, picking the down from each ripened flower-head and prodigally scattering the seeds upon the weed-grown soil where once had bloomed the odorous Roses of Paestum that the poets loved.

Sitting thus amid the silence and solitude of a city half as old as Time itself, we were unexpectedly aroused by a gruff salutation proceeding from a little distance behind the temple. Turning quickly in the direction of the sound, we perceived the figure of a tall bearded man dressed in conical hat, with goat-skin trousers and cross-gartered legs, who but for the gun slung across his shoulders by a stout leathern strap might well have been mistaken for an apparition of

the god Pan himself returned to earth. Vague recollections of the brigand Manzoni, the scourge of the
neighbourhood and the murderer of more than one
unhappy visitor to the ruins of Paestum in the good
old *vetturino* days, flashed through our mind, as we
surveyed the muscular frame and the fowling-piece
of the strange being before us. It was with a sigh
of relief that we noted upon the straight stretch of
white road leading to the Little Temple in the distance
the presence of two royal *carabinieri* majestically
riding at a foot's pace, their tall forms enveloped in
long black cloaks whose folds swept over their horses'
tails. We felt reassured, and when for a second
time the guttural voice addressed us in unintelligible
patois, we perceived the innocent object of this
mysterious visit. Searching in a capacious goat-skin
bag, a species of Neapolitan sporran, this descendant
of the Poseidonian Greeks produced and held up to
our gaze three birds that he had shot in his morning's
hunting. For the modest sum of three lire the game
exchanged hands, and the sportsman departed, well
satisfied with his luck. Next evening we feasted
royally in our inn at Salerno upon a succulent wood-
cock fattened upon the berries of the wood of Persano,
and upon a couple of snipe that had grown plump
amongst the Neptunian marshes. Nor was this dainty
addition to our supper that night altogether un-
deserved ; for having decided in a momentary fit of
enthusiasm to forego the usual basket of hotel food
at the time of starting from Salerno, in order to follow
the advice of old Evelyn " to diet with the natives,"
we had preferred to take our chance of midday re-
freshment at the solitary *osteria* within the ruined

city wall. The good people of the inn did what they could to regale the two *gran' signori Inglesi*, whose unexpected presence had the effect of creating some stir within their humble walls. No little time was expended in bustling preparations, before a flask of red wine, some coarse bread, a dish of fried eggs and a plateful of cold sausage were placed before us upon the rough oak table, well scored with knife-cuts. Eggs, wine and bread are usually tolerable everywhere throughout Italy, no matter how mean the inn that provides them ; but the Lucanian sausage, though interesting as a relic of classical times, is positive poison to the Anglo-Saxon digestion. For the Lucanian sausage of to-day is the *Lucanica* unchanged ; the same tough, greasy, odoriferous compound, in fact, that Cicero describes as " an intestine, stuffed with minced pork, mixed with ground pepper, cummin, savory, rue, rock-parsley, berries of laurel, and suet." And we have only to add that mingling with the above-mentioned condiments there was an all-pervading flavour of wood-smoke, due to the sausage's place of storage, a hook within the kitchen chimney. But if the fare was rough, it was cheap and smacked of classical times, and our reception by the Paestani of to-day was most cordial.

We left Poseidonia late in the afternoon, casting back many regretful glances at the three giant sentinels of the plain, looming preternaturally large in the rapidly fading light of a starless evening. At that hour we felt we could understand and sympathise with the poor untutored peasant's fear and avoidance of these lonely ruins, for superstition is often as much the result of chance environment as of crass ignorance.

CHAPTER X

SORRENTO AND ITS POET

IT has been said of more than one spot on this globe, that it was so beautiful in summer the marvel was to think any one could die there; and so wretched in winter, it was a miracle for its inhabitants to survive. Sorrento may be said to belong to this class of place, for the climate of its short winter is one of the most trying and inclement that can possibly be imagined, whilst during spring, summer and early autumn it well merits its local reputation as *il piccolo paradiso* of the Bay of Naples, and its air is considered by Neapolitans as the " balm in Gilead " for every evil to which human flesh is heir. The Lactarian Mountains protect the plain of Sorrento in summer from the scorching rays of the sun, and lay their beneficent shadow for several hours of the long hot summer's day over the many thousands who dwell on the fertile Piano di Sorrento at their base. But in winter these same hills intercept the blessed sunshine, which is what most travellers speed southwards to obtain, and leave the coast line from Castellamare to the Punta di Sorrento with its northern aspect wrapped in shade and moisture, whilst the remainder of the Bay is still basking in the genial warmth, so that anything more miserable than a mid-winter sojourn in Sorrento it would be impossible to conceive.   There are of course calm warm days to be met with even in December and January, but these are occasional and by no means dependable blessings, and the visitor who persists in taking up his abode here at this season of the year must prepare himself to experience cold, damp, wind and rain, without any of the contrivances or comforts of a northern winter.   " One swallow does not make a summer," and on the same principle a southern latitude and the presence of orange groves do not necessarily imply a salubrious climate ; indeed, the sub-tropical surroundings seem to add an extra degree of chilliness to the place.   To sit at Christmastide in a large lofty room before a meagre fire of sputtering smoky logs, with Vesuvius wrapped from crest to base in a white mantle of new fallen snow, and with an icy *tramontana* from the bleak Abruzzi howling round the house, bending the bay trees and penetrating into every corner of the chamber, is by no means the ideal picture of a winter in the Sunny South ; yet this is only what the traveller must be prepared to face, and is very likely to obtain.   Nor is the cold compensated for by any advantages in the neighbourhood itself, for there is but the high road from Castellamare which passes through the town and leads above the seashore to Massa Lubrense.   It is all very well in its way, but in wet weather its surface is one sheet of slippery mud, and the streams pouring down the hillside make it chilly and damp for all who are not quick walkers.   Besides this not very attractive and soon exploited walk, there are only the *vicoletti*, the narrow steep rocky paths running up hill, which make rough going and give little pleasure, for they are almost all bounded on either side by high stone walls that jealously exclude the view. So much for Sorrento in its winter dress. But when the spring comes, here truly is a transformation from cold and torpor! The soft warm air is redolent of the penetrating fragrance of orange blossom, of stocks, of jessamine, of wallflower, and of a hundred odorous plants and shrubs from each garden and grove behind the many obstructing walls. The balconies and gate-pillars are draped in scented masses of the beautiful wistaria, which in Italy produces its long pendant bunches of purple flowers before putting forth its bronze-coloured leaves. Cascades of white and yellow banksia roses fall over each confining barrier, or else their stems may be seen climbing like huge serpents up the trunks of pine and olive, to burst forth amidst the topmost boughs into floral rockets against the cloudless sky. The ravines with which the whole of the Piano di Sorrento is intersected are filled with a perfect jungle of fresh spring foliage, amidst whose varied tints of green appear here and there the bright red shoots of the pomegranate trees bursting into leaf. In the heavily perfumed air at dusk, or when the bright moonlight is flooding the whole scene and is turning the Bay into a mirror of molten silver, the song of the innumerable nightingales can be heard resounding from all sides ; alas! too often sweet songs of sorrow for nests despoiled by the ruthless hands of young Sorrentine imps, as in the days of the Georgics.

> Qualis populeâ mærens Philomela sub umbrâ
> Amissos queritur fetus, quos durus arator
> Observans nido implumes detraxit, at illa
> Flet noctem, ramoque sedens miserabile carmen
> Integrat, et mœstis late loca questibus implet.

(At nightfall hear sad Philomel upraise
Her mellow notes amid the dark-leaved bays,
Mourning her babes and desecrated bower,
Which some rough peasant robbed in evil hour ;
She tells her story of despair and love,
Until her plaintive music fills the grove.)

All is fragrant, warm, genial, and peaceful, save for the melancholy notes of poor ill-used Philomel, who is foolish enough to visit a cruel country, wherein every bird is merely regarded as a toothsome morsel for the family pot. We bird-lovers of Britain, with our Selborne Societies and our Wild Birds' Protection Acts, find it extremely difficult to understand the utter indifference displayed by Italians of all classes towards the feathered race. The whole of the beautiful country with its cypress hedges and olive groves lies almost mute and lifeless, for on every festival the fields and lanes are patrolled by bands of *cacciatori* with dogs and guns on the look-out for game, if blackbirds and sparrows can be accounted such. In some districts it is even dangerous for pedestrians to use the roads on a Sunday, for fear of a stray bullet, since all, as a rule, fire recklessly at any creature within and out of range. Nor is this senseless war of extermination carried on merely with guns, for trapping is used extensively, and very ingenious and elaborate are some of the arts employed in this wretched quest. Every country house has its *uccellare*, or snare for the securing of small birds for the table, whilst many of the parish priests in the mountain districts add to their scanty incomes by catching the fledglings which the young peasants sell in the neighbouring market. The result is what might only naturally be expected—a scarcity of birds and an almost complete absence of song, for the whole countryside has been practically denuded of blackbirds and thrushes ; even the nightingale has escaped destruction rather on account of its nocturnal habits than of its tiny size and exquisite notes. It is positively sickening to observe the quantities of slaughtered wild birds in an Italian market at any season of the year, for the work of devastation proceeds apace equally in spring time. Basketfuls of thrushes and blackbirds, and strings of smaller varieties—linnets, sparrows, robins, finches, even the diminutive goldfinches, most beautiful, most gay, and most innocent of all songsters—are being hawked about by leathern-lunged *contadini*, who, alas! always manage to find customers in plenty. No matter how melodious, how lovely, or how useful to the farmer a bird may be, no Italian, high or low, seems to have any sense or appreciation of its merits except as an article of food ; it is merely a thing that requires to be caught, killed, cooked and eaten, and Providence has decreed its existence for no other purpose ; even gold-finches in the eye of an Italian look better served on a skewer than when they are flying round the thistle-heads, uttering their bright musical notes and enlivening the dead herbage of winter with their gay plumage. *Che bel arrosto !* (what a glorious dish!) sigh the romantic peasants, as they glance upward for a moment from their labour in the fields at the sound of the larks carolling overhead ;. and though an educated Italian would probably not give vent to so vulgar a remark, he would much prefer the *bel arrosto* to the " profuse strains of unpremeditated art "

P

that so entrance the northerner, who is in reality far
more of a poet by nature than the more picturesque
dweller of the South. *Tantum pro avibus.*

As summer advances, the delight of bathing in the
limpid waters of the Bay is added to the other attractions of Sorrento, whilst many pleasant and profitable
hours can be passed in reading or writing during the
long midday rest in the cool airy carpetless and
curtainless rooms, where on the frescoed ceilings there
plays the green shimmer of light that penetrates
through the closed bars of the *persiani*, the outside
heavy wooden shutters that let in the sweet air, but
somehow seem to exclude the intense heat. With
the approach of sunset and the throwing open of
casements to catch the westerly breeze, there comes
a delightful ramble, perhaps an excursion on mule-
back to the famous convent of the Deserto or some
other point of interest ; or else a row upon the glassy
waters at our feet, to explore " Queen Joanna's Bath,"
or some strange caverns beyond the headland of
Sorrento, well known to our boat-men. That is the
true life of *dolce far niente*, but such an ideal existence
can only be indulged in during summer time or in
late spring ; to pass a winter at Sorrento the heaviest
of clothing, abundance of overcoats and rugs, hot-
water bottles, cough drops, ammoniated quinine and
all the usual adjuncts of a northern yule-tide must
be carefully provided before-hand by the traveller,
who is bold enough to tempt Providence by turning
what is essentially a warm weather retreat into a place
of winter residence.

In early autumn also the place has its charms, in
the days when the market is filled with stalls heaped

with glowing masses of fruit, many of them unknown to us wanderers from the north.   There are peaches that resemble our own fruit at home, and there are also great yellow flushed velvety globes, like the sun-kissed cheeks of a fair Sorrentina, that appear tempting to the eye, but are in reality tough as leather, for they are the *cotogni* or quince-peaches of Italy, which to our feeble palates and digestions seem only fit for cooking, though the experienced native contrives to, make them edible by soaking the fruit in wine.   The moment he sits down to table, he carefully pares his *cotogne* and cuts it into sections, which he drops into a glass of red wine where they repose until the meal is finished ; by this time the fruit has become thoroughly saturated, and it is then eaten with apparent relish.   There are hundreds of apples, some of a shining rich crimson and others of dull yellow peppered over with tiny black specks, the *renati*, highly prized by the natives for their delicate flavour and soft flesh.   There are of course loads of grapes, varying from the little honey-tasting purple sort, that has been introduced from California, to the huge but somewhat insipid bunches of the white *Regina* ; we note also the quaintly shaped " Ladies' Fingers," which are especially sweet.   The figs, massed together in serried layers between fresh vine leaves and costing a *soldo* the dozen, stand around in glossy purple pyramids, so luscious that their sugary tears are exuding from their skins, and so ripe that they seem to cry to be eaten before noon.   Here is a barrow piled high with the little green fruit, each separate fig being decorated with a pink cyclamen stuck in its crest ; and here is a smaller load of the black *Vescovo*,

which is said to obtain its ecclesiastical name from
the fact that the parent stock of this highly esteemed
variety originally flourished in the bishop's garden at
Sorrento. No one who has not visited the shores of
the Mediterranean in September or early October can
realize the luscious possibilities of the fig ; for there
seems nothing in common between the freshly-picked
fruit of the south, bursting its skin with liquid sugar,
and the dry sweetish woolly object which tries to
ripen on the sheltered wall of an English garden and
is eaten with apparent gusto by those who know not
its Italian brother. Being autumn, we have missed
one prominent feature of the fruit market, the great
green-skinned water-melons (*poponi*) with their rose-
coloured pulp and masses of coal-black seeds, which
form the favourite summer fruit of the people, who
find both food and drink in their cool nutritious
flesh. But even gayer and more striking than the
fruits are the piles of vegetables, arranged with a fine
appreciation of colour to which only an Italian eye
can aspire. Carrots, turnips, tomatoes, purple-headed
cauliflowers, all the broccoli and many others to be
observed are old familiar friends, but who in England
ever saw such gorgeous objects on a coster's stall or
in a green-grocer's shop as the yellow, scarlet and
shining green pods of the *peperoni*, or the banana-
shaped egg-plants of iridescent purple, or the split
pumpkins, revealing caverns of saffron-hued pulp
within ? Truly, the Sorrentine market contains a
feast of colour to satisfy the craving of an artist !

At vintage time the whole Piano di Sorrento reeks
with the vinous scent of the spilt juice, that is carelessly thrown on to the stone-paved roads by the

jolting of the country carts which bring in the great wooden tubs, so that the very streets seem to run with the crimson ooze. Slender youths in yet more slender clothing, with legs purple-stained from treading the grapes (for in the South wine is still made on the primitive plan), are to be met with on all sides, playing at their favourite game of bowls on the public road, in order to relieve their brains of the pungent fumes of the fermenting grape juice. Somehow at the very thought of a Campanian vintage with its long hot dusty days, its bare-legged brown-skinned peasants treading the pulp, and its all-pervading aroma of wine-lees, there rise to memory the truly inspired lines of John Keats :

> " O for a draught of vintage, that hath been
> Cool'd a long age in the deep-delved earth,
> Tasting of Flora and the country-green,
> Dance, and Provençal song, and sun-burnt mirth !
> O for a beaker full of the warm South,
> Full of the true, the blushful Hippocrene,
> With beaded bubbles winking at the brim,
> And purple-stained mouth."

But all these joys of odorous gardens made musical by nightingales, of morning plunges into the blue Mediterranean, of the wealth of southern fruit and the novel delights of the vintage are not for the winter traveller, who had far better spend the December or January days of his visit to the Bay in a steam-heated Neapolitan hotel, rather than face the cold and wet in a Sorrentine inn on its overhanging cliff. Nevertheless the warm autumn often extends itself into a continuous St Martin's summer, that lasts almost until the New Year, before skies grow clouded and the snow-flakes descend upon the vineyards and the lava streams of Vesuvius. Nothing can be pleasanter in fact than some of the long walks in a sharp exhilarating air, and though days are short and nights are often chilly, one can sometimes linger on comfortably in Sorrento, though it is as well to be prepared for departure in case of a sudden spell of stormy weather, for winter sunshine is a necessity, not a luxury, on the Piano di Sorrento.

Unlike other towns upon the Bay of Naples, Sorrento is divided into two distinct portions; the city on the cliffs, with its streets and squares, its cathedral and ancient walls, its villas and gay gardens; and the Marina, lying at the mouth of the gorge below, close to the water's edge. The population of Upper Sorrento is agricultural and labouring, whilst that of the lower consists entirely of fisher-folk and sailors; it is needless to add that the latter are far less prosperous than their fellow-citizens who live over-head. Until recent times little communication between these two sets of Sorrentines took place and intermarriages were rare, for the sea-faring population only ascended to the town above and intermingled with the people of Upper Sorrento on the great occasions of local festivals, such as the enthronement or funeral of a bishop. Nor has the levelling spirit of the age as yet broken down the deep-rooted feeling of local clannishness; although it cannot be long before time-honoured customs and prejudices will be swept away in the tidal wave of modern development. One of the chief industries of the place is the manufacture of scarves and sashes of rich silk woven in cross bars of strong contrasting colours, so that the Sorrentine silk work strongly

AFTERNOON, SORRENTO

resembles the well-known Roman variety. Equally popular with visitors are the various articles made of olive wood and decorated in *tarsia*, the art of inlaying with pieces of stained wood, which is a speciality of the place. There are two kinds of this Sorrentine inlaid work; one consisting of figures of peasants dancing the *tarantella*, of Pompeian maidens in classical drapery, of *contadini* or priests bestriding mules, and of similar local subjects; and the other, of fanciful patterns made up of tiny coloured cubes of wood, much in the style of the old Roman stone mosaics. The designs employed vary of course with the fashion of the day, for there is a local school of art supported by the municipality, which professes to improve the tastes of the *tarsiatori*, but most persons will certainly prefer the trite but characteristic patterns of the place.

But the main industry of Sorrento consists in the culture of the orange; and the dark groves, covered with their globes of shining yellow fruit, " like golden lamps in a green light," to quote Andrew Marvell's charming conceit, constitute the chief feature of its environs. Even the coat-of-arms of the medieval city, showing a golden crown encircled by a wreath of the dark glossy leaves, attests the antiquity of this industry here. The cultivation of the orange in Southern Italy is by no means an easy pursuit, though under favourable conditions it may prove a very lucrative one, even in a spot so subject to sudden changes of temperature as Sorrento in winter time, when a continuance of severe weather, like that experienced around Naples in the opening months of the year 1905, means total destruction of the fruit crop and temporary ruin to the owners.

The fruit of commerce is propagated by means of grafting the sweet variety on to the stock of the bitter orange—said on doubtful authority to be indigenous to this district—which is fairly hardy and can be grown in the open as far north as Tuscany, so that every *aran.iaria* ought to possess a nursery of flourishing young sweet-orange shoots, ready in case of necessity.   For eight long years the grafted tree remains as a rule profitless, but having survived and thriven so long, it then becomes a valuable asset to its proprietor for an indefinite period ;—as a proof of the longevity of the orange under normal conditions we may cite the famous tree in a Roman convent garden, which on good authority is stated to have been planted by St Dominic nearly six hundred years ago.   As to the amount of fruit yielded, the growers of Sorrento commonly aver that one good year, one bad year and one mediocre year constitute the general cycle in the prospects of orange farming.   Two crops are gathered annually, the principle one in December and the other at Eastertide, the fruit produced by the later and smaller crop being far finer in size and flavour than those of the Christmas harvest.   Mandarin oranges are gathered on both occasions, but the large luscious loose-skinned fruit of March and April—*Portogalli* as they are commonly termed—are far superior to the small hard specimens that appear in December, and seem to consist of little else than rind, scent and seeds. The oranges begin to form in spring time, almost before the petals have fallen, when the peasants anxiously draw their conclusions as to the expected yield.   But however valuable the fruit, the wood of the tree is worthless for commerce, except to make walking-sticks, or to serve the ignoble purpose of supplying hotels and cafés with tooth-picks! Lemons, which are far more delicate than oranges and require to be kept protected by screens and matting during the sharp winter nights, are less common at Sorrento than on the warmer shores of the Bay of Baia or the sunny terraced slopes of the Amalfitan coast.

With the ripening of the oranges on the trees appear those strange creatures from the wilds of the Basilicata or Calabria, the *Zampognari*, who visit Naples and the surrounding district in considerable numbers. They usually arrive about the date of the great popular festival of the Immaculate Conception (December 8th) and remain until the end of the month, when they return to their homes with well-filled purses. In outward aspect these strangers resemble the stage-brigands that appear in such old-fashioned operas as *Fra Diavolo*, for they wear steeple-crowned hats with coloured ribands depending, shaggy goat-skin trousers, crimson velvet waistcoats, blue cloaks, sandalled feet and gartered legs. Their pale faces are unshorn, and their hair hangs in great tawny masses over neck and ears, which are invariably adorned with golden rings. These fellows come in pairs, one only, properly speaking, being the *zampognaro*, for it is he who carries the *zampogna* or classical bag-pipe of Southern Italy, whilst his companion is the *cennamellaro*, so called from his ear-splitting instrument, the *cennamella*, a species of primitive flute. The *zampogna* may be described as first cousin to the historic bag-pipes of Caledonia, for the sounds emitted strongly resemble the traditional "skirling" of the pipes; but no Scotch-man even could pretend to delight in the shrill notes

of the *cennamella*. The former at least of these two
popular instruments of southern Italy was well known
to the omniscient author of the Shakespearean plays,
for in *Othello* we have a direct allusion to the uncouth
braying music still made to-day by these outlandish
musicians.

"Why, masters, have your instruments been in
Naples, that they speak i' the nose thus? . . . Are
these, I pray you, wind instruments? . . . Then put
up your pipes in your bag, for I'll away: go; vanish
into air; away!"

In the midst of their instrumental duet the two
shaggy mountaineers are apt to break into a harsh
nasal hymn in honour of the Virgin, to visit whose
shrines at this season of the orange harvest is the main
object of their Christmas migration to the Neapolitan
shores. Very tastefully decorated are many of the
Madonna's little sanctuaries in or near the orange
groves, when the arrival of the *zampognari* is considered
imminent. The tiny lamps are well trimmed and
shine brightly, whilst heavy garlands composed of
masses of bay or laurel or ilex leaves, interspersed
with some of the golden clusters of the ripening fruit
are suspended round the alcove that holds the figure
of the Virgin. This effective but simple form of
ornamentation will at once suggest the beautiful glazed
and coloured terra-cotta wreaths of fruit and foliage
that are to be seen so frequently in Tuscan churches;
indeed, it is possible that the members of the Della
Robbia family may have originally borrowed the
decorative schemes for their famous plaques and
lunettes from the rustic shrines thus simply but tastefully embellished. Nominally, the two performers

are supposed to sing and make music on nine different days at the houses of all their patrons in order to make up the total number of the *novena*, but the extent of their performances is generally calculated in accordance with the depth of the householder's purse, the sum given for their services varying from a few *soldi* to a five *lire* note.   All classes of society employ the *zampognari*, for it is with the first appearance of the lovely golden fruit, essentially *the* winter fruit of the Italians, that the arrival of these picturesque strangers has been associated from time immemorial. The *zampognari* are in fact as much of a national institution with the Neapolitans at Christmastide as are the waits or carol-singers in our own country, so that to the majority of these people *Natale sensa zampogna e cennamella* would seem no true Christmas at all.

Closely connected with the life of the people of the Piano di Sorrento is the famous dance known as the *Tarantella*, which may be witnessed by the curious at almost any time—for money.   Even when performed by professional dancers, tricked out in spick and span stage-peasant finery, the Tarantella is a most graceful exhibition of movement, although the dance naturally gains in interest when it takes place in the days of vintage or on the popular festivals of the Church, without the presence of largesse-giving strangers. The origin of the name has always puzzled antiquarians, although in all probability the dance derives its curious appellation from the Greek city of Taranto, whence the Tarentines introduced its steps and action into other parts of Italy.   But vulgar belief is very strong, so that this graceful dance is still closely associated in the popular mind with the *tarantula*, a kind of poisonous spider found in the neighbourhood of Taranto, the effects of whose bite are said to yield to violent exercise followed by profuse perspiration. In order to excite the proper amount of exertion necessary for the cure, the person afflicted, *il tarantolato*, is induced to leap and caper by the sound of music, with the result that there exist a number of tunes specially connected with this wild species of dancing. The real explanation of this fable seems to lie in the extremely excitable nature of the Tarentines themselves, assisted by the exhilarating music and by frequent pulls at the wine barrel. The two lines sung to the air of one of the tunes employed :

> " Non fu Taranta, ne fu Tarantella,
> Ma fu la vino della carratella : "

("It was neither the taranta, nor the tarantella, but it was the wine from the cask.")

sums up pretty accurately the real cause of these strange Tarentine orgies, which have really nothing whatever in common with the rhythmical dance that is still so popular in the environs of Naples. Nevertheless the theory of *tarantella* and *tarantismo* has been gravely discussed by old Italian writers, and a certain learned prelate of the fifteenth century, Niccolo Perotto, Archbishop of Siponto, alludes to the malignant cause of this dance-cure as "a species of speckled spider, dwelling in rents of the ground caused by excessive heat. It was not known in the time of our fore-fathers, but now it is very common in Apulia . . . and is generally called *Tarantula*. Its bite seldom kills a man, yet it makes him half

stupid, and affects him in a variety of ways. Some,
when a song or tune is heard, are so excited that
they dance, full of joy and always laughing, and do
not stop till they are entirely exhausted; others
spend a miserable life in tears, as if bewailing the
loss of friends. Some die laughing, and others in
tears."

Such is the curious legend concerning the origin of
the Tarantella, which is still danced with something
of the old spirit by the holiday-making crowds of
Naples, though it is at the *festa* of San Michele, the
patron of Procida, that the Tarantella can now be
seen to best advantage. Of the three islands that lie
close to Naples, Procida is the least known or visited
by strangers, so that when the Tarantella is danced by
the Procidani, the old-fashioned popular orchestra is
employed to give the necessary music. This consists
of five quaint instruments (obviously of Oriental origin
as their counterparts can still be seen amongst the
Kabyles of Northern Africa): the first being a fife
(*siscariello*); the second a tin globe covered with skin
pierced by a piece of cane (*puti-puti*); the third a
wooden saw and a split stick, making a primitive bow
and fiddle (*scetavaiasse*); the fourth an arrangement of
three wooden mallets, that are rattled together like a
gigantic pair of bones (*tricca-ballache*); and the fifth a
Jew's harp (*scaccia-pensieri*). A tarantella danced to
the accompaniment of so weird a medley of instruments and by real peasants full of gaiety is naturally a
thing altogether diverse from the stilted, though graceful and decorous performance that can be observed
any day for payment in a Sorrentine or Neapolitan
hotel; yet it must ever be borne in mind that the

Tarantella proper, whether danced *con amore* by Procidan peasants or performed for lucre by costumed professionals, is no vulgar frenzied *can-can*, but a musical love-dance expressive of primitive courtship.

"The Tarantella is a choregraphic love-story, the two dancers representing an enamoured swain and his mistress.   It is the old theme—'the quarrel of lovers is the renewal of love.'   Enraptured gaze, coy side-look, gallant advance, timid retrocession, impassioned declaration, supercilious rejection, piteous supplication, softening hesitation ; worldly goods oblation, gracious acceptation ; frantic jubilation, maidenly resignation. Petting, wooing, billing, cooing.   Jealous accusation, sharp recrimination, manly expostulation, shrewish aggravation ; angry threat, summary dismissal.   Fuming on one side, pouting on the other.   Reaction, approximation, exclamation, exoneration, reconciliation, osculation, winding up with a grand *pas de circomstane*, expressive of confidence re-established and joy unbounded.   That's about the figure of it ; but no word-painting can give an idea of the spirit, the ' go ' of the tarantella when danced for love and not for money." *

On a modest scale Sorrento can lay claim to be called an eternal city, for the Surrentum of the ancient Romans was a place of no small importance, filled with villas of wealthy citizens and boasting a fair-sized population, as its numerous remains of antiquity can easily testify ; whilst its crumbling ivy-clad walls and towers point to its prosperity during the Middle Ages, when Sorrento shared the political fortunes of Naples. It is now a busy thriving little cathedral town, and

* W. J. A. Stamer : *Dolce Napoli.*

the possessor of silk and *tarsia* work industries, so
that like Imperial Rome it can boast a continuous
existence as a city from remote times to the present
day.   Its chief local Saint—for what Italian town
does not boast a special patron?—is Sant' Antonio,
whose most famous feat is said to have been the
administering of a severe drubbing to Sicardo, Duke
of Benevento, for daring to interfere with the liberties
of his city in the ninth century.   It would appear
from the legend that all arguments as to ancient
rights, the quality of mercy and the honour of keeping
faith having been vainly exhausted upon the cruel and
obstinate prince, Bishop Antonio came forward with
a stout cudgel and belaboured the tyrant in order to
obtain a favourable answer to the people's petition.
The sanctity of the pugnacious prelate and the force
of this *argumentum ad baculum* were evidently too
much for the Duke of Benevento, who at once conceded
the popular demands, whilst Antonio's name has
deservedly descended to posterity as the capable protector of his native city.

    .   .   .   .   .   .

But the name which above all others Sorrento will
cherish as her own, "so long as men shall read and
eyes can see," is that of the famous Italian poet, Torquato Tasso, whose interesting but melancholy life-
story is closely associated with this, the town of his
birth.   Tasso is reckoned as the fourth greatest bard
of Italy, ranking after Dante and Petrarch, and being
esteemed on a level with rather than below his rival
and contemporary, Ludovico Ariosto.   In one sense
however he may be described as the most truly national
poet of this immortal quartet, for his career is con-

nected with his native country as a whole, rather than
with any one of the little cities or states then comprising that "geographical expression" which is now
the Kingdom of Italy.   His father's family was
of Lombard origin, having been long settled in the
neighbourhood of Bergamo, where a crumbling hill-set
fortress known as the Montagno del Tasso still recalls
the name of the poet's ancestors.   His mother, Porzia
de' Rossi, was Tuscan by birth, her family haling from
Pistoja at the foot of the Apennines, but owning property near Naples ; whilst the poet himself was
destined to spend his years of childhood at Sorrento
and at Naples, his youth at Rome and Verona, his
brilliant period of fame and prosperity at Ferrara and
the Lombard courts, and again some of his closing
years of disgrace and disappointment amidst the
familiar scenes of his infancy.   Of good ancient stock
the Tassi owed their acquisition of wealth to the re-
establishment of the system of posting throughout
Northern Italy in the thirteenth century, when the
immediate progenitor of the poet, one Omodeo de'
Tassi, was nominated comptroller, and it is curious to
note that owing to this circumstance the arms of the
family containing the posthorn and the badger's skin
—*Tasso* is the Italian for badger—continued to be
borne for many centuries upon the harness of all
Lombard coach-horses.   Torquato's father, Bernardo
Tasso, himself a poet of no mean calibre and the
composer of a scholarly but somewhat prolix work, the
Amadigi, formed for many years a prominent member
of that brilliant band of literary courtiers within the
castle of Vittoria Colonna, the Lady of Ischia, of whom
we shall speak more fully in another place.   But for

the overwhelming and all-eclipsing fame of his distinguished son, Bernardo might have been able to claim
a high place in the list of Italian writers of the
Renaissance; as it was, the father's undoubted talents
were quickly forgotten in the blaze of his own beloved
" Tassino's " popularity, so that he is now chiefly remembered as the sire of a poetic genius, as one of the
the great Vittoria's favourite satellites and as the author
of an oft-quoted sonnet to his intellectual mistress.
Bernardo Tasso did not marry until the somewhat
mature age of forty-seven, when, as we have already
said, he espoused the daughter of the Tuscan house of
Rossi, by whom he had two children; a daughter,
Cornelia, and the immortal Torquato, who was born in
1544, three years before the death of the divine
poetess of Ischia.

But Bernardo was not merely a bard and a courtier,
for he was also, unfortunately for himself and his ill-
fated family, a keen politician in an age when politics
offered anything but a safe pursuit, and as his views
invariably coincided with those of his chief friend and
patron, the head of the powerful Sanseverino family,
Tasso the Elder found himself in course of time an
exile from Neapolitan territory on account of his
dislike of the new Spanish masters of Naples. The
poet-politician therefore took up his abode at Rome
whilst his wife and two young children continued to
reside at Naples and Sorrento. The boy was a born
student, almost an infant prodigy of learning, and so
great was his desire for knowledge that he would
insist upon rising long before it was day-light, and
would even make his way to school through the dark
dirty streets of Naples, conducted by a servant with a

Q

torch in his hand. The Jesuits, who had just set up their first academy at Naples, soon discovered in the future poet an ideal pupil, and not only did they impart to the child all the lore of ancient Greece and Rome, but they also imbued his mind, at an age when it was "wax to receive and marble to retain," with their own peculiar theological tenets. It is obvious indeed that the faith implanted by the Fathers in his tender years was largely, if not wholly answerable for the unswerving belief and firm religious convictions that ever stood Tasso in good stead throughout the whole of his chequered career. "Give me a child of seven years old," had once declared the great Founder of the Society of Jesus, "and I care not who has the after-handling of him"; and in this case the Jesuit professors did not fail to carry out Loyola's precept. But his home life with his mother, whom he loved devotedly, and his course of study at the Jesuit school were suddenly interrupted when he was barely ten years of age, for the elder Tasso was anxious for his little son to join him in Rome, there to be educated under his own eye. The boy left his mother, but after his departure the Rossi family brutally refused to allow their sister access to her absent husband, who had lately been declared a rebel against the Spanish government and deprived of his estates. Thus persecuted by her unfeeling brothers, Porzia Tasso sought refuge together with Cornelia in a Neapolitan convent, where, deprived of her erratic but beloved husband and pining for her absent son, the poor woman died of a broken heart a year or two later. As for Cornelia, she became affianced when of a marriageable age to a gentleman of Sorrento,

the Cavaliere Marzio Sersale, and consequently
returned to live in the home of her childhood.

Of Tasso's many adventures, of his universal literary
fame, of the honours heaped upon him by his chief
patron, Duke Alfonso of Ferrara, and of his subsequent
disgrace and imprisonment for daring to lift his eyes
in love to a princess of the haughty House of Este,
we have no space to speak here. Let it suffice to say
that he was one of the most charming, virtuous,
brilliant, manly figures, as he was also almost the last
true representative, of the great Italian Renaissance,
the end of which may be described as coinciding with
his decease. According to his biographer Manso, the
author of the *Gerusalemme Liberata* was singularly
noble and refined in appearance, though always
possessed of an air of melancholy ; he was well-built,
strong, active and resourceful, anything in fact but a
carpet-knight who spent his days in writing verse and
dallying with Italian court beauties :

> " Colla penna e colla spada,
>   Nessun val quanto Torquato ; "

sang the populace of Ferrara in honour of their
illustrious Sorrentine guest, for the Ferrarese delighted
in the handsome stranger who could in an emergency
wield the sword as skilfully as he could ply his
quill. Twice only however did Tasso revisit the city
of his birth, and each return home was occasioned
by deep tragedy. In 1577, wounded by the attacks
of his literary rivals and humiliated by the Duke
Alfonso's discovery of his infatuation for the Princess
Leonora d'Este, the unhappy poet travelled southward, reaching Sorrento in the disguise of a shepherd.

Making his way to the Casa Sersale, the house of his sister, now a widow with two sons, Torquato passed himself off as his own messenger, and so eloquently did he relate the story of his own grief and wrongs, that the tender-hearted Cornelia fainted away at this recital. Having satisfied his mind as to his sister's genuine affection, the pseudo-shepherd now revealed his true character, whereupon the pair embraced with transports of joy, though it was deemed prudent not to acquaint their friends with the arrival of Torquato, who was represented to the good people of Sorrento as a distant relative from Bergamo. Cornelia Sersale now entreated the poet to take up his abode permanently in her house, and to forget the rebuffs of the cruel world without in the enjoyment of family ties and affections ; and well would it have been for Torquato, had he accepted his sister's advice and passed the succeeding years in simple rural pleasures. But restless and inconsequent despite all his virtues, the poet must needs return to Ferrara to bask in the presence of his beloved Leonora, with the dire and undignified result that all the world knows. Tasso's second visit took place not long before his death, when his strength was rapidly failing, so that it seems strange that he did not decide to end his days amidst these lovely and well-remembered scenes of his early boyhood, instead of deliberately choosing for the last stage of his earthly journey the Roman convent of Sant' Onofrio, where the death-chamber and various pathetic relics of the poet are still pointed out.

Students of Tasso's immortal epic are apt to overlook the immense influence exercised on its author by his early Sorrentine days and surroundings. The

Gerusalemme Liberata contains, as we know, a full
account of the First Crusade and constitutes an
apotheosis of Godfrey de Bouillon, first Christian King
of Jerusalem ; but it is also something more than a
mere poetical description of a departed age of chivalry.
For there can be little doubt that the poet aspired to
be the singer of a new movement which should wrest
back the Holy City from the clutches of the Saracens,
and set a second Godfrey upon the vacant throne of
Palestine. To this important end the experiences of
his infancy and his training by the Jesuits had undoubtedly tended to urge the precocious young poet.
The servants of his father's house at Sorrento must
many a time have regaled his eager boyish mind with
harrowing tales of the infidel pirates who scoured the
Tyrrhene Sea within sight of the watch-towers on the
coast; within ken, perchance, of Casa Tasso itself, perched
on the commanding cliff above the waters. Scarcely
a family dwelling on the Marina below but was mourning one or more of its members that had been seized
by the blood-thirsty marauders, perhaps to be brutally
slain on the spot or to languish in the dungeons of
Tripoli and Smyrna, eking out a life of slavery that
was far worse than death itself. Stories of tortured
Christians, like that of the pious Geronimo of Algiers
who was tied with cords and flung into a mass of soft
concrete, were common enough topics among the
Sorrentine folk, all of whom lived in constant dread
of a successful raid by the Barbary pirates. For,
despite the efforts of the great Emperor Charles the
Fifth to protect his maritime subjects, the swift galleys
of Tunis and Tripoli out-stripped the Imperial men-
of-war, and continued to carry on their vile commerce

of slavery. Such a state of terrorism must have
appeared intolerable to the highly romantic, deeply
religious spirit of the young poet; and his Jesuit
preceptors, working on the boy's imagination, were
soon able to instil into his youthful brain the notion
of a new Crusade which would not only sweep the
infidel ships from off the Italian seas, but would also recapture the Holy City itself. The Church, beginning
at last to recover from the effects of Luther's schism,
was once more in a position to re-assert its ancient
authority over Catholic Christendom, and in Torquato
Tasso it found an able trumpeter to call together the
scattered forces of the Faithful, and to reunite them
in a holy war. Astonished and delighted, all Italy
was swept by the golden torrent of Tasso's impassioned
verses, that were intended to urge the Catholic princes
of Europe to the inauguration of a new Crusade. Nor
were the times unpropitious for such an event. Tunis,
that hot-bed of infidelity, piracy and iniquity, was in
the hands of the Christians; and the fleets of the
Soldan had been well-nigh annihilated by Don John
of Austria at the glorious battle of Lepanto :—to
convince a doubting and hesitating world that the
actual moment had come wherein to recover the city
of Jerusalem was the main object of the author of
the *Gerusalemme Liberata*. And it was his infancy
spent upon this smiling but pirate-harassed coast that
was chiefly responsible for this desired end in the epic
of the Crusades ; it was Tasso's early acquaintance
with the Bay of Naples, combined with his special
training by the Jesuits, that forced the poet's genius
and ambition into this particular channel.

It is pleasant to think that Sorrento is still appreciative of its honour as the birth-place of the great Italian poet. The citizens have erected a statue of marble in one of their open spaces ; they have called street, hotel and *trattoria* by his illustrious name ; and can the modern spirit of grateful acknowledgment go further than this? His father's house has perished, it is true, through " Nature's changing force untrimmed," for the greedy waves have undermined and swallowed up the tufa cliff which once supported the old Tasso villa. But there is still standing in Strada di San Nicola the old Sersale mansion, wherein the good Cornelia received her long-lost brother in his peasant's guise, an unhappy exile from haughty Ferrara. Of more interest however than the old town house of the Sersale family is the ancient farm, known as the Vigna Sersale, which once belonged to Donna Cornelia, and supplied her household with wine and oil. It is a lovely sequestered spot lying on the breezy hill-side not far down the Massa road, facing towards Capri and the sunset. Hallowed by its historic connection with the poet and his devoted sister, the Vigna Sersale can claim perhaps to be one of the most interesting and beautiful places of literary pilgrimage upon earth. Ascending by the steep pathway that leads upward from the broad high road, it is not long before we reach the old *podere*, amidst whose olive groves and vineyards the poet was wont to sit dreamily gazing at the glorious view before him. Here are the same ancient spreading stone-pines, the same gnarled olive trees that sheltered the gentle love-lorn poet, whilst Cornelia and her sons sate beside him in the shade, endeavouring—alas ! only too vainly—by their caresses to detain the roving Torquato in their midst. Could not, we ask ourselves, the erratic poet have been content to remain in this spot, "in questa terra alma e felice" as he himself styles it, instead of plunging once more into the dangers and dissipation of that Vanity Fair of distant Ferrara? Why could he not have brooded over his ill-starred infatuation for the highborn Leonora in this soothing corner of the earth, allowing its quiet and beauty to sink into his soul, until the recollection of his Innamorata declined gradually into a fragrant memory that could be embalmed in never-dying verse? But like his own favourite hero, the Christian King of Jerusalem, the poet must in his inmost heart have preferred a changing storm-tossed life to the ideal existence of rustic ease; and had he not returned to the treacherous splendours of Alfonso's court, how much less entrancing would his own life-story have appeared to after ages! Unconsciously he seems to have composed his own epitaph in describing Godfrey's death ; for the crusading king lived and died like a true Christian knight, for whom the world has afforded many adventures, and but few intervals of peace until the final call to endless rest.

> "Vivesti qual guerrier cristiano e santo,
> E come bel sei morto : ei godi, e pasci
> In Dio gli occhi bramosi, o felice alma,
> Ed hai del ben oprar corona e palma."

con-
na e
)nce
nity
ave
gh-
th,
ul,
xl
te
n
n
t.

FARAGLIONI ROCKS, CAPRI

CHAPTER XI

CAPRI AND TIBERIUS THE TYRANT

LYING between the classic capes of Misenum and Minerva, the island of Capri appears like a couched lion, guarding the entrance of the Bay of Naples; his majestic head being formed by the stupendous cliffs of the Salto that face the sunrise, whilst his back and loins are represented by the long broad slope which stretches from the summit of Monte Solaro to the most westerly headland of Vitareta. Nor is it only as a guardian to their Bay that Capri serves the Neapolitans, for it also presents them with a gigantic natural barometer. In fine settled weather a soft haze invariably lies over the sea, so that Capri is only faintly visible from the shores of Parthenope, save at sunrise and sunset, when for a short time the graceful form of the islet looms out clear-cut like a jagged amethyst upon a sapphire bed ; but before rain or storm it yields up its inmost secrets to the public gaze of Naples. The northern Marina, the towns of Capri and Ana-Capri, even the little terraced fields become discernible to the naked eye : " It will be wet to-morrow," augur the weather-wise of Naples, and the prediction is rarely falsified.

It is an easy matter to cross from Sorrento to the

island, whether it be by the little steamer that plies daily between Naples and Capri, putting in at Sorrento on its journeys backwards and forwards, or—far pleasanter if somewhat slower way—by engaging a boat with four rowers, who on a calm day ought to make the Marina of Capri in less than two hours. Nothing can be more delightful or exhilarating than this old-fashioned method of transit; and it gives also a feeling of superiority over less enterprising persons who prefer the quicker passage on a smoky steamer, crammed with tourists and attendant touts. It is the very morning for a row on the cool glassy water, as we step joyfully into our boat with its four stalwart Phrygian-capped sailors in attendance:

> " Con questo zeffiro
> Cosi soave,
> Oh, com' e bello
> Star su la nave !
> Mare si placido,
> Vento si caro,
> Scordar fa i triboli
> Al marinaro."

Bending with a will to their oars, our genial mariners quickly impel our barque round the first jutting headland, so that the thickly populated Piano di Sorrento is at once lost to view. Making good headway over the clear water, it is not long before we find ourselves passing beneath the wave-washed precipices of the Salto, and well within our time limit of two hours we reach the roadstead of the Marina, to find ourselves in a bright and busy world of traffic and pleasure. Between the houses coloured coral-pink, white, blue, and yellow, and the pale green transparent water lies a long stretch of beach covered with every sort of craft that sails the Mediterranean, and with a motley crowd of fishermen, tourists and noisy children; whilst the whole atmosphere rings with raucous voices raised in giving directions, in quarrelling, or in addressing the many perplexed strangers. We disembark, and cross the intervening beach with its sea-weed veiled boulders and masses of tawny fishing nets; we reach the village, and here we meet with our first disappointment in romantic Capri. It was not so very many years ago, barely thirty in point of fact, that this island was roadless, and in those primitive days the visitor was met at the Marina Grande by tall strapping Capriote women, who were wont to seize the traveller's pieces of baggage as though they had been light parcels, and to march up the old stone staircase poising these burdens on their heads with the carriage of an empress. The stranger's own entrance into Capri was less dignified, for either he had to toil painfully in the blazing sun up that steep picturesque flight of steps and reach the plateau above, perspiring and probably out of temper; or else he was compelled to bestride a miserable ass which a bare-footed damsel steered upward by means of the quadruped's tail. Nowadays, we are spared this original and somewhat humiliating manner of arrival at our journey's end. There are little *carrozzelle*, drawn by clever black Abruzzi cobs awaiting us, and even one or two hotel conveyances. We find ourselves being driven rapidly up the excellent winding road constructed only a quarter of a century ago, past the domed Church of San Costanzo, the patron Saint of the Caprioti, past hedges of aloe and prickly pear, until we gain the saddle of the island-mountain, where stands the small capital perched upon a ledge that overlooks the Bay of Naples to the north, and to the south the endless expanse of the unruffled Tyrrhene.

It is evident even to the most casual untrained eye, that this huge mass of sea-girt rock whereon we stand must in remote ages have formed part of the mainland opposite, until some fierce convulsion of nature, common enough in this region that is ever changing its outward face through subterranean forces, tore what is now Capri asunder from the Punta della Campanella, and placed the sea as an eternal barrier between the riven headlands of continent and new-formed island. The charm of this rocky fragment, thus placed in mid ocean by volcanic action, was first discovered by the great Emperor Augustus, who chancing to visit the island for some obscure reason was greatly affected by the spectacle of a withered ilex tree, that revived and burst into foliage at the auspicious moment of his setting foot at the Marina. Flattered at the compliment paid by Nature's self to his august presence and drawing a happy omen from the incident, the Emperor at once proposed to the people of Neapolis, who then owned the island, that they should exchange barren Capreae for the larger and more fertile imperial appanage of Aenaria (Ischia)—a bargain to which the shrewd Neapolitans readily agreed. Here then in a spot at once so salubrious and so convenient for the management of affairs of state, the Emperor sought rest and relaxation at such times as he could escape the cares of government. At his bidding villas and

pleasaunces were constructed ; roads were carried by
means of viaducts across the airy plateau lying between
the Salto and the Solaro; and the able bodied inhabitants of the island were enrolled as a sort of
honorary bodyguard for the person of Augustus during
his occasional visits. In this secluded, yet accessible
retreat, the ruler of the Roman world could easily lay
his finger, as it were, upon the beating pulse of his
mighty empire, for Capreae was at no great distance
from Rome itself, and from the heights of the island
note could be made of the movements of the Imperial
fleet lying at Baiae or of the arrival of the corn ships
from Egypt and Asia Minor. But the name of the
good Augustus is scarcely remembered in connection
with Capreae, which alone recalls its association with
Tiberius the Tyrant, who spent the last nine years
of his reign upon the rocky islet that was so beloved
of his predecessor. To this spot " Timberio" (as the
natives invariably misname the Emperor) feeling the
rapid approach of senile decay, weary of the thankless
task of ruling an ungrateful people, sick of family dis-
sensions and of court intrigue, at last came in the
cherished hope of spending the few remaining years of
his life in cultured leisure and in comparative solitude.
An enthusiastic student of astronomy and of its sister
science, or rather pseudo-science, astrology, Tiberius
proposed to study the heavens in the company of
chosen mathematicians and soothsayers. Twelve
buildings—palaces, villas, pavilions, call them what
you will—were now constructed for the special examination of the planets, and in consequence the whole
of the island, whose limited area after all is exceeded
by many an English park, was practically turned into

one vast maritime residence, for all the Imperial
pleasure-houses seem to have been connected with each
other by means of viaducts or secret stair-ways.   Yet
whilst immersed in astronomy and occultism, the aged
Emperor contrived to find time for the routine of
public business, and, like Augustus, he was still able
to direct from his rocky retreat the policy of the
Empire.   The reports of governors of provinces, for
example, were received, read, and commented upon by
Tiberius in his Capriote home, and amongst these
there must have been included a certain official
document from one Pontius Pilatus, Procurator of
Judaea, relating how a Jewish prophet from Nazareth
had been condemned, scourged and crucified by his
orders at the special request of the Jews themselves.
How eloquent is this bald statement of a simple fact,
that here in this tiny barren islet was brought the
casual news of the death of Jesus Christ to the then
ruler of the Roman world!   Surely an historical
incident such as this is of more value than all the
hazy legends or pointless miracles of St Januarius or
of San Costanzo, upon which the imagination of the
islanders has been fed for generations.

Remnants of Tiberius' palaces, all of which are said
to have been razed to the ground by order of the
Roman Senate at his death, are scattered thick as
fallen leaves in Vallombrosa over the whole surface of
the island, and it is to the ruins of the Villa Jovis at
its eastern crest that the visitor will in all probability
first direct his steps.   The way thither from the little
city of Capri leads through narrow lanes along a stony
but populous hill-side, to which the flat-roofed dazzling
white houses with their small iron-barred windows lend

CAPRI FROM THE VILLA JOVIS

an oriental aspect ; an illusion that is aided by the
appearance of an occasional date-palm over-topping
some low wall, and by clumps or hedges of the prickly
pear. This latter plant, of Indian extraction as its
name of *Ficus Indica* betrays, grows in profusion over
the sun-baked rocky slopes of southern Italy, especially
in the neighbourhood of the sea. The peasants find
it most useful, for it makes impenetrable hedges, and
its coarse pulpy leaves when pounded up afford good
provender for their goats and donkeys. The fruits of
the prickly pear, those quaint crimson or yellow knobs
attached to the edges of the leaves, are likewise
gathered and eaten by the people, or else cleaned of
their protecting layers of spiny hairs and despatched
in baskets to Naples, where the cactus-fruit forms an
important item of the popular fare. The fruit itself
has a lovely colour and a fragrant scent, which give
promise of a better flavour than it actually possesses,
for it is hopelessly insipid to the taste, although the
Neapolitans declare that the pulp, when mashed up
into patties and iced, is very palatable.

A long up-hill ramble over rough paths leads eventually to the Villa of Jupiter, perched on the Salto—
the *Saltus Caprearum*, the " Wild Goats' Leap," of the
ancients. There is little of interest to be seen in the
existing portions of Tiberius' chief villa, for the building has been despoiled centuries ago of its rich marbles,
its slabs of *giallo* and *verde antico*, its pillars of red
porphyry and *serpentino*, some fragments of which may
be found imbedded in the pavement of the mosque-like
little Duomo of Capri. But it is evident from the
immense extent of its substructures, now used for
humble enough purposes, that the Villa Jovis must

have been a palace of remarkable size. A hermit who offers sour wine, a fat middle-aged woman, a figure of fun in her gay be-ribboned dress who begins languidly dancing a *tarantella*, and a vulgar pestilent guide who produces a spy-glass usually haunt these caverns on the look-out for any chance visitor. Buy them off, O stranger! with *soldi*, is our advice, for you cannot otherwise escape their importunities, and then mounting to the highest point, peer down into the clear depths of the water nearly a thousand feet below. For it was here, if we can credit serious Roman historians, that the Imperial tyrant, half crazy with terror and ever thirsting for human blood, was wont to hurl the objects of his hate into the sea ; " from this eminence," Suetonius gravely tells us, " after the application of long drawn-out and exquisite tortures, Tiberius used to order his executioners to fling their victims before his eyes into the water, where boats full of mariners, stationed below, were waiting in readiness to beat the bruised bodies with oars, in case any spark of life might yet be left in them." The terrible legend fits in aptly with the appearance of this forbidding dizzy precipice, especially on a dark stormy afternoon, when the dull roar of the waves dashing against the cliffs below, mounts upward to the Villa Jovis like the angry bellowing of some insatiable sea-monster.

It was whilst brooding here after the death of Sejanus in Rome, that the Emperor, not daring to move beyond the walls of his palace, shunning the society of all save his familiar friends and attendants, and with his face disfigured by an eruption of the skin of which he was painfully sensitive, that there took place an incident (which may or may not be true) mentioned by Suetonius. In the privacy of this villa Tiberius was one day surprised by an ingenious Capriote fisherman, who in ignorance or defiance of the Emperor's wishes had managed to scale with his naked feet the steep cliffs from the sea below, in order to present a fine mullet for the imperial table, and of course to earn a high reward for his "gift." Terrified at the mere notion of anybody being able thus to penetrate into his most secret domain, the irate Emperor at once gave orders for the intruder's face to be scrubbed with the mullet he had brought, a sentence that the imperial minions performed without delay. The intrepid fisherman might have congratulated himself on so mild a punishment for having disturbed a tyrant's repose, had he not been possessed of an unusually strong sense of humour. For at the close of the mullet-scrubbing episode, the foolish fellow remarked by way of a jest to the officer on duty, that he was thankful he had not also offered the emperor a large crab which he had likewise brought in his basket. This imprudent speech was immediately reported to Tiberius, who thereupon commanded the man's face to be lacerated with the aforesaid crab's claws ; but whether this pleasing incident ended with a cold plunge from the Salto, the Roman historian does not relate.

Other tales of Timberio's vices and cruelties have been handed down from generation to generation, so that the dark deeds committed at the Salto have almost passed into a local article of faith ; and such being the case, it would seem almost a pity to pronounce these picturesque horrors untrue or exaggerated.

R

Nevertheless, of recent years there has arisen amongst scholars a certain degree of scepticism as regards these highly coloured anecdotes of Roman historians known to be prejudiced. The Emperor was nearly seventy years old at the time he came to reside in Capreae, and until that date his life had been orderly and above reproach ; it is not likely therefore, argue these modern writers, that Tiberius should suddenly, at so extreme an age, have flung himself into a whirl of vices and crimes that he had hitherto shunned. The thing is of course possible, but it sounds improbable. That he was moody and morose ; that he loved solitude and hated formal society in the spot he had especially chosen as the retreat of his declining years ; that he practised certain of the mystic arts, as well as studied astronomy, are all likely enough conjectures ; and these circumstances probably formed the foundation for the extravagant legends which now surround the Emperor's memory. Very shocking and reprehensible were the doings at Villa Jovis, if they really occurred there, but to try and dispute their authenticity would be a task quite outside the scope of this work.*

If, despite the negative theories held to-day concerning the private life and character of the second Emperor of Rome during his residence on Capreae, the traveller be still inclined to trace the sites of the remaining eleven Imperial villas, he will find little difficulty in meeting with numberless Roman remains scattered over all parts of the island. On the beach, for example, a little to the west of the Marina Grande,

* For an able defence of the Emperor Tiberius, the reader is referred to Mr J. C. Tarver's *Tiberius the Tyrant*, chap. xviii.

are clearly visible the sunken foundations of the great sea-palace, which in the Roman manner jutted into the water and ranked probably second in size to the Villa Jovis. The neighbourhood of Ana-Capri also, and in fact the whole western portion of the island, is likewise plentifully besprinkled with ancient ruins, one of which is still known by the suggestive title of Timberino. But most people will prefer to explore the unrivalled natural beauties of Capri, rather than to make themselves acquainted with its archaeological points of interest.

First and foremost of the many wonders that Capri has to show must be ranked the Grotta Azzurra. The pleasantest way of reaching this world-famous cavern is by small boat from the Marina, rather than by the daily steamer from Naples; and a perfectly calm and bright morning must be selected for the expedition, for if the surface of the sea appears in the least degree ruffled by northerly winds, it becomes impossible for any craft to make the low entrance of the grotto. Capriote boatmen are as a rule intelligent and pleasant to deal with, and not a few of the denizens of the Marina own to some knowledge of English, or rather of American, since several of the inhabitants are the sons of emigrants who have settled in the cities of the United States or the Argentine, but whose love for their island home is still so strong that they contrive to send their children back to Capri, in order that they may retain their Italian citizenship and be ready to serve their expected term of years in the Army.

Past the gay-coloured shipping of the noisy Marina, past the wave-washed halls of Tiberius' *palazzo a mare*, our boat swiftly glides over the pellucid expanse until it reaches those vast towering cliffs of limestone that spring almost perpendicular from the waters' edge to the plateau of Ana-Capri, fully a thousand feet above our heads. Clumps of palmetto, of cytizus, and of various hardy shrubs manage to sprout and to exist in the crannies of this sheer wall of rock ; and on some of the larger ledges, far out of reach of a despoiling human hand, we see masses of the odorous narcissus, though whence they draw their sustenance it is hard to tell. At length we reach the entrance of the Grotto, and here, at a signal from our boatman, we crouch down low in the body of the boat, whilst our rower, skilfully taking advantage of a gentle surging wave, guides our craft with his hands through an opening in the sheer wall, so low that the gunwales grate against the rocky surface of the natural arch. At once we find ourselves in a scene of mystical beauty, in an extravagant voluptuous dream of loveliness, such as the Arabian Nights alone could dare to suggest. Above us, around us, behind us, before us lies a luminous azure atmosphere, which produces the effect of a gigantic molten sapphire, whose secret blue fires we have actually tracked to their lurking-place in the very heart of the gem. Against the all-pervading shimmering light our own forms stand out distinct of an intense and velvety blackness, yet the blades of the oars that cleave the melted sapphire of the water, the tips of our fingers that dabble in the celestial liquid, appear as if coated with tiny globules of silver. Our boatman's son, a picturesque lad of fifteen or thereabouts, has, we notice, been engaged in hastily casting off his scanty attire ; for a moment his slight graceful figure is outlined against the blue light like some antique bronze of Pompeii or Herculaneum, and then there is a splash as the youthful form, diving into the pool, is instantaneously changed by the genius of the place into a silver-glistening sea-god, the very image of the fisherman Glaucus sung of old by Ovid, who became an Immortal and dwelt ever afterwards, according to the ancient myth, in an azure palace beneath the sea. As the stripling rises to the surface all glittering to breathe the air, his head turns from frosted silver to ebon blackness, as does likewise his hand, raised from the water to clasp the boat's prow.   Slowly we are propelled round the lofty domed cavern, and are shown the little beach at its further extremity with its mysterious and unexplored flight of stone steps, down which, so our mariner informs us, the wicked Timberio used to descend from his villa at Damecuta, hundreds of feet overhead, to take a plunge in these enchanted waters.   The Emperor and his friends may or may not have gambolled in this jewelled bath ; but certain it is that Tiberius knew of the existence of this unique cavern ; and equally certain that an artistic but demented potentate of our own days was so smitten with the idea of owning a secret staircase descending to a blue grotto, that he must needs construct within the walls of a fantastic castle in the highlands of Bavaria an artificial counterpart of the Grotta Azzurra, with metal swans moved by clockwork swimming thereon !

Our genial boatman beguiles the time of our returning by a long story, told him in his boyhood by his old grandfather, of how two English *Signori* had managed to rediscover the entrance to the Blue

Grotto, which had been lost since the days of the Emperor Timberio, and how in expectation of the Englishmen's reward a plucky sailor, named Ferrara, had made his way all round the island in a cask, trying to force an entrance into every possible cavern, until at last he hit upon the mouth of the Grotta Azzurra itself, and thus gained the prize.   But as a matter of fact the existence of the Grotto was never wholly forgotten, for its beauties were certainly known to the old Italian chronicler Capaccio.   Yet doubtless during the long period of the Napoleonic wars, when Capri from its strategic position became a choice bone of contention between French, English and Neapolitan forces, there were few if any persons who possessed the courage or curiosity to visit the cavern ; with the result that its *exact* locality became temporarily lost.   It was known, however, to exist somewhere at the base of the great northern cliff, so that only a very small portion of the coast-line had to be explored, before its tiny inconspicuous entrance could be re-discovered.   A far more exciting event than the re-finding of the Blue Grotto was the genuine discovery of the beautiful Grotta Verde on the southern side of the island by two Englishmen, Mr Reid and Mr Lacaita, in the summer of 1848.   This grotto, esteemed the second in importance of the many caves that Capri boasts, consists of a huge natural archway formed in the cliffs wherein the water and rocks appear of an emerald hue, contrasting strangely with the opaque blue of the sea beyond, and suggesting in its dual colouring the marvellous combination of dark blue and iridescent green in the peacock's tail.

Capri is a pleasant enough place of residence for a

IN THE BLUE GROTTO, CAPRI

short time, particularly if one invests in a pair of the rope-soled shoes affected by the people, which enables the wearer to follow with greater ease the rough stony tracks, often at a dizzy height above the sea, that form the only walks in the eastern portion of Capri, except the villa-lined Tragara road leading to the Guardiola, now become the fashionable promenade of the many foreign residents upon the island. There are some delightfully peaceful nooks to be sought near the water's edge, not far from the Faraglioni, that picturesque trio of rocks lying off the south-eastern corner of Capri. Here we can find a sheltered corner, unfrequented alike by the pestering native or by the ubiquitous tourist ; perchance the deserted hall of some maritime villa, for the caverns near the Piccola Marina abound in traces of Roman architecture. In such a retreat, with a book on one's knees and with one's own thoughts for sole company, how fascinating it is to lie

> . . . on Capri's rocks, close to their snowy streak
> Of ambient foam, and watch the restless sea
> Tossing and tumbling to Eternity,
> Feeling its salt kiss fall upon the cheek.

But to those who prefer to take long tramps afield rather than to linger in meditation on the sunny beaches near the Piccola Marina, there is always the ascent to Ana-Capri by the broad smooth winding road that affords a fresh view of the Bay of Naples at every one of its many twists and turnings. Over a ravine filled with masses of ilex and myrtle; past the fragment of the pirate Barbarossa's aerial castle, perched on a rocky pinnacle and looking like some fantastic creation of Gustave Doré's brush ; the broad ribband of road leads across the steep northern flank of Monte Solaro, until it ends at Ana-Capri with its white houses nestling round a domed church.   It is an easy ascent, taking no great space of time, yet strange to relate, well within living memory the only approach to this hill-set village was by means of the interminable stone staircase with some five hundred steps that connected it with the Marina Grande below.   A charming writer on Nea-politan life and character thus shrewdly sums up the general opinion concerning this altered aspect of conditions with regard to Ana-Capri, now brought at last into close touch with modern civilization and its accruing benefits :

"Before the culminating point is reached, the road crosses the old staircase, which has unfortunately been almost completely destroyed by the huge masses of rock dislodged from the cliff above by the workmen. It makes one sad to look at it, and almost regret that the new road ever was constructed.   Were every invective that has been vented on those same steps turned into a paving-stone, there would be more than sufficient to pave the streets of Naples anew ; were every drop of sweat that has fallen upon them collected, there would be enough water to flood them.   And yet now that this dreadful staircase has been superseded by a good macadamised road, every one seems to regret the change.   Says the heavily laden *contadina* : ' The old way was the shortest ; ' says the artist : ' It was infinitely more picturesque ; that new parapet wall is a dreadful eye-sore ; ' says the archaeologist : ' It had the merit of antiquity ; it is not everywhere that one can tread in the footprints of a hundred generations.' Even those whose every step in the olden time was accompanied by a malediction, can remember how of Naples. Thus the rasping red liquid that appears on the table of a London restaurant, and the scented strong-tasting white stuff that is sold in the hotels of the island itself or of Naples under the name of Capri, have little in common with the pure unadulterated product of these sunny breezy vineyards. But besides wine and oil, the island is likewise celebrated for its beautiful and varied flora, and it is amongst the olive groves and lanes of the western side of the island that the wild flowers can be found in the greatest profusion. Amongst the tender green shoots of the young springing corn are set myriads of brilliant hued anemones, purple, scarlet, and white with a crimson centre; and even in January can be found in warm sheltered nooks the pretty mauve wind-flower, one of the earliest of spring blossoms in Italy. The grassy pathways that intersect the various holdings are gay with rosy-tipped daisies, white "star-of-Bethlehem," dark purple grape-hyacinth, and the tiny strong-scented marigold, that seems to bloom the whole twelve-month round. Amongst the loose stone-work of the walled lanes, where beryl-backed lizards peep in and out of every crevice, can be found fragrant violets and the delicate fumitory with its pink waxy bells. In moist places flourish patches of the wild arum or of the stately great celandine, the "swallow-wort" of old-fashioned herbalists, who believed that the swallow made use of the thick yellow juice that runs in the veins of this plant to anoint the eyes of her fledge-lings! And with the disappearance of the anemones as the season advances, their place is taken by blood-red poppies, by golden hawkweeds and by masses of tall magenta-coloured blooms of the wild gladiolus, the

"Jacob's Ladder" of our own English gardens. Strange enough amongst these familiar homely flowers appear the sub-tropical clumps of prickly pear, and the hedges of aloe which here and there have thrown up a gigantic spike of blossom eight or ten feet in height, a triumphal favour of Nature that the plant itself must pay for by its subsequent death.

From Ana-Capri we ascend to the peak of the lofty Solaro, by no means an arduous climb from this point, for we have but to follow a narrow goat-track leading across slopes covered with coarse grass and some low thickets of stunted lentisk and myrtle. The rosemary too grows plentifully on the dry wind-swept soil, and the soft sea breeze wafts its refreshing scent to our nostrils. There is a pretty legend of the people which relates the cause of this plant obtaining its perfume of unearthly sweetness :—how the Madonna one day hung the swaddling clothes of the Infant Christ to dry upon a common pot-herb in the garden at Nazareth—the rosemary is freely used in Italian cookery, and its taste is as unpleasant as its scent is delicious—whereupon the humble plant thus honoured was ever afterwards endowed with the delicate odour that is so highly prized. And beyond this, the rosemary was likewise permitted to put forth masses of flowers of the Madonna's own colour of blue, concerning which a tradition—Celtic, not Italian—avers that on Christmas morning upon every plant of rosemary will be found by those who care to seek them expanded blooms in honour of St Joseph, the Virgin and the Holy Child. Reaching the crest of the Solaro, we are well rewarded for our climb over the stony slopes by a wide-spreading view. Owing to the central position of the island, we can from its airy summit, some sixteen hundred feet above sea-level, command a glorious panorama of the three bays of the Neapolitan Riviera, each teeming with a thousand associations of classical or modern history. Upon those dancing waters of the Bay of Naples appeared in the dim ages of the heroic world the Trojan galleys that were bearing the founder of the Roman race towards the beach by Cumae yonder, where dwelt the venerable Sibyl; the fleets of ancient Rome and Carthage, the war-ships of the great Emperor Charles V., the pirate galleys of the Soldan's vassals, the men-of-war of Nelson have all rode and fought upon the bosom of the bay beneath us. What a marvellous perspective of the whole naval history of the Mediterranean does a survey of the Bay of Naples suggest!

Exquisite and inspiring as is the view on a clear cloudless day, with the keen *tramontana* off the distant Abruzzi flecking the azure waves with streaks of creamy foam and driving the white-sailed feluccas merrily towards the open sea, the landscape is even more impressive in dull lowering weather, when the inky clouds that envelop the sky give promise of the approaching hurricane. At such times a striking phenomenon, said to be peculiar to the Parthenopean shores, may be observed. From out the purple threatening masses that fill the heavens there suddenly falls a shaft of rosy light, as though directed by some vast celestial lens fixed aloft in the sky, upon a small portion of the opposite shore. The plateau of Sorrento with its many white hamlets first becomes illuminated; then the light rapidly passes towards Vesuvius, which is instantly revealed with marvellous clearness, whilst

Sorrento returns to its former dark brooding shadows.
For some moments we watch the circlet of towns that
fringe the base of the burning mountain and Camaldoli
erect on its wooded height, and then our gaze is
diverted towards Naples, so clearly revealed that one
can almost fancy it possible to detect the carriages
driving along the white line of the Caracciolo.   From
the city this weird fairy-like light glides swiftly towards
the headland of Posilipo and the great sombre mass
of Ischia, and then finally seems to vanish altogether
in the leaden-hued expanse of the watery horizon.
Storm, rain, wind, hail and thunder will certainly
follow the appearance of this fantastic rose-coloured
glow, and the visitor to Capri may in consequence be
compelled to remain willy-nilly upon the island until
such time as communication with Naples shall be
once more restored, for rough weather on Capri means
complete isolation from the mainland and the outside
world.   A spell of four or five days without a letter
or a newspaper may in certain cases be restful and
even beneficial, but it can also be highly inconvenient.

.   .   .   .   .   .

Comparatively few persons are aware that in the
history of Capri is to be found a page, not a particularly glorious one perhaps, of the annals of our own
nation.   In the spring of 1806, the year after Trafalgar,
whilst our fleet was blockading Naples on behalf of its
worthless monarch, King Ferdinand, then skulking in
cowardly ease at Palermo, Admiral Sir Sidney Smith,
the hero of Acre, managed to capture the island after
a sharp struggle with the French troops then holding
it in the name of Joachim Murat, King of Naples
and brother-in-law of the great Napoleon.   Sir Hudson

(then Colonel) Lowe — afterwards famous as the Governor of St Helena during Buonaparte's captivity—was now put in command of the newly conquered island with some 1500 English and Maltese troops at his disposal. Lowe and his second in command, Major Hamill, at once set to work to put the place into a strong state of defence, and so satisfied were they with their work of fortification, that Lowe in his confidence nick-named the islet "Little Gibraltar." For more than two years the Union Jack floated in triumph from the fort-crowned heights of Capri, much to the annoyance of the monarch on the mainland, who finally determined at all costs to recapture the stronghold facing his capital. Fancying himself perfectly secure in his "Little Gibraltar," now deemed impregnable by a combination of art and nature against any hostile descent, Lowe made light of any possible expedition from Naples, and when Neapolitan warships actually appeared as though making to land troops at the Marinas on either side of the saddle of the island, the British commandant was delighted at the ease with which these attempts were repelled. But whilst the garrison was busied in thwarting the movements on the Marinas, which in reality only constituted a feint on Murat's part, transports were engaged in disembarking at the low cliffs of Orico, the western extremity of the island, boat-loads of men, who quickly swarmed up the terraced slopes towards Ana-Capri and surprised its garrison. On the following day, October 6th 1808, in spite of Lowe's efforts, Ana-Capri with its eight hundred men surrendered to the French and Neapolitan troops led by General Lamarque, who at once set up a battery on the crest of the Solaro, so as to command the town of Capri and the English head-quarters, fixed at the Convent of the Certosa that lies between the Tragara Road and the southern shore. The eastern half of the island still of course remained in the hands of the British; and failing to reduce the town itself and the Convent of the Certosa by bombardment from above, General Lamarque decided upon taking the place by storm, so as to forestall the arrival of the English fleet, which was hourly expected to come to the rescue of the beleaguered garrison. As we have already mentioned, there was no road existing upon the whole island in those days a hundred years ago, so that in order to attack the capital, the French general had to march his victorious troops by the precipitous flight of stone steps down to the Marina Grande and then try to carry the position from below. Before however the Frenchmen, now further aided by supplies sent by Murat's order from Sorrento, could arrange for the projected assault upon the town, the delayed British fleet suddenly appeared in the offing, evidently with the intention of bearing down upon the island. But on this occasion the luck was all on the side of the French, for scarcely had the eagerly expected ships hove in sight, than the besieged garrison had the mortification to see their hopes of succour overthrown by the uprising of one of those sudden squalls, so common on the Mediterranean, which drove the warships southward. More than one assault was repulsed with heavy loss by the small English garrison, which had already been deprived of half its numbers at Ana-Capri, including the gallant Major Hamill, whose death is commemorated in a marble tablet set in the little piazza of the town. But with the re-

tirement of the relieving fleet and the continuance
of foul weather, Colonel Lowe deemed it useless to
resist further, and like a sensible man decided to
capitulate on the best terms he could obtain. In
return for his immediate surrender of Capri the British
commandant accordingly stipulated that his garrison
should be allowed to embark and sail for Sicily unmolested, and that the persons and property of the
islanders, who seem to have appreciated the British
occupation, should be respected. But Lamarque, on
communicating Colonel Lowe's request to King Murat,
received peremptory orders to demand an unconditional
surrender, whereupon an aide-de-camp of the King's, a
certain Colonel Manches, was sent to interview Lowe
with the royal letter in his pocket. Had the missive
been delivered to him, the British Governor would in
all probability have decided to fight to the bitter end
rather than to submit to such severe and humiliating
conditions. Happily so terrible a catastrophe, which
must have involved heavy loss of life on both sides,
followed by a sack of the town, was unexpectedly,
averted at the last moment, for whilst Manches was
actually advancing with a flag of truce, the approach
of the British fleet was again signalled from the look-
out on the hill now called the Telegrafo. Before the
Governor could be made aware of this piece of
news, Colonel Manches, cunningly keeping his master's
imperious letter in his pocket, told Colonel Lowe that
King Murat was ready to accept the terms of surrender
offered. The weather being propitious, the British fleet
would have been able this time to reach the island,
but its nearer approach was prevented by Colonel
Lowe himself, who sent to acquaint the Admiral,

s

much to his chagrin, of the compact already concluded with the besiegers, a compact which, as Hudson Lowe himself very properly pointed out, was binding upon the British Government. On October 26th, three weeks from the date of the first attack, the English troops embarked for Sicily, and the island was formally handed over to the French and Neapolitan forces, who held it undisturbed until the close of the Napoleonic Wars.

good a glass of very inferior wine tasted on reaching Ana-Capri." *

But whether Ana-Capri has or has not been really benefited by the Italian Government's finely engineered road, there can be no doubt that the primitive charm of the island, which in by-gone days constituted one of its chief attractions, has greatly declined with the wholesale introduction of modern conventions and improvements. With the sudden influx of wealthy strangers, Anglo-Saxon, German, French and Russian, it is not surprising to learn that the islanders have become somewhat demoralized under the changed conditions of life, and that not a small proportion of them have grown venal and grasping. The happy old days when artists and inn-keepers, peasants and such chance visitors as loved the simple unsophisticated life, hob-nobbed together on terms of equality are gone for ever. Fashion, that merciless deity, has annexed the Insula Caprearum to her ever-growing dominions ;—there are smart villas on the Tragara road and even at Ana-Capri ; there are British tea-rooms and Teutonic *Bierhälle* in the town. At the present time the tourists and foreign residents form the chief source of wealth to the islanders, now that the quails have more or less deserted these shores. Instead of awaiting in due season with nets ready prepared the advent of the plump little feathered immigrants from the African coast, the modern Caprioti are continually on the look-out for the steamers that bear hundreds of money-spending tourists to the Marina, and these they proceed to enmesh with proffered offers of service. And, speak-

* W. J. A. Stamer : *Dolce Napoli.*

ing of the quails, in the days before breech-loading guns and reckless extermination had injured this valuable source of revenue, the arrival of the birds winging their way northward was the signal for every sportsman on the island to hasten to collect the annual harvest of game. High poles, supporting nets twenty feet broad and sixty feet long, were erected on the grassy slopes of the Solaro or in the plateau of the Tragara, towards which, by dint of judicious scaring and shouting from expectant watchers stationed at various points, the flight of the on-rushing birds was directed. Dashing themselves with force against this wall of netting, the poor quails fell stunned to the ground, where they were easily taken by hand, whilst scores of guns were levelled ready to bring down such birds as had escaped the snare prepared for them. From the thousands of quails thus captured the islanders were enabled to pay their taxes to the Bourbon Government, as well as to provide the income of their Bishop—for in those distant days a prelate dwelt at Capri—who in allusion to his chief source of income was jocularly known at the Roman court as " Il Vescovo delle Quaglie."

From Ana-Capri to the western shore extends the most fertile stretch of land in the island : a broad slope set with vineyards and groves of silver-grey olives, that are interspersed here and there with clumps of almond and plum trees. Fine oil is yielded by the *poderi* of Ana-Capri and Damecuta, whilst the grapes produce the highly prized red and white Capri vintages, choice wine of which the casual traveller rarely tastes a good sample, for it is usually doctored and " improved " for purposes of keeping by the wine-merchants

of Naples. Thus the rasping red liquid that appears
on the table of a London restaurant, and the scented
strong-tasting white stuff that is sold in the hotels of
the island itself or of Naples under the name of Capri,
have little in common with the pure unadulterated
product of these sunny breezy vineyards. But besides
wine and oil, the island is likewise celebrated for its
beautiful and varied flora, and it is amongst the olive
groves and lanes of the western side of the island that
the wild flowers can be found in the greatest profusion. Amongst the tender green shoots of the
young springing corn are set myriads of brilliant hued
anemones, purple, scarlet, and white with a crimson
centre; and even in January can be found in warm
sheltered nooks the pretty mauve wind-flower, one of
the earliest of spring blossoms in Italy. The grassy
pathways that intersect the various holdings are gay
with rosy-tipped daisies, white "star-of-Bethlehem,"
dark purple grape-hyacinth, and the tiny strong-
scented marigold, that seems to bloom the whole twelve-
month round. Amongst the loose stone-work of the
walled lanes, where beryl-backed lizards peep in and
out of every crevice, can be found fragrant violets and
the delicate fumitory with its pink waxy bells. In
moist places flourish patches of the wild arum or of
the stately great celandine, the "swallow-wort" of
old-fashioned herbalists, who believed that the swallow
made use of the thick yellow juice that runs in the
veins of this plant to anoint the eyes of her fledge-
lings ! And with the disappearance of the anemones
as the season advances, their place is taken by blood-
red poppies, by golden hawkweeds and by masses of
tall magenta-coloured blooms of the wild gladiolus, the

"Jacob's Ladder" of our own English gardens. Strange enough amongst these familiar homely flowers appear the sub-tropical clumps of prickly pear, and the hedges of aloe which here and there have thrown up a gigantic spike of blossom eight or ten feet in height, a triumphal favour of Nature that the plant itself must pay for by its subsequent death.

From Ana-Capri we ascend to the peak of the lofty Solaro, by no means an arduous climb from this point, for we have but to follow a narrow goat-track leading across slopes covered with coarse grass and some low thickets of stunted lentisk and myrtle. The rosemary too grows plentifully on the dry wind-swept soil, and the soft sea breeze wafts its refreshing scent to our nostrils. There is a pretty legend of the people which relates the cause of this plant obtaining its perfume of unearthly sweetness :—how the Madonna one day hung the swaddling clothes of the Infant Christ to dry upon a common pot-herb in the garden at Nazareth—the rosemary is freely used in Italian cookery, and its taste is as unpleasant as its scent is delicious—whereupon the humble plant thus honoured was ever afterwards endowed with the delicate odour that is so highly prized. And beyond this, the rosemary was likewise permitted to put forth masses of flowers of the Madonna's own colour of blue, concerning which a tradition—Celtic, not Italian—avers that on Christmas morning upon every plant of rosemary will be found by those who care to seek them expanded blooms in honour of St Joseph, the Virgin and the Holy Child. Reaching the crest of the Solaro, we are well rewarded for our climb over the stony slopes by a wide-spreading view. Owing to the central position

of the island, we can from its airy summit, some
sixteen hundred feet above sea-level, command a
glorious panorama of the three bays of the Neapolitan
Riviera, each teeming with a thousand associations of
classical or modern history. Upon those dancing
waters of the Bay of Naples appeared in the dim ages
of the heroic world the Trojan galleys that were bearing the founder of the Roman race towards the beach
by Cumae yonder, where dwelt the venerable Sibyl ;
the fleets of ancient Rome and Carthage, the war-ships
of the great Emperor Charles V., the pirate galleys of
the Soldan's vassals, the men-of-war of Nelson have
all rode and fought upon the bosom of the bay beneath
us. What a marvellous perspective of the whole naval
history of the Mediterranean does a survey of the Bay
of Naples suggest !

Exquisite and inspiring as is the view on a clear
cloudless day, with the keen *tramontana* off the distant
Abruzzi flecking the azure waves with streaks of
creamy foam and driving the white-sailed feluccas
merrily towards the open sea, the landscape is even
more impressive in dull lowering weather, when the
inky clouds that envelop the sky give promise of the
approaching hurricane. At such times a striking phenomenon, said to be peculiar to the Parthenopean shores,
may be observed. From out the purple threatening masses that fill the heavens there suddenly falls a
shaft of rosy light, as though directed by some vast
celestial lens fixed aloft in the sky, upon a small
portion of the opposite shore. The plateau of Sorrento
with its many white hamlets first becomes illuminated ;
then the light rapidly passes towards Vesuvius, which
is instantly revealed with marvellous clearness, whilst

Sorrento returns to its former dark brooding shadows. For some moments we watch the circlet of towns that fringe the base of the burning mountain and Camaldoli erect on its wooded height, and then our gaze is diverted towards Naples, so clearly revealed that one can almost fancy it possible to detect the carriages driving along the white line of the Caracciolo. From the city this weird fairy-like light glides swiftly towards the headland of Posilipo and the great sombre mass of Ischia, and then finally seems to vanish altogether in the leaden-hued expanse of the watery horizon. Storm, rain, wind, hail and thunder will certainly follow the appearance of this fantastic rose-coloured glow, and the visitor to Capri may in consequence be compelled to remain willy-nilly upon the island until such time as communication with Naples shall be once more restored, for rough weather on Capri means complete isolation from the mainland and the outside world. A spell of four or five days without a letter or a newspaper may in certain cases be restful and even beneficial, but it can also be highly inconvenient.

.   .   .   .

Comparatively few persons are aware that in the history of Capri is to be found a page, not a particularly glorious one perhaps, of the annals of our own nation. In the spring of 1806, the year after Trafalgar, whilst our fleet was blockading Naples on behalf of its worthless monarch, King Ferdinand, then skulking in cowardly ease at Palermo, Admiral Sir Sidney Smith, the hero of Acre, managed to capture the island after a sharp struggle with the French troops then holding it in the name of Joachim Murat, King of Naples and brother-in-law of the great Napoleon. Sir Hudson (then Colonel) Lowe — afterwards famous as the Governor of St Helena during Buonaparte's captivity— was now put in command of the newly conquered island with some 1500 English and Maltese troops at his disposal. Lowe and his second in command, Major Hamill, at once set to work to put the place into a strong state of defence, and so satisfied were they with their work of fortification, that Lowe in his confidence nick-named the islet " Little Gibraltar." For more than two years the Union Jack floated in triumph from the fort-crowned heights of Capri, much to the annoyance of the monarch on the mainland, who finally determined at all costs to recapture the stronghold facing his capital. Fancying himself perfectly secure in his " Little Gibraltar," now deemed impregnable by a combination of art and nature against any hostile descent, Lowe made light of any possible expedition from Naples, and when Neapolitan warships actually appeared as though making to land troops at the Marinas on either side of the saddle of the island, the British commandant was delighted at the ease with which these attempts were repelled. But whilst the garrison was busied in thwarting the movements on the Marinas, which in reality only constituted a feint on Murat's part, transports were engaged in disembarking at the low cliffs of Orico, the western extremity of the island, boat-loads of men, who quickly swarmed up the terraced slopes towards Ana-Capri and surprised its garrison. On the following day, October 6th 1808, in spite of Lowe's efforts, Ana-Capri with its eight hundred men surrendered to the French and Neapolitan troops led by General Lamarque, who at once set up a battery on the crest of the Solaro,

so as to command the town of Capri and the English
head-quarters, fixed at the Convent of the Certosa that
lies between the Tragara Road and the southern shore.
The eastern half of the island still of course remained
in the hands of the British ; and failing to reduce the
town itself and the Convent of the Certosa by bombardment from above, General Lamarque decided upon
taking the place by storm, so as to forestall the arrival
of the English fleet, which was hourly expected to come
to the rescue of the beleaguered garrison.   As we
have already mentioned, there was no road existing
upon the whole island in those days a hundred years
ago, so that in order to attack the capital, the French
general had to march his victorious troops by the
precipitous flight of stone steps down to the Marina
Grande and then try to carry the position from below.
Before however the Frenchmen, now further aided by
supplies sent by Murat's order from Sorrento, could
arrange for the projected assault upon the town, the
delayed British fleet suddenly appeared in the offing,
evidently with the intention of bearing down upon the
island.   But on this occasion the luck was all on the
side of the French, for scarcely had the eagerly expected ships hove in sight, than the besieged garrison
had the mortification to see their hopes of succour
overthrown by the uprising of one of those sudden
squalls, so common on the Mediterranean, which drove
the warships southward.   More than one assault was
repulsed with heavy loss by the small English garrison,
which had already been deprived of half its numbers
at Ana-Capri, including the gallant Major Hamill,
whose death is commemorated in a marble tablet set
in the little piazza of the town.   But with the re-

tirement of the relieving fleet and the continuance
of foul weather, Colonel Lowe deemed it useless to
resist further, and like a sensible man decided to
capitulate on the best terms he could obtain. In
return for his immediate surrender of Capri the British
commandant accordingly stipulated that his garrison
should be allowed to embark and sail for Sicily unmolested, and that the persons and property of the
islanders, who seem to have appreciated the British
occupation, should be respected. But Lamarque, on
communicating Colonel Lowe's request to King Murat,
received peremptory orders to demand an unconditional
surrender, whereupon an aide-de-camp of the King's, a
certain Colonel Manches, was sent to interview Lowe
with the royal letter in his pocket. Had the missive
been delivered to him, the British Governor would in
all probability have decided to fight to the bitter end
rather than to submit to such severe and humiliating
conditions. Happily so terrible a catastrophe, which
must have involved heavy loss of life on both sides,
followed by a sack of the town, was unexpectedly,
averted at the last moment, for whilst Manches was
actually advancing with a flag of truce, the approach
of the British fleet was again signalled from the look-
out on the hill now called the Telegrafo. Before the
Governor could be made aware of this piece of
news, Colonel Manches, cunningly keeping his master's
imperious letter in his pocket, told Colonel Lowe that
King Murat was ready to accept the terms of surrender
offered. The weather being propitious, the British fleet
would have been able this time to reach the island,
but its nearer approach was prevented by Colonel
Lowe himself, who sent to acquaint the Admiral,

S

much to his chagrin, of the compact already concluded with the besiegers, a compact which, as Hudson Lowe himself very properly pointed out, was binding upon the British Government. On October 26th, three weeks from the date of the first attack, the English troops embarked for Sicily, and the island was formally handed over to the French and Neapolitan forces, who held it undisturbed until the close of the Napoleonic Wars.

A GATEWAY, CAPRI

CHAPTER XII

ISCHIA AND THE LADY OF THE ROCK

EMBARKING at Torregaveta, the little terminus of the *Ferrovia Cumana*, which traverses the classic district of the Phlegraean Fields, we are quickly transported in a small coasting steamer past the headland of Misenum to the island and port of Procida, the "alta Prochyta" of Virgil. Although the poet calls the island lofty, it is remarkably flat considering its volcanic origin, for Procida and Ischia were undoubtedly one in remote ages, as the learned Strabo rightly conjectured. Its only eminence is the Rocciola, the castle-crowned hillock to the north-east of the island, but as this hill must first have caught the expectant eye of Aeneas' steersman, perhaps the epithet is after all not so misplaced as would appear at first sight. Carefully tilled and densely populated, the island produces a large proportion of the fruit, vegetables, and olive oil, that are sold in the Naples market, and as it possesses no remains of antiquity, no medieval churches, no works of art, and but few beauties of nature to recommend it for inspection, Procida is rarely visited by strangers. Its inhabitants, who are chiefly husbandmen, are hard working and independent, and content also to retain the manners and customs of their frugal forefathers, and

even to a certain extent to continue the use of
their national dress, so that the festivals of Procida
have more interest and local colour than those
observed in tourist-haunted Capri or Sorrento. Unconcerned at the progress of the world without, unspoiled
by the gold of the *forestiere*, the Procidani pursue the
even tenor of their old-fashioned ways, unenvious of
and unenvied by their neighbours on the mainland.

> " O fortunatos nimium, sua si bona nôrint,
>   Agricolas ! "

We halt at the port of Procida, with its flat-roofed
gaily coloured houses lining the quay and ascending
the gentle slope towards the Rocciola. Thence, skirting
the low-lying fertile shores of the island, and passing
the olive-clad islet of Vivara, we soon come in sight of
the steep headland on which are perched the grey masses
of the Castle of Ischia, " the Mount St Michael of Italy."

Covered from base to summit with fume-weed,
lentisk, aromatic cistus, and every plant that loves
the sun, the wind and the salt foam of the
Mediterranean, the huge solitary cliff rises majestically from the deep blue water. Whether viewed
in brilliant sunshine under a cloudless sky, or in
foul weather, when the sea is hurling its waves over
the stone causeway that connects the isolated crag
with the little city of Ischia, the first sight of this
historic castle is singularly impressive. Nor is its
grandeur lessened on a near approach, for the ascent
to its topmost tower takes us through a labyrinth
of staircases and mysterious subterranean passages,
through vaulted chambers and curious hanging
gardens to an airy platform, which commands a
glorious view in every direction over land and sea.

Built by Alphonso V. of Aragon in the fifteenth century, this massive pile, half-fortress and half-palace, is famous in Italian annals for its long association with the noble poetess Vittoria Colonna, Marchioness of Pescara. Born in the old Castle of Marino, near Rome, one of the strongholds of the great feudal house of Colonna, the poetess, who was great-great-niece to Pope Martin V., was betrothed in her infancy at the instigation of King Ferdinand of Naples to the youthful heir of the d'Avalos family, hereditary governors of the island of Ischia. The elder sister of Vittoria's affianced husband, Constance d'Avalos, the widowed Duchess of Francavilla, was the "châtelaine" of Ischia during her brother's minority, so that it was but natural that his Colonna bride-elect should be sent to dwell with Constance in this castle. Here Vittoria under her sister-in-law's excellent tutelage grew up to womanhood amidst the intellectual atmosphere of the Italian Renaissance, and here she was trained to develop into one of the most learned, the most interesting and the most attractive figures that all Italy produced at this period. Childless in her early marriage at eighteen, and with her husband frequently, not to say usually, engaged in military expeditions on the mainland, Vittoria had every opportunity of cultivating her mind and of filling her sea-girt palace with men of genius. The poets Cariteo and Bernado Tasso (the father of Torquato Tasso), were frequent visitors at this

"Superbo scoglio, altaro e bel ricetto,
   Di tanti chiari eroi, d' imperadori,
   Onde raggi di gloria escono fuori,
   Ch' ogni altro lume fan scuro e negletto."

Strange to relate, her husband, the Marquis of Pescara, was destined to forestall his learned lady in the matter of poetry, for during his imprisonment at Milan in the year 1512, he composed a " Dialogo d'Amore " to send to his sorrowing wife at Ischia, a production which the learned Paolo Giovio, the historian and bishop of Nocera, pronounced as being " summae jucunditatis," though in reality it seems to have been feeble enough.   But however halting and commonplace the warrior's verses, Pescara's composition had the immediate effect of opening the flood-gates of his wife's poetic temperament, for she replied at once to her spouse's effort with an epistle conceived in the *terza rima* employed by Dante, and though the poem is turgid in diction and shallow in thought, full of classical names and allusions, "a parade of all the treasures of the school-room," it exhibits the graceful ease and high scholarship which mark all Vittoria's writings.   Meanwhile, unblest with offspring of her own and ever separated by the cruel circumstance of war from the husband she seemed perfectly content to admire from a distance, Vittoria did not expend all her time at Ischia in sacrificing to Apollo and the Muses, for she now undertook the education of her husband's young cousin and heir, Alphonso d'Avalos, Marchese del Vasto, whose manhood certainly did credit to his instructress, for del Vasto under her influence grew up to be a brave soldier and a tolerable scholar.

After sixteen years of married life with a husband who, although professing deep devotion to his brilliant and virtuous consort, was almost invariably absent from her side, Vittoria found herself left a widow shortly after the great battle of Pavia in 1525 wherein Francis I. of France surrendered to the Emperor Charles V. The Marquis of Pescara, after the usual career of blood-thirsty adventures which passed in those days for a life of knight-errantry, died at Milan towards the close of this year, leaving behind him an unenviable reputation for treachery towards his master. But however hard were the things said of the deceased Fernando d'Avalos by the outside world, no breath of suspicion seems ever to have penetrated to the heart of the faithful if placid Vittoria, who mourned bitterly if somewhat theatrically over her departed hero. The Lady of the Rock was now in her thirty-fifth year, and her beauty, so we are told, still remained undimmed; in fact it was rather improved by a tendency towards plumpness, for sorrow and poetry are not necessarily associated with a meagre appearance. Spending her time partly in the great Italian cities, but chiefly on her beloved *scoglio superbo*, the widow of Pescara now set herself to write that series of sonnets in memory of her dead husband which have rescued his unworthy name from oblivion and have rendered her own famous in Italian literature. For the sonnets of Vittoria Colonna, though appearing cold classical and pedantic to our northern ideas, evidently appeal to the Italian temperament, so that the praises of Pescara and his widow's stilted complaints, couched in the elegant language of the Renaissance, are still read and appreciated to-day by her compatriots. As time passed, and the ghost of sorrowful remorse was supposed to be decently laid, the sonnets contain somewhat less of hero-worship, and assume a religious and speculative character. Some critics have even gone so far as to affect to perceive a latent spirit of Protestantism underlying the graceful platitudes and commonplace but grandly expressed ideas. Very likely the Lady of the Rock dabbled in the fashionable heterodoxy of the hour, as it is at least certain that she was on terms of intimacy with the celebrated Princess Renée, the "Protestant" Duchess of Ferrara. On the other hand, several of her acquaintances and correspondents were amongst the most prominent of the unyielding Churchmen of the day ; in their number being, it is interesting to note, Cardinal Reginald Pole, great-nephew of King Edward IV. of England and after-wards Queen Mary's Archbishop of Canterbury, who was certainly not likely to encourage Vittoria's un-orthodox or reforming tendencies. "The more opportunity," so writes the poetess to Cardinal Cervino, afterwards Pope Marcellus II., "I have had of observing the actions of his Eminence the Cardinal of England, the more clear has it seemed to me that he is a true and sincere servant of God. Whenever, therefore, he charitably condescends to give me his opinion on any point, I conceive myself safe from error in following his advice." And on the strength of Cardinal Pole's astute counsels, Vittoria promptly broke off all com-munication with the leading reformer, Bernardino Ochino, and (a thing which does not strike us as par-ticularly honourable) forwarded his letters to her-self unopened to his spiritual adversaries. But it is evident that Vittoria's "Protestantism" was a mere pose, assumed at a time when adverse criticism from all sides was being levelled at the political abuses of the Papacy and at the various scandals in the Church which were patent to the eyes of all onlookers. In short her religious verses are if anything more frigid and artificial than those which compose the *In Memoriam* to her husband, her *Bel Sole*, as she usually terms him. Whilst admitting considerable merit in Vittoria's compositions, we find it at this distance of time very difficult to understand the extravagant praise which was showered upon her poems by the Italian critics of the day, or to conceive how a sonnet from the gifted pen of the Marchioness of Pescara could possibly have been considered an important event in the literary world by cardinals, princes, poets, wits and scholars. From Naples to Rome, from Rome to Ferrara, from Ferrara to Mantua and Milan, the precious manuscript containing the last-born sonnet of the illustrious Lady of Ischia was eagerly passed along. Court poets read aloud amidst breathless silence the divine Vittoria's fourteen lines of jejune sentiment draped in folds of elegant verbiage; nobles and prelates applauded, hailing the authoress as a heaven-sent genius. Sincere to a certain extent this strange admiration undoubtedly was, although the homage was paid perhaps in equal proportions to the excellence of the verse and to the high rank of the author. She was a Colonna by birth; she was the widow of a petty despot; she was governor of a large island;—any literary production, however indifferent, from so high a personage would have been received throughout Italy with respect or flattery. But Vittoria was no mean or careless aspirant to fame; it was the fault of an artificial age rather than the lack of her own natural ability that has made her poetry cold and soulless, for under healthy conditions of life and thought, "the Divine Vittoria" was doubtless capable of producing something warmer and more human than the lifeless but graceful sonnets that bear her name.

It is chiefly through her close connexion with the great literary movement of the Italian Renaissance and her intimacy with its leading artists and writers, rather than through her own reputation as a poetess, that the name of Vittoria Colonna herself is remembered outside the borders of Italy. With her wealth, her culture, her virtue and her unique position in the world of rank and of letters, it is nothing marvellous that so fortunate and gifted a mortal should have become the idol of the leading persons of her day. She belonged, in fact, to a brilliant and famous group of which she was the soul and centre ; of which she was at once the patron, the disciple and the teacher. That great master of Italian prose, Pietro Bembo, set a high value on her powers of criticism ; other men, almost as distinguished as the Venetian cardinal, besought her for advice on literary subjects. Foremost in her circle of admirers appears of course the great Michelangelo, with whom the immaculate Vittoria condescended to indulge in one of those cold platonic pseudo-passions which constituted the true *divino amore* of the idealists of the Renaissance. So here was nothing to cavil at, nothing to arouse base suspicion. Considered the greatest man and the greatest woman in all Italy, both were of mature age, he in the sixties and she in the forties, when Michelangelo first professed himself seized with a pure but unquenchable love and devotion for the widowed Lady of the Rock.

The last days of Vittoria, which were chiefly spent within the walls of the Convent of Sant' Anna at

Rome, were clouded by ill-health and sorrow. The death of the young Marchese del Vasto, " her moral and intellectual son," was an irreparable loss, for which her boundless fame and popularity could offer little real consolation. At length the poetess, feeling death approaching, moved to the house of Giulia Colonna, her relative, and there expired in February 1547, in the fifty-seventh year of her age. To the last her death-bed was surrounded by sorrowing and adoring friends, amongst them being Michelangelo, who is said to have witnessed with his own eyes the last moments of his beloved Lady. And the famous sculptor, painter and poet—perhaps the most stupendous genius the world has yet produced—is reported to have bitterly regretted in after years that on so solemn an occasion he had not ventured to imprint one chaste kiss upon the forehead of the woman he had adored so ardently, yet so purely during life. By her expressed wish the body of the poetess was buried in San Domenico Maggiore at Naples, the finest and least spoiled of all the Neapolitan churches, where a velvet-covered coffin containing the ashes of the Divine Vittoria and her " Bel Sole," and surmounted by the sword, banner and portrait of Fernando d' Avalos, is still pointed out to the stranger, resting on a shelf in the sacristy of the church. We cannot but regret that Vittoria's body did not find a final resting-place in her *superbo scoglio*, where all her happiest years were spent and where her memory still survives so fresh.

Sadly deserted appear to-day the historic buildings, which are fast falling into hopeless decay; even the large domed church of the Castle has been desecrated and turned into a stable.

Tocsins from yon bleak turrets never ring ;
No knight or pages pace those galleries,
So sombre and so silent : ever cling
To that cold church and palace draperies
Of glaucous fume-weed ; sea-birds ever sing
The vanished glories with low mournful cries.

Ischia itself is a quaint, dirty, straggling town, possessing a small cathedral of ancient foundation, but modernised within and without, its sole object of interest being a curious font resting on marble lions. The charm of the city lies chiefly in the busy scenes to be witnessed daily on its sandy beach and on the stone causeway that leads to the Castle, where a large part of the population seems to spend most of its time in mending the deep brown fishing nets or in attending to the gaudily painted boats.

Almost adjoining the outskirts of the little capital of the island is Porto d'Ischia, with a deep circular harbour that was once the crater of an extinct volcano, wherein every variety of Mediterranean fishing craft is to be seen at anchor. Close to the port, embowered among groves of orange and lemon trees that in winter time are laden with bright or pale yellow fruit, stands a fine old villa of the Bourbon kings of Naples, once a favourite summer retreat of his Majesty King Bomba. Royalty has long abandoned Ischia, and the villa has now been converted into a bath house. Beyond its neglected park stretches an extensive pine forest, carpeted in spring time with daisies, marigolds and anemones, and even in February gay with yellow oxalis and redolent with the scent of hidden violets.

The road from Ischia to Casamicciola, a distance

of four miles, leads along the base of Monte Epomeo
through olive groves and vineyards, the whitewashed
walls of the domed cottages, the flat roofs and cisterns,
and the frequent clumps of aloe or prickly pear giving
an Eastern aspect to the scenery, though the sharp
tinklings of the goat bells among the thickets of
white heath and dark myrtle scrub on the hill-sides
and the continual murmur of the waves breaking on
the rocks below, serve to remind us we are upon the
Neapolitan Riviera. Our destination at length is
reached, the roadway crossing the deep valley of the
Gurgitello with its sulphur baths, which once had a
wide reputation and are still much frequented in the
summer months by the people of Naples. Although
the sources of the springs were certainly damaged by
the earthquake of 1883, new bathing establishments
have been built, and a fair number of patients are
once more availing themselves of these beneficent
waters, which of course are warranted to heal every
bodily evil under the sun. A course of the Ischian
waters therefore applied externally and internally (so
the local doctors inform us)

" Muove i paralitici,
  Spedisce gli apopletici,
  Gli asmatici, gli asfitici,
  Gl' isterici, i diabetici
  Guarisce timpanitidi,
  E scrofule e rachitidi."

Formerly the most populous and prosperous town-
ship of the whole island, Casamicciola consists to-day
principally of a mass of shapeless ruins, together with
a number of dismal corrugated iron huts grouped
round an ugly modern church, nor can its exquisite

views and luxuriant gardens make amends for the settled air of melancholy which continues to brood over this unlucky spot. Every reader will doubtless remember the story of the terrible earthquake of July 28th 1883, when almost without warning the whole town, then crowded with its usual influx of summer visitors, was overthrown and engulfed in the space of a few seconds of time. Hotels, villas, churches, cottages, all suffered equally, and though the exact number of those who perished of all classes will never be known, the most moderate accounts put the figure as high as 3000 souls. Several English people lost their lives in that brief but terrible upheaval, and as many of the bodies as were recovered from the wreckage were laid to rest in the little cemetery outside the town, a plot of ground overhanging the sea, and shaded by cypress and eucalyptus trees. Many and impressive are the stories still to be heard from the lips of the present inhabitants, who are wont to date all events from that fearful night of darkness and destruction, and who all have piteous tales to tell of relations killed and houses shattered. The English landlady of the *Piccola Sentinella*, who herself had an almost miraculous escape on the occasion, gave us a most vivid and heart-rending description of how her hotel and most of its inmates were overwhelmed on that awful July night, and how the existing inn is literally built upon foundations that are filled with many unrecovered bodies of victims. It was on a dark sultry night after the evening meal had been finished, when the many guests of the *Piccola Sentinella* were sitting in the public rooms or on the terrace overlooking the hotel gardens. In the *salon* a young Englishman, an accomplished musician, had been playing for some time on the piano, when suddenly and unexpectedly he plunged into the strains of Chopin's *Marche Funèbre*, which had the immediate effect of scattering his audience, since many of his listeners, not caring for so melancholy a piece of music, deserted the room for the garden. Lucky indeed were those persons driven forth by the strains of Chopin's dirge, for a few moments later came the earthquake, when in a trice the whole hotel was swallowed up in the yawning chasm of the earth. Everybody inside the walls was killed, and the body of the poor pianist was actually discovered later amidst the wreckage, crushed down upon the instrument which had struck the warning notes of impending disaster. The horrors of that night still linger vividly in the memory of the people, and many are the terrible incidents, and many also, we are glad to say, the acts of bravery which are recorded of it. One elderly English lady, who owned a small villa on the slope above the hotel, rushed at the first suspicion of the catastrophe into the stone archway of a window, whence she beheld the whole of her house collapse like a castle of cards around her. Nothing daunted by the spectacle, this gallant woman, as soon as the shock had ceased and the clouds of dust rising from the ruin had cleared away, left her own dismantled home, of which nothing but the one wall that had sheltered her remained standing, and joined the *parroco*, the parish priest of Casamicciola, in the task of succouring the living and comforting the dying. To the darkness of the night was now added a heavy rainfall, yet the good priest and this noble woman traversed together the altered and devastated scene amidst the wet and gloom on their errand of mercy. It is some satisfaction to learn that this piece of unselfish heroism and devotion on the part of the priest was officially acknowledged, for the humble curate of Casamicciola was afterwards made a prelate by Pope Leo XIII. in recognition of his signal services. Even to-day people are inclined to be somewhat chary of spending any length of time in this unfortunate spot, where the ruined streets and shapeless mounds of earth, only too suggestive of a latter-day Pompeii, speak so eloquently of terrible experiences in the past and of possible dangers in the future. Nevertheless, if one can triumph over these gloomy feelings, Casamicciola affords a delightful centre whence to explore the whole island, and many are the pleasant walks to be found on the overhanging slopes of Mont' Epomeo, and many the boating expeditions to be made from the Marina below the upper town.

It is a two-mile walk through stony lanes overhung by branches of fig and orange from Casamicciola to Lacco, a large village well situated on a little bay which is distinguished by a curious mushroom-shaped rock, aptly nicknamed " Il Fungo " by the natives. This place, which also suffered severely in the earthquake of 1883, is the head-quarters of the straw-plaiting industry of the island, the women and children noisily beseeching every chance visitor to buy their wares in the guise of baskets, hats and fans ; the pretty coloured tiles (*mattoni*), which are used with such good effect in the churches and houses of the island, are likewise manufactured here. Lacco is particularly associated

ON THE PICCOLA MARINA, CAPRI

with the great annual festival of St Restituta on May
17th, which is always marked by religious processions
and by universal merry-making, followed by illuminations and fireworks at nightfall. This saint, of whom
an early mosaic portrait still exists in her ancient chapel
within the Neapolitan Cathedral, was once the patroness
of the city of Naples, but since medieval times she has
been honoured as the special guardian of this island,
whither her body (so the legend runs) was miraculously
conveyed from Egypt in a boat rowed by angels. A
local tradition also asserts that on her landing by the
beach of Lacco, an Egyptian lotus bloom was found
in the saint's hand, as fresh as when it had been
plucked months before from the banks of the Nile.

Leaving the little bay with its sulphur-impregnated
sands, and turning inland, we proceed along a road
across an ancient lava-stream over-grown with pine
trees, wild caper and a tangle of aromatic brushwood,
to Forio, which with its white domed houses, its palm
trees, and its stately bare-footed women bearing tall
pitchers on their heads gives at first acquaintance the
full impression of an Oriental city. There is little to
be seen in Forio itself, with the exception of some fine
vestments of needlework that are preserved in the
sacristy of its principal church, but no traveller should
fail to visit its wonderfully picturesque Franciscan
monastery, a barbaric-looking pile of dazzling white
walls and cupolas set against a background of cobalt
waters, which stands outside the town on a rocky platform jutting into the Mediterranean and is approached
by a broad flight of marble steps adorned with most
realistic figures of souls burning in brightly painted
flames of Purgatory. This point too commands a

T

good view of the extreme north-eastern promontory of the island, a tall cliff known as the Punta del Imperatore in honour of the great Emperor Charles the Fifth, beyond which visitors rarely penetrate owing to the roughness, or rather non-existence of roads, though the southern side of the island, which lies between this cape and the castle of Ischia, is fully as beautiful as the northern portion just described.

The chief attraction, however, of a visit to Ischia is the ascent of Mont' Epomeo, an easy expedition on foot to the active, and feasible to the weak or lazy on mule-back. This extinct volcano, whose broad lofty summit is visible from many points of the Bay of Naples, is naturally rich in classical associations, the ancients believing that within it lay imprisoned the giant Typhoeus, whose agonised movements were wont to cause the frequent eruptions of the crater that eventually drove away the early Greek settlers from this island—the Aenaria or Inarime of antiquity—and in later times accounted for the neglect of Ischia as a winter resort by the luxurious Romans, in spite of its near presence to fashionable Baiae. So destructive of life and property were these convulsions of nature, that for long periods, notwithstanding its fertile soil and its lucrative fisheries, the island remained uninhabited, and an old tradition, mentioned by Ovid, derives one of its ancient names, Pithecusa, from a race of apes (*pithēkoi*) that dwelt on its abandoned shores. Since the great eruption of 1302, the effects of which can still be traced among the large pine woods near Porto d'Ischia, the mountain has been quiescent, and the population of the island has increased considerably, although the constant shocks of earthquake have always made a permanent residence in Ischia somewhat insecure. Nor can we rest assured that Typhoeus himself is truly dead, not merely sleeping, but ready to renew his fierce efforts after his long spell-of slumber, and to change the face of nature as unexpectedly as did the Demon of Vesuvius in the reign of Titus.

Like the great volcano of Etna, which the Ischian mountain somewhat resembles on a tiny scale, Epomeo contains three distinct climatic zones. The lowest is that of the coast line with its rich sub-tropical vegetation, the early part of the ascent leading by steep stony paths through sun-baked vineyards which produce the white wine of Ischia, wholesome and light but somewhat acid in taste. For the storing of this vintage the peasants make use of the numerous old stone towers, that once served as safe retreats for the terrified inhabitants in times when the Barbary pirates frequently descended on the Italian coasts to plunder and enslave. Very curious it is to step out of the blinding sunlight into the interior of one of these medieval buildings, where in the icy gloom stand great barrels of the new white wine, each carefully inscribed with a prayer in praise of St Restituta, from one of which the swarthy *contadino*, in expectation of a few pence, draws a glassful of the sour chilly liquid to offer his visitor. Leaving behind this region of houses and of cultivation, the zone of forest is reached, covered with woods of chestnut and oak, with a thick undergrowth of heather, myrtle, laurustinus and sweet-scented yellow coronella ; there is grass under our feet, and long-stemmed daisies, violets, mauve anemones and small fragrant marigolds everywhere. Through the trees comes the nasal but not unmelodious singing of an unseen charcoal-burner, or the plaintive note of the little goat-herd's rustic pipe, accompanied by the musical jingling of his goat-bells; —for a moment we try to fancy ourselves in the pastoral Italy of Theocritus, where nymphs and shepherds, peasants and dryads, lived together on terms of amity in the woods. But soon the chestnut trees appear stunted, and the groves become less thick, and we finally gain the last zone, the desolate expanse of naked rock and dark lava deposits of the summit, where only a few hardy weeds can thrive. Here in some damp mouldy chambers dwells a hermit, for nearly all the classic mountains of Southern Italy are tenanted by an anchorite, generally an old and ignorant, but pious peasant, of the type of Pietro Murrone, the holy recluse of the Abruzzi, who was finally dragged from his cell to be invested forcibly with the pontifical robes and tiara as Celestine the Fifth. The present hermitage on Mont' Epomeo dates however from comparatively modern times, for its first occupant is said to have been a German nobleman, a certain Joseph Arguth, governor of Ischia under the first Bourbon king, who in consequence of a solemn vow made in battle deliberately passed his last years of existence on the topmost peak of the island he had lately ruled. His example has been followed and his cell filled by many successors, who have endured the spring rains, the summer heats, the autumn storms and the winter chills upon this airy height, where the glorious view may be found a compensation for eternal discomfort, if hermits condescend to appreciate anything so mundane as scenery. The shrine and cell are dedicated to St Nicholas of Bari, and to this circumstance is due the local uninteresting name of Monte San Niccolò to the entire mountain, whose crest, some 3000 feet above sea-level, we finally gain by means of steps roughly hewn in the lava.

The view from this height, embracing two out of the three historic bays of the Parthenopean coast, is one of the noblest and most extensive in Southern Italy. Looking southward, the fantastic cliffs of Capri are seen to rise abruptly from the ocean; beyond them appears the graceful outline of Monte Sant' Angelo, with the crater of Vesuvius beside it, veiling the clear blue sky with volumes of dusky smoke. Beneath extends the broken line of shore, stretching north and south as far as the eye can travel, with its classic capes and islands basking in the strong sunshine; whilst behind the foam-fringed boundary of land and sea rises the jagged line of the Abruzzi Mountains with the huge snow-clad mass of the Gran Sasso d'Italia towering above the lower peaks. At our feet is spread the beautiful and fertile island, in outward appearance little changed since the days when the good Bishop Berkeley "of every virtue under Heaven" penned its description nearly two centuries ago in a letter to Alexander Pope, wherein he described Ischia as "an epitome of the whole earth."

In spite of the good Bishop's eloquent tribute to the genial climate and the natural beauty of Ischia, it must be borne in mind that a residence on the island possesses one or two serious drawbacks. Apart from the ever-present fear of earthquakes, which hangs like the sword of Damocles above the heads of the inhabitants, there is yet another disadvantage, prosaic but very real, in the lack of pure water, every well and rivulet on Ischia being more or less impregnated with sulphur, with the result that water for drinking (and in summer even for domestic) purposes has to be conveyed by boat from Naples. It is bad enough to be dependant on a distant city for a food supply (which is to some extent also the case here), but the possibility of enduring a water famine through storms or mis-adventure would be a far more serious calamity; nevertheless as casual visitors to this charming and little-known island, we can easily afford to smile at such supposititious misfortunes.*

* A portion of this chapter has already appeared in an article by the Author, entitled *The Island of Ischia*, in the *Westminster Review*, December 1905.

CHAPTER XIII

PUTEOLI AND THE GRANDEUR THAT WAS ROME

PASSING along the noisy thronged street of the Chiaja and plunging thence into the chill gloomy recesses of the ancient grotto of Posilipo, we emerge at its further side into a new world, as it were, into a district where " there is scarcely a spot which is not identified with the poetical mythology of Greece, or associated with some name familiar in the history of Rome." In truth, the headland of Posilipo presents a wonderful landmark in the history of Naples, for it forms a barrier between the busy world of to-day and the departed civilisation of the ancients : at the latter end of this tunnel, the fierce life and movement of a great commercial city ; at its western exit, a tract of land teeming with recollections of the glorious past.

As our carriage emerges once more into the warmth and sunlight, we find ourselves in the miserable village of Fuorigrotta, which, by a strange coincidence, is associated with the memory of a famous Italian poet. For if the name and verses of Sannazzaro cling to Piedigrotta and the Parthenopean shore on the eastern side of the hill, the genius of Count Giacomo Leopardi sheds its melancholy radiance over the unlovely purlieus of Fuorigrotta. Here in the vestibule of the parish

church of San Vitale, lie the ashes of that unhappy
writer, the Shelley of Italian literature, who so bewailed
the Austrian and Bourbon fetters that enchained his
native land.   Poor Leopardi !   It was but eleven years
before the first great movement of the *Risorgimento*
swept over Italy in 1848 that he passed away ; his
poems were indeed songs before sunrise, a sunrise of
which he failed to detect the far-off glimmering, so
that he could only lament without hope the sad
condition of his dismembered country, once the
mistress and now the play-thing of the world, and
the abject slave of hated Austria :

> " O patria mia, vedo le mure e gli archi
> E le colonne e i simulacri e l' erme
> Torri degli avi nostri,
> Ma la gloria non vedo ;
> Non vedo il lauro e'l ferro ond' eran carchi
> I nostri padri antichi."

It is a flat dusty stretch of road that lies between
Fuorigrotta and Bagnoli ; the high walls give only
occasional glimpses of well-tilled *parterres* — one
cannot call these tiny patches of cultivation fields—
with thriving crops of brilliant green corn, of claret-
red clover, of purple lucerne, and of the white-flowered
" sad lupin," which Vergil has immortalised in verse.
The round bright yellow beans of the lupin crop, known
locally by the name of *spassa-tiempt* (time-killers),
afford an article of food to the very poorest of the
population.   A quaint story runs that one day an
impoverished philosopher, reduced to making his
dinner off a handful of these beans, and imagining
himself in consequence the most wretched wight in
existence, was cheered and comforted by observing

himself followed by a still more miserable fellow-mortal, who was engaged in picking up and eating the husks of the beans that, *more italiano*, he had thrown carelessly on to the pathway after their insipid farinaceous contents had been sucked out!

Above us to the right are the heights of Monte Spina, covered with groves of the umbrella pine, the typical tree of Naples ; to our left extends the verdant ridge of Posilipo, ending in Cape Coroglio, beyond which the massive form of Nisida rises proudly from the blue expanse of water. All the landscape shows somewhat hard in the glare of noontide, and we find the enveloping clouds of fine white dust very oppressive and disagreeable. From time to time a lumbering country cart is passed with its attendant bare-footed peasant ; otherwise there is little sign of life on the high road. The bright sunlight flashes upon the horse's polished brass harness, and upon the elaborate erection of charms placed thereon, with the avowed object of averting the dreaded Evil Eye, that ever-lasting bugbear of all dwellers upon these southern shores. On his poor drooping head the worn-out old steed carries a large bell with four jingling clappers and two brazen crescents, the horns of one of which point upwards and of the other towards the ground. On the off-side of the headgear is a bunch of bright-coloured ribbands or woollen tassels, from which depends the single horn, the invaluable Neapolitan talisman that is supposed to protect every man, woman, child or beast, from the chance glance of a passing *jettatore*. Above this glowing mass of colour some three or four feathers of a pheasant's tail are stuck, apparently with no ulterior purpose

than that of ornament; but beside the bunch of
ribbands there is also fixed a piece of wolf's skin,
to give strength to the jaded animal, for, remarks
the sapient Pliny, "a wolf's skin attached to a horse's
neck will render him proof against all weariness."
Personally, we should think a little more consideration and some elementary knowledge of farriery
would have been of more service to the ill-used
beasts round Naples than the excellent Pliny's
highly original receipt.   Besides this powerful battery
of charms to intercept the *jettatura*, there is the light
brass headpiece engraved with sacred figures, so
that any evil glance must be fully absorbed, baffled
or exhausted, before it can fix itself upon the animal.
In addition however to this shining mass of head-
gear, the horse carries on his back one of those
curious high pommels that are peculiar to Southern
Italy and Sicily.   The front of the pommel itself is
of well-polished brass, and covered with a number of
studs, whilst at its back is fastened a miniature
barrel, upon which there stands erect the figure of
some local saint, generally that of San Gennaro.
The exact part that the barrel and the row of studs
play in this mystic battle against the Evil Eye is
unknown, but the two revolving flags of brass that
swing and creak above the pommel itself are believed
to represent "the flaming sword which turned every
way," and finally expelled Adam and Eve from the
Garden of Eden.   Certainly this shimmering metal
has the appearance of a flaming sword in the bright
sunshine, so that it ought to prove efficacious in
catching and averting any baleful glance.   A second
patch of wolf skin on the crest of the pommel, and

some red worsted wound round the spindle of the flags complete the list of strange charms that are considered necessary to protect a Neapolitan horse from the pernicious influence of a casual passer-by.

We soon reach the sea-shore at Bagnoli, a little watering-place much frequented by Neapolitans of the middle classes, and on looking back we obtain a charming view of the headland of Posilipo and of stately Nisida, the Nesis of the ancients, with its memories of Brutus, "the noblest Roman of them all," who on this little island bade farewell for ever to his devoted Portia. A very different tenant from the chaste Portia, however, who once possessed a villa in this sea-girt retreat during the Middle Ages, was Queen Joanna the Second, the last member of the Durazzo branch of the Angevin royal house, and sister and heiress of King Ladislaus II., whose splendid monument in San Giovanni a Carbonara is one of the chief artistic treasures of Naples. It is of course unnecessary here to remark that there were two Queens of Naples, both Joanna by name, and that the first of these, the contemporary of Petrarch (whose proper feeling she contrived to shock) was certainly not a pattern of female virtue, but that she shone as a moral paragon when contrasted with her name-sake and successor, the sister of King Ladislaus. Of this second Queen, tradition more or less accurate relates a host of stories, none of them to her credit; how she dabbled in necromancy and was immersed in love intrigues, the most celebrated of which was her amour with the handsome "Ser. Gianni," Giovanni Caracciolo, head of an eminent family that has figured prominently in Neapolitan history from the days of Angevin monarchs to those of King Ferdinand.   Little good did the fickle Queen's favour do Ser. Gianni, who suffered an ignominious fate for having one day boxed Joanna's ears during a lovers' tiff.   Murdered secretly by four assassins, Caracciolo's body was laid to rest in the family chapel in San Giovanni a Carbonara beneath a splendid monument which is surmounted by the luckless favourite's effigy.   Joanna the First with all her faults was never guilty of such light conduct as this, but the peasant mind is always impatient of dry details of fact, so that in the popular imagination to-day both Queens are blended into one personage, whose character, it is needless to say, is about as vile as can be conceived. "Siccome la Regina Giovanna," is a form of peasant execration around Naples that has some historical affinity with the time-honoured Irish maledicton of the "Curse o' Cromwell."

Turning our backs on the island with its memories of Portia the Perfect and of Queen Joanna the Improper, we pursue our course along the sea-shore with rocks of ancient lava above us to the right, now heavily overgrown with brushwood and plants, amongst which we notice tufts of the pretty wild asparagus, that the observant Pliny centuries ago found flourishing in this district.   As an early herb, coming into season long before its cultivated cousin is fit for cutting, this succulent vegetable is highly prized in the South, and its flavour though somewhat bitter is most palatable, so that an omelette *aux pointes d'asperges sauvages* is a dish not to be despised by those who get the opportunity of testing this local delicacy.   Before us lies our goal, Pozzuoli, with its ancient citadel jutting into the placid waters and backed by the classic headland of Misenum, above which in turn towers the crest of distant Epomeo.

Pozzuoli in recent years has been much neglected by strangers, so much so that no inn worthy to be called an hotel now exists, and such *trattorie* as the place offers are all equally extortionate and detestable. Some time ago there was a comfortable *pension* at the edge of the town on the road to the Amphitheatre, but its English landlady has long since migrated elsewhere, and the comfortable " Hotel Grande Bretagne " is no more ; whilst nowadays there are to be found no visitors hardy enough to endure a prolonged sojourn in the wretched hostelries of the town itself. The electric tram and the rail-road have in fact killed Pozzuoli as a winter resort, more's the pity, for it is not only a spot of singular interest in itself, but its climate is certainly superior to that of Naples, for the great headland which shuts off the city from the Phlegrean Fields serves also to act as a buffer against the icy *tramontana* that sweeps along the Chiaja in winter and early spring. Invalids used at one time to inhabit Pozzuoli on account of its mild atmosphere, and even to visit the Solfatara daily on mule-back, in order to inhale its sulphureous fumes, which were then believed to be good for weak chests. But medical fashions vary like all others, and consumptive patients now seek other places then Pozzuoli for their cure.

Many are the walks outside the town, and none are without beauty or interest, for, the neighbourhood of Syracuse excepted, we can think of no place in Italy wherein one is brought so closely into touch with the classical past. Nature has long clothed the ruined area of the ancient city with her kindly drapery of foliage and flowers, so that the crumbling masses of tawny brick that we come across in our rambles are all swathed in garlands of clematis, myrtle, honey-suckle and coronella. It is a delight to speculate upon the original use and appearance of these shapeless blocks of creeper-clad masonry, which attract the eye on all sides amidst the vineyards and orange groves, where the peasants delving in the rich soil frequently alight upon treasures of the antique world. What a delight it is to wander through the Street of Tombs—alas, long rifled of their contents ! —where the gay valerian and the pink silene sprout from every fissure of the soft tufa rock, and lizards of unusual size and brilliancy play games of hide-and-seek in the warm sunshine. We moderns are afraid of graveyards and the paraphernalia of the dead : many a stout-hearted Englishman objects to passing through a church-yard at night ; not so the pagan Romans, who placed their cemeteries in public places and were wont to proceed through lines of tombs as they entered the city of the living : a very salutary and practical reminder of the transitory nature of life itself. The whole neighbourhood in short is sprinkled with these memorials of Imperial Rome ; there is not an orange or lemon orchard but stands above some forgotten villa, not an acre of tilth but must conceal some hidden mine of classical associations. Charming too are the walks by the sea-shore—now sadly disfigured by the *Cantiere Armstrong*, with its smoke and ugliness looking like a dirty smudge upon the delicate landscape of the Bay—for here again we find endless traces of the Imperial age. There can be no more fascinating employment than to wander along the beach after one of the heavy winter storms that so often vex the quiet of the Bay of Naples, and to search for fragments of precious marbles that have been spied by the waves amidst the sunken foundations of Roman villas, and thence idly flung upon the shore. Pieces of the choicest white Parian, squares of speckled Egyptian porphyry, of *verde*, *rosso* and *giallo antico*, of the coal-black *Africano*, all wet and glistening from the waves, can be picked up by the quick-sighted, and the gathering of these beautiful trifles, cut and polished by skilled hands nearly two thousand years ago, makes an interesting occupation. Nor is its classical lore the only feature of the Bay of Baiae, for though its actual scenery cannot compare with the grandeur of Capri nor its vegetation with the rich luxuriance of Sorrento, yet these shores have a quiet beauty of their own. Vine, olive and almond abound on all sides, and everywhere we see the groves of orange and lemon that in spring time scent the air with their perfumed blossoms. And in the early months of the year every patch of warm-coloured, up-turned earth is gay with sheets of that beautiful but rapacious weed, hated of the peasant, the oxalis, with its clusters of pale yellow flowers : a species of sorrel that is allied to our own white-blossomed variety. From many a point on the little ridges that rise behind Pozzuoli magnificent views can be obtained, whilst to those who care to study the scientific results of volcanic action the Phlegraean Fields afford endless occupation and interest. Every one of course visits the Solfatara, that curious semi-extinct crater, the *Forum Vulcani* of Strabo, which has remained for over seven hundred

years in its present condition of languor. A strange
experience it is to enter the heart of a volcano that is
still comparatively active, and to observe woods of
poplar and a large pine tree beneath which grow
masses of spring flowers—bright blue bugloss, the
crimson vetch, starch hyacinths, purple self-heal, and
golden spurge—and to pass from these thickets on to
a space of bare white-coloured ground that trembles
and sways under the feet like a sheet of insecure ice.
Beyond, one sees the little fissures (*fumaroli*) emitting
fumes of sulphur, and the guides take us to stifling
caverns in the hill-side where we are shown the
beautiful primrose-coloured crystals. The Solfatara,
the Amphitheatre and the Temple of Serapis, these
are the recognised " sights " of Pozzuoli, which strangers
visit to-day in the space of an hour or two, and then
return to Naples comforted with the feeling that they
have exhausted the attractions of the place. Certainly their reception in the town is not likely to
inspire them with a wish to return, for the guides and
touts swarm here more than in any other spot in
Italy ; " until he has spent half an hour in Pozzuoli,"
says the author of *Dolce Napoli*, " let no man say that
he understands the signification of the verb to pester."

Putting aside even the objectionable habits of so
many of its citizens, it cannot be said that the town
itself of Pozzuoli to-day is particularly attractive,
although its situation on the Bay of Baiae is charming
and its quays are full of picturesque life and movement. Lines of irregular yellow-washed buildings,
with faded green *persiani* and balconies draped
with the domestic washing, with here and there a
domed rococo church, look down upon the clear tide-

less waters that gently lap the ancient stone-work of
the Mole, whilst a mixed crowd of fishermen with
bare bronzed limbs, of chattering women with gay
handkerchiefs tied over their thick black hair, and of
blue uniformed dapper little customs officers,—*lupi
marini* (wolves of the sea) as the poor people face-
tiously term these revenue officials of the coast—loiter
in the sunlight amidst the piles of tawny fishing nets
or the pyramids of golden oranges. From the quay
we make our way to the Largo del Municipio, a
typical square of a provincial town in the South,
enclosed by shabby houses and adorned by a couple
of stunted date-palms and a battered marble fountain,
around which numberless children and some slatternly
women noisily converse or dispute. There is an old
proverb in the South, that a good housewife has no
need to know any thoroughfares save those leading to
her church and her fountain, and as conversation cannot well be carried on in the former, it is the daily
visits to the well that usually afford the required
opportunity for exchange of gossip or for the picking
of quarrels. Two statues decorate this unlovely but
not uninteresting space; one is that of a Spanish bishop,
Leon y Cardeñas, one of King Philip the Third's
viceroys, which serves as a reminder of the many
vicissitudes this classic land has experienced in the
course of history:—Phoenician, Greek, Carthaginian,
Roman, Barbarian, Norman, German, French, Spanish
conquerors have all left "footprints on the sands of
Time" in the coveted land of the Siren, which all have
possessed in turn but none have held in perpetuity.
His Excellency the Bishop Cardeñas stands therefore
in the open as a solid memento of the glory that once

U

was Spain, when half Europe and all America owned
the sway of the Catholic King. The second statue,
though not a thing of beauty, has always had the
attraction of an unsolved puzzle, for we cannot
decide whether it proves a complete absence or an
abundant superfluity of humour in the Puteolani of
to-day. It is the figure of a Roman senator, vested
in his flowing toga, and owning (as the ancient inscription informs us) the grandiose name of Quintus Flavius
Mavortius Lollianus, whose marble trunk was one of
the earliest archaeological "finds" made in the
excavations at Pozzuoli some two hundred years ago.
Since the statue lacked a head and was otherwise of
no especial value as a work of art, the Viceroy of
Naples very generously presented this object to the
place of its discovery, whose citizens, doubtless
thinking the appearance of the headless statue uncanny,
popped a stray antique occiput (of which a goodly
number, more or less mutilated, are constantly brought
to light by the peasants) upon Lollianus' vacant
shoulders. Anything more comical and at the same
time more repellent than this hybrid statue it would be
impossible to imagine, yet Lollianus of the unknown
head remains a favourite with the people of Pozzuoli.
Leaving the Largo del Municipio, with its weird senator
and its dusty palms, we ascend by a zigzag lane
between tall featureless houses to the Cathedral of
San Proculo, which occupies the site of a temple of
Augustus, that once dominated the ancient city and
harbour below. Within, the cathedral of Proculus,
who was a companion of St Januarius and a fellow-
martyr, is gaudy and painted, one of those dismally
gorgeous ecclesiastical interiors that are such a dis-

ON THE BEACH

appointment to the antiquarian in Southern Italy. In opposition to the memorial of Spanish conquest in the square below, we find here an elaborate monument to a French viceroy, the Duke of Montpensier, who served for some time as Governor of Naples after Charles VIII.'s capture of the city. Except the tomb of the young musician Pergolese, who composed the original *Stabat Mater*, there is little else to see, and we gladly ascend the tower in order to gain a bird's eye view of the town from a point of vantage whither noisy coachmen, troublesome beggars and impudent ragamuffins cannot pursue. Captured by the Greek colonists of Cumae, who gave the city the name of Dicoearchia instead of its ancient one of Puteoli,—a corruption, perhaps, of the Syriac word *petuli* (contention)—this old Hellenic settlement was rechristened Puteoli by the conquering Romans, under whose beneficent rule the place rapidly aspired to wealth and prosperity. With the rise however of Naples, the fame of Puteoli began to grow dim, and its importance to decline, although throughout Imperial times it ranked after Ostia as the chief victualling port of Rome. And of the two celebrated cities which adorned the shores of this Bay in classical times, Puteoli was the seat of commerce, and Baiae the resort of pleasure and luxury ; yet both were doomed to dwindle and almost perish in the disastrous years that followed the break-up of the Empire. The invading hordes of Germany, the raids of Saracen pirates, and the constant presence of malaria on this deserted coast were sufficient causes in themselves to reduce in the course of time the thriving port of Puteoli to the squalid town of to-day. From our lofty post we can easily distinguish the limits of

the city in the days of Tiberius and Caligula, for to
the north we turn our faces towards the ruined bulk
of the Amphitheatre, now lying amidst fields and
gardens, but well within the town walls at the time
when Nero entertained the Armenian king Tiridates
and shocked his Asiatic guest by himself descending
into the arena and deftly performing the usual dis-
gusting feats of a professional gladiator.   To westward
lies the Bay of Baiae, a semi-circle of glittering water
surrounded by low hills amidst which the Monte
Nuovo, unknown to the ancients, stands conspicuous.
How completely have all traces of splendour and
extravagance disappeared from these shores !   At
fashionable Baiae across the Bay there is nothing visible
save a few shapeless ruins over the identity of which
scholars dispute ; at busy Puteoli there survive to-day
but the ruined Amphitheatre, the Temple of Serapis,
and the arches of the famous Mole, to prove to
wondering posterity how great were the wealth, the
population and the magnificence of a spot which is
closely associated with all the power and culture of
the Roman Empire in its zenith.

Of the various fragments of antiquity that are still
standing in this district of the Phlegrean Fields, the
Mole of Puteoli is undoubtedly the best preserved and
the most interesting. So splendidly constructed is
this relic of the past, that but for continuous shocks of
earthquake the whole breakwater must have survived
intact ; as it is, more than half the Mole has withstood
the wear and tear of centuries of wind and storm.   It
is built on the model of a Greek pier, a series of arches
of massive masonry, acting at once as a barrier against
the force of the invading waves and as a means of

preventing the silting of the sand. Formed of brick, faced with stone, and cemented with the local volcanic sand, which is consequently known as *puzzolana*, this wonderful breakwater must originally have stretched out into the Bay a total length of twenty-five arches, its furthest extremity being crowned by a light-house. If we could only call up in imagination the Bay of Baiae in the days of the Empire, when its shores were fringed by sumptuous villas of famous or infamous Romans and its expanse was thickly covered with every variety of vessel of pleasure or merchandise, instead of the few fishing boats that now and again flit across its glassy surface, we might better be able to realise the extraordinary episode which is connected with this classical fragment in the little port of Pozzuoli below us. For it was from the Mole of Puteoli to the spit of land we see on the western shore opposite that the demented tyrant, Caius Caligula, constructed his historic bridge of boats across the Baiaean gulf. Every large vessel in the surrounding harbours had been pressed into the service of the Emperor for this gigantic piece of folly, so that the inhabitants of Rome were seriously inconvenienced by the detention of their corn ships, and loud in consequence were the complaints of the Roman populace, for whose anger, it is needless to state, the Emperor cared not a fig. " History," says Gibbon, " is but a record of the crimes, follies and misfortunes of mankind ; " and this smiling Bay of Baiae will ever be memorable as the scene of what was perhaps the worst exhibition of tyrannical caprice that the world has yet witnessed.

Using a double line of vessels well yoked together as a compact and solid base, the Emperor now gave orders for a military road of the usual Roman type to be constructed of planks of timber covered with earth and paved with hewn stones. When this stupendous work was completed, the usual station-houses were erected at various intervals, and fresh water was laid on by means of pipes connected with the Imperial cisterns at Misenum. Upon this broad road, laid across the Baiaean Gulf, the young Emperor now advanced on horseback, followed by his whole army clad in array of battle. Caligula on this occasion wore a historic coat of armour studded with rare gems that had once belonged to Alexander the Great ; a jewelled sword was fastened to his thigh, and a crown of oak leaves bound his temples. Solemnly the Emperor and his army crossed the broad expanse of water on dry land and entered Puteoli with mock honours of war. After remaining a day in the port to refresh his victorious troops, the Emperor was driven back in a splendidly equipped chariot, which was surrounded by a number of pretended captives of rank, some noble Parthian hostages being utilised for the occasion. At the centre of the bridge the procession halted, and the crazy prince next indulged in an absurd bombastic harangue, wherein he congratulated his soldiers on their glorious campaign just concluded, and declared to them that the famous feats of Xerxes and Darius had at length been surpassed. Finally, he invited his troops to a magnificent banquet upon this bridge of boats, an entertainment which lasted till far into the night and was accompanied by lavish illuminations by land and sea. As might only have been expected, the feast soon degenerated into a drunken orgy, wherein every guest from the Master of the Roman world to his meanest soldier became intoxicated, whilst many persons in their cups lost their balance and fell into the waters, so that the sounds of music and revelry throughout the midnight hours were mingled with groans and cries of drowning men close at hand.

Apart from its senseless extravagance and innate folly, the story of the bridging of the Baiaean Gulf, of this harnessing of old Ocean, affects us moderns with astonishment at the extraordinary thoroughness of all the ancient Roman feats of engineering ; had this high road across the Bay been intended to serve any useful purpose, instead of merely to satisfy the passing whim of a selfish tyrant, we could have had no choice but to admire the marvellous speed of the artificers and the completeness of the scheme undertaken.

Quarter of a century later, and the Mole of Puteoli was destined to become the scene of another event in the world's history, which has left a far more enduring impression on mankind than the so-called miracle of Caligula. In the early spring of the year 62 A.D. there dropped anchor in the port a certain Alexandrian corn-ship, the *Castor aud Pollux*, coming from Malta after touching at Syracuse and Rhegium (Reggio) on her way northward. Unnoticed amidst the vast phalanx of shipping that lined the Mole and filled the broad harbour of Puteoli, the vessel emptied her cargo on the quay, whilst there also disembarked from her hold a number of prisoners of no great social consequence, who were on their way to Rome under the guardianship of a kindly old centurion, named Julius, belonging to the cohort *Prima Augusta Italica.*

Amongst the persons under Julius' charge was a Jew named Paul, who was accompanied by three of his friends, Timothy, Luke and Aristarchus of Thessalonica, and all four, thanks to the kindness of the centurion, who was evidently much attached to his exemplary captive, were permitted to remain at this spot for seven days. Paul himself was anxious to tarry at this spot, for of all the Italian ports Puteoli was most frequented by men of his own nation, so that the city possessed its little community of Christians, who naturally were eager to detain the Apostle. So hopelessly intermingled are truth, tradition and legend concerning the various places on Italian soil that St Paul is known to have visited, that we cannot be too grateful for the undoubted link with his journey to Rome that we possess in the existing Mole of Puteoli, whose surface has undoubtedly been trodden by the sandalled feet of the great Apostle of the West. Here Paul landed amid the haughty scenes of Roman pride and power; above him he saw the pagan Temple of Augustus, all gleaming with marble and gilded bronze that were mirrored in the calm waters of the port: along this famous causeway he passed, unmarked by the busy crowd, except perhaps to be mocked by some idler for his nationality or his halting speech. Guided by Christian compatriots, the Apostle with his three faithful friends was led through the noisy jostling concourse of all countries that thronged the great Roman city to the humble dwelling of his host. Where he lodged in that mighty city we know not, but we do know for a certain fact that he landed on the Mole, and that he passed along it to the shore; it is not much, perhaps, but that little is very precious.

What a contrast do these two incidents connected with the Mole of Puteoli afford! The Roman Emperor, glittering like the morning star in purple mantle and jewelled cuirass, riding on his charger across the solid road that to humour his own caprice had been flung across the buoyant waters, accompanied by soldiery, by music, and by bands of wealthy sycophants ; and the Apostle, poor, in bonds, a despised prisoner in an alien land, meekly threading his way through the crowds towards his mean lodging. Where is the proud Temple of Augustus that beheld these two strange scenes, that occurred with no great interval of time apart ? Where are the villas and quays that lined the Bay of Baiae ? The very ruins of the palaces and warehouses are swept away ; the gorgeous temple is a Christian Cathedral dedicated to a follower of the despised Jewish captive ; the name of Caligula lives but in human execration, whilst that of the Apostle is. enshrined in the hearts of the whole Christian world.

. . . . . .

It is but a three-mile walk along the beach from Pozzuoli to Baiae, passing beside the Lucrine Lake and the southern slope of the Monte Nuovo, which always seems to us a far more wonderful freak of Nature than the Solfatara. Here we have a miniature mountain, a mile and a half round its base and nearly five hundred feet high, that was made in the course of a single night, and is to-day less than four hundred years old! The presence of this brand-new intruder on the shore of the Baiaean Gulf must ever remain a wholesome warning to all dwellers on these coasts, that their tenure of King Pluto's dominions is very insecure. One morning towards the close of September 1538, after some days of earthquake shocks, "Pozzuoli awoke," says the flippant Alexandre Dumas, "and on looking about did not recognise herself! She had left a lake the evening before, and lo! she found a mountain; where she had owned a forest, she found ashes; and last of all, where she had left a village, she perceived no trace!"

In one sense Dumas' facetious description is correct: the New Mountain was born with extraordinary celerity, and woods, lake and village—familiar and beloved landmarks to the people of Baiae and Pozzuoli—disappeared at its birth. But the event was no peaceful act of Nature; on the contrary, it was accompanied by loud rumblings, by showers of red-hot stones, by clouds of smoke, by torrents of scalding water, and by the retreating of the sea, which left thousands of fish lying helpless on the exposed shore. The village of Tripergola, a summer pleasaunce of the Angevin kings of Naples, and many traces of ancient Roman villas and engineering works, all perished in this notable cataclysm. Four eye-witnesses have left us details of this strange scene of desolation, whilst only a few days after Mother Earth had brought forth this new mountain, one of them, the Spanish Viceroy of Naples, the valiant Don Pedro of Toledo, owned sufficient pluck and curiosity to make the ascent of the Monte Nuovo, still smoking hot and reeking of sulphur. Who can tell when this *parvenu* volcano may spout forth fire and ashes? Would any sane person have the courage ever to settle within range of a possible eruption? No, the Phlegrean fields are interesting to visit, but he must require a strong nerve who would fain dwell beneath the shadow of this dormant crater.

It is a very short walk from the base of the Monte Nuovo to the "golden shores" of Imperial Baiae, which is certainly not an imposing place in these days. What with the destroying hand of time and the still more obliterating action of the neighbouring volcano, there is little left for the fancy to build upon ; certainly the three ruined shells that are called temples by courtesy, but served probably a much humbler purpose than that of worship, are not particularly striking. It requires not only a good classical knowledge, but also no small amount of imagination to picture the Baiae of the Roman poets.

"If Pozzuoli has gone down in the world, still more so Baiae. It does not require any more sinking ; it is low enough as it is, so low that some of its ancient villas and palaces can only be visited in a diving-bell. So dreary and deserted is the site, that at first glance the visitor feels mightily inclined to question the veracity of the historian, and to doubt whether Baiae—Baiae the gay, the fashionable, the dissolute, the beloved of emperors, statesmen and poets—ever existed. But when he is shown the enormous sub-structures lying under water, and the masses of solid masonry wherewith the surrounding hills are over-spread, incredulity gives place to amazement. What towns of lath and plaster are Brighton, Newport and Trouville, when compared with this 'Rome by the sea,' where the materials used for the foundations of a single villa would more than suffice for the construction of a dozen 'genteel marine residences' of the modern style! What would a Roman architect think of the card-board streets and squares, and the stucco crescents and terraces, of an English watering-place? of those 'eligible family

mansions' wherein dancing is dangerous, and to venture
on whose balconies is perilous in the extreme? Echo
answers : 'What!'"*

Here on this desolate strip of sea-shore, now
dominated by the Spanish viceroy's frowning fortress
on the hill above, the great and opulent of ancient
Rome founded a city composed wholly of palaces.
Here were no noisy market-places to annoy aristocratic nerves ; no slums to afflict plutocratic nostrils ;
no families of the proletariat to disturb the refined
senses of the jaded pleasure-seekers who retired hither
in the winter months. A writer, from whom we have
just quoted, makes comparison between Baiae and
Brighton or Trouville ; but in reality the fashionable
American resort of Newport has more in common
with the old classical watering-place than any modern
European sea-side resort. The hot sulphur baths on
the Lucrine shore formed of course only a shallow
excuse for the annual migration of Roman fashion-
ables to Baiae, where blue-blooded senators and
pushing plutocrats indulged in fierce social struggles
for individual pre-eminence. Yet certain of the
natural warm springs had been enclosed in splendid
buildings, and were used by the luxurious citizens, so
that even to-day the Thermae of Nero (Stufe di
Nerone) are pointed out by the local guides. " Quid
Nerone pejus ? Quid thermis melius Neronianis ? "
(what is worse than Nero ? yet what more beneficent
than his baths?) asks the poet Martial, whose name
will ever be bound up with the tales of luxury and
vice that are associated with this spot. Baiae in
winter, Tibur (Tivoli) in summer, the two names stand

* W. J. A. Stamer : *Dolce Napoli.*

for the beau-ideal of a Roman existence, the cynosure of every wealthy citizen.

But let us ascend out of the close and enervating air of low-lying Baiae to the breezy heights of Misenum, which has immortalised the name of the Trojan trumpeter whose end was mourned by the tears of pious Aeneas himself. In gaining its summit and in gazing upon the landscape spread around us, we have penetrated, so it seems, into the very heart of Italy : not the Italy of Roman history, but the land of Ausonia itself, the fabled shore that the Trojan hero sailed at his goddess-mother's bidding to discover, when all the world was young and the high dwellers of Olympus still condescended to take a personal interest in the affairs of favourite mortals. Surely the vine-clad terraces of Lake Avernus, the pools of the Lucrine and the Mare Morto, the verdure-clad hillocks lying beneath us must conceal the true secret of the antique Tyrrhenian country, in whose history the rise and fall of Roman power afford but one amongst many epochs. Looking to northward, beyond the little landing-stage of Torregaveta, we behold the heights of Cumae, that was a flourishing city with harbour and citadel hundreds of years before a certain Romulus built a wall of mud near the banks of Tiber and slew his brother Remus for leaping over his handiwork. The founding of Rome is enveloped in impenetrable clouds of legend ; the building of Cumae is a fact :—here then we obtain a key to Italian history. Rome, whose origin is lost in mists of obscurity, is a flourishing modern capital ; Cumae is but a shapeless mass of crumbling ruins, overgrown with ivy and cytizus, and inhabited by lizards and serpents. But both cities, dead Cumae and living Rome, present but passing events in the long slow progress of the centuries, which have witnessed successive phases of civilisation and destruction in this

> "Woman-country, wooed, not won,
>   Loved all the more by Earth's male lands,
>   Laid to their hearts instead."

Is the Genius of Italy, the Sibyl of Cumae, still living, we wonder, in some dim recess, some secret cavern of Cimmerian gloom, beneath those decaying heaps of the ancient Greek city? She was old, very old, we know, when pious Aeneas found her shrieking her strange prophecies, and that was long ages before Hellenic wanderers raised a fortress upon the wooded heights above the dread lake of Avernus.—Venerable Mother of Italy! dost thou still survive muttering thy strange warnings in some sunless labyrinth, that the rapacious guides of Baiae have yet failed to penetrate? Art thou, like King Arthur of romantic Wales, still keeping watch over the destiny of thy country, ever ready to assist in the hour of need?

> "Thy cave was stored with scrolls of strange device,
>   The work of some Saturnian Archimage,
> Which taught the expiations at whose price
>   Men from the gods might win that happy age
> Too lightly lost, redeeming native vice;
>   And which might quench the earth-consuming rage
> Of gold and blood—till men should live and move
> Harmonious as the sacred stars above."

For Italy has not wholly forgotten her ancient guardian and soothsayer, who welcomed the founder of the victorious Roman race; nor did the artists of the revived glories of the Renaissance neglect to honour the mysterious priestess of the Cimmerian shore. With prophetic mien the Sibyl of Cumae, that Michelangelo depicted, watches ever the come-and-go of humanity from her lofty post within Pope Sixtus' Chapel, bidding all remember her ancient prophecy of the Judgment Day, which the Roman Church has included in one of its most solemn canticles :

> " Dies Irae ! Dies illa !
> Solvet saeclum in favilla,
> Teste David cum Sibylla."

INDEX

X

PRINTED BY
TURNBULL AND SPEARS
EDINBURGH

PSIA information can be obtained
www.ICGtesting.com
Printed in the USA
VOW06*1718131217
502720BV00001B/2/P